PREFACE

Do-It-Yourself Choices

As you can imagine, while putting together the book that you hold in your hands, we did a lot of thinking about the term *do-it-yourself*, and what it means to homeowners. And now, as we cross the last t's and dot the last i's, it becomes even more clear that *do-it-yourself* is a flexible, malleable term that can connote everything from patching a nail hole in a wall, to building your own kitchen cabinets, to fixing a hinge on a door, to replacing a leaking water heater entirely without outside help.

Do-it-yourself gained a solid foothold as a word in our language in the mid- to late-Seventies when the first of the baby boomers found new housing scarce and immersed themselves in the renovation of older existing homes to make up for the shortage. The term soon came to describe the rapidly growing ranks who were taking on projects themselves instead of having them hired done.

By the early Eighties, *do-it-yourself* references had often become abbreviated to the acronyms *D-I-Y* and *D-I-Yers*. Since then, the terms have been applied to everything from simply buying a product to actually completing a major home project without help from professionals. It is used as a label for those of us who carefully select a roofer to re-roof our home, as well as those of us who buy and put on the shingles ourselves.

If do-it-yourself terms seem somewhat clumsy today, it is because they are asked to cover a lot of territory. This is partly because, as relatively affluent homeowners, we have the ability to pick and choose what we want to do ourselves, as compared to early pioneers, who had to do everything on their own because there was no other choice. With more cash available, we have unprecedented choices in what projects we do in and around the home. Because of this, the overriding goal in assembling this year's *Do-It-Yourself Yearbook* has been to reflect this new age of do-it-yourself choices.

Do-it-yourself decisions must be made across a broad spectrum. A few examples include whether you choose to use your time to:

- concentrate on such areas as wiring, plumbing, or maintenance and repair to keep home systems in top shape;
- make time for more enjoyable projects, such as building decks, fixing up the boat, or building a piece of furniture or a birdhouse in the home shop;
- work at making home improvement projects more efficient by acquiring and using new time-saving products and materials;
- reduce the cost of acquiring such luxuries as whirlpool baths, attractive new doors, swimming pools, and additions, or
- become a better home manager by searching out the best prices and quality on the financing, products, materials, and services you need.

As you look through the contents of this book, keep in mind that the first stage of becoming a do-it-yourselfer is deciding what you must do, can do, or want to do yourself. Our goal has been to show you the wide range of do-it-yourself choices you can make.

Because time is always short, we begin to make do-it-yourself choices when we decide to hire a lawn service to mow the grass, for example, so that we can have time to fix the clothes dryer. Or, when we buy microwaveable food so that we can have more time for gardening or landscaping. The blueprint of do-it-yourself choices for each of us would require hundreds of pages of diagrams, and it would take a super computer to track the factors which result in the decisions we each make every week.

However, one choice most of us have already made is to accept the basic responsibilities of protecting the investment we have in our homes, including the hiring and supervising of professionals to help us with inevitable emergencies, repairs, and improvements. That's where every homeowner, regardless of inclination, begins to become a do-it-yourselfer.

Gene Schnaser, Editor

CONTENTS

Setting Up A Shop   12

Making Fine Furniture   80

Building With Logs   56

Updating Exterior Doors 117

Rigging The Perfect Boat 160

CONCEPTS

Photo: Marlyn Rodi

The
DO-IT-YOURSELF
PAYOFF

Sure, You Can Save Big Money Doing It Yourself,
But The Real Benefit May Be The Intangibles

Most recent figures show that do-it-yourselfers account for a good two-thirds of the $80 billion now being spent each year on home improvements in this country. Surprising? Not if you're one who has been shelling out endless sums of hard-earned cash lately just to keep up — to say nothing of improving — the family homestead.

Periods of skyrocketing real estate prices, soaring building costs, spiraling labor rates, and raging inflation over the past three decades have left the U.S. homeowner backed against a wall. During the 1970s, for example, the cost of acquiring and maintaining a home doubled, and in many cases tripled or even quadrupled. The 1980s brought some relief, but like a rachet wrench home expenses in most areas headed in only one direction — up.

Faced with this avalanche of higher costs, today's homeowners have two choices: 1) keep paying others to maintain, repair, and improve their home, or 2) acquire the know-how and tools necessary to become more self-sufficient. Millions of Americans are opting for the latter. And they have become part of a quiet movement that could be labeled the Do-It-Yourself Revolution.

It's been a subtle phenomenon that has altered life-style habits as much as the personal fitness, anti-smoking, and save-the-earth movements. It has received little fanfare, yet has wrought major changes in how we get what we believe we deserve. Our willingness to roll up our sleeves, in turn, has brought big changes in the way tools and materials used in home projects are packaged, distributed, and sold.

The roots of the movement began when Americans began to react against escalating charges made by professionals ranging from basement remodelers to roofers. Alvin Toffler wrote in his best-selling book *The Third Wave* that as recently as 1970 fully 70% of all power tools were bought by professionals. Just 10 short years later the figures had dramatically flip-flopped: only about 30% were bought by tradesmen; the rest were being grabbed up by homeowners bypassing professionals to take on the projects themselves.

And for good reason. Some simple arithmetic shows that in many cases homeowners can pocket well over $50 for each hour they spend on home-related projects. But saving money is only part of the do-it-yourself reward. Learning to become more self-sufficient not only can save you a small fortune over the years, but also can throw several side benefits your way.

One payoff is that by handling more home projects yourself you are able to get more things done without having to first earn the money, having it taxed, then paying help with *after tax* dollars. Because of this added bonus, you can often save significantly more than the hourly charge you'd pay hired professionals.

Example: Let's say that a section of copper piping breaks next weekend and sprays water all over your bathroom. Instead of calling a plumber who might charge $128 to repair the pipes, you could go to a home center and spend $25 for new copper tubing, the tools you need, and a booklet on how to make solder joints. Let's guess it would take the plumber two hours to make the repairs, but might take you twice as long, or four hours.

The total savings to you for making the repairs would appear to be $128 minus $25, or $103. That's a payback of $25.75 per hour.

But your savings actually would be greater because the $128 you would have paid the plumber would have been *after-tax* money.

Let's say you and your spouse file returns as a married couple with a taxable income of about $64,000 a year. Using the assumptions in the chart, opposite, you would have had to earn $202 before taxes to get the $128 after-tax money to pay the plumber. Because we're taking taxes into account, we also should figure that you would need to earn about $39 in pre-tax money to pay for $25 worth of supplies. But even subtracting $39 from $202 still leaves you with a savings of $163 for four hours of work, or $40.75 per hour.

In addition, by doing the job yourself, you would have armed yourself with the know-how, tools, and materials to get the job done for even less the next time a similar problem occurred. The next time you might not have the $39 pre-tax cost for supplies, and the job might only take you two hours instead of four. In this case, the return would be approximately $82 per hour.

Do-it-yourself projects — even relatively minor ones — can add up to big-buck savings. You can do many jobs for 30% to 80% less than a contractor would charge you. Some examples:

Painting Projects. Usually at least three-fourths of the cost of painting jobs, whether interior or exterior, is for labor. For $75 worth of paint and supplies, you can do a job that would easily cost $300 — and probably more — if you hired it done. On a large house-painting job, the savings would be much greater.

Doing The Roof. About half of the

As former hire-it-done homeowners will attest, accomplishing even smaller do-it-yourself projects can help you feel more in control of your life.

cost of putting on new shingles often goes for labor. So, on a small $1,000 roof project, you could save as much as $500 by going the do-it-yourself route — and much more for larger roofs. (Whether you do it yourself may depend on safety factors, however; if the roof is very steep or complex, you may decide to concentrate on other home project opportunities.)

Installing Air Conditioning. Because the cost of equipment runs high on this project, labor may only account for about a third of the total cost. Even so, putting in a central air conditioning system yourself could save you from $300 to $500 or more. And, if you invest your savings in a more energy-efficient unit, you will reap a payback every time it's turned on.

Making Siding Repairs. It doesn't take much to run up a big expense in re-siding a house, and labor will again make up about half the cost of such

project. Even on a partial re-siding or repair project, you should be able to easily save at least $250 by doing it on your own.

Another factor adding to do-it-yourself savings is that you can avoid paying markups and overhead costs that help your contractor drive that shiny new pickup. Any contractor you hire may mark up both labor and materials from 10% to 25% or more. At 25% on a $5,000 project, for example, you could end up paying $1,000 in markups.

Over the past few decades, a mountain of excellent how-to information has been amassed by magazine and book publishers, as well as home video producers. Suppliers of tools and materials also have responded with gusto to the growing army of nonprofessional home improvers. Every time the new-home building market dries up, such companies begin courting the do-it-yourself homeowner with new fervor.

It wasn't that long ago that you had to show many of these firms a union card to do business with them. Today, the tables have turned, and the homeowner has become a prized customer. The result has been a tidal wave of new products, specially packaged with instructions for the do-it-yourselfer, including everything from prepasted wallpaper to assemble-your-own kitchen cabinets. Home centers have sprung up across the country, increasingly staffed with friendly, trained salespeople.

By becoming more knowledgeable about home projects, you also become less vulnerable to shady purveyors of home repair services. While most such businesses are honest, the sad fact is that thousands of unsuspecting homeowners are still gypped by home improvement hucksters every year. Studies show that as much as $1 out of every $15 we spend to repair and refurbish our homes may get into the hands of con artists and peddlers of "miracle" materials that simply do not work. You can lose hundreds, or even thousands of dollars, on home non-improvements.

Common homeowner gyps include "bait and switch" advertising hoaxes, "bargain" driveway resurfacing and chain-referral home siding sales, "crew switching" (one crew quotes highly inflated prices, followed by another quoting lower prices), unscrupulous basement waterproofing, phony furnace inspections, fake repairs, termite swindles, swimming pool scams, as well as landscaping and gardening frauds.

If you don't know how things should be done, or what kind of materials should be used, you can become an easy target for any of these swindlers who might happen your way.

Do-it-yourself skills can pay dividends another way, too. By doing the work yourself and keeping costs down, you are more likely to make home improvements that will save on future operating costs. Let's say you decide to install a water-saving showerhead yourself. It's a small

project, but if you pay 8 cents per KWH for electricity for your water heater and pay $1 per thousand gallons for water, installing it might save you nearly $150 a year.

The do-it-yourself bottom line, however, includes more than saving money; it also allows you more control over where you spend the money you earn. Being more self-sufficient gives you choices. Instead of having to pay $128 of your hard-earned pre-tax money to a plumber, you might decide to do the job yourself and use the money saved to take your family on a much-needed weekend trip.

The do-it-yourself movement has had a major impact on how Americans relate to technology in the home. If we make little or no effort to understand technology, we are often at a loss as to how to correct it when it fails. And we feel victimized. Indeed, most who begin to learn how home technology works seem to command a new confidence in themselves. As former "hire-it-done" homeowners will attest, accomplishing even smaller do-it-yourself projects can help you feel more in control of your life.

THE ULTIMATE PAYBACK

The biggest payoff for becoming more self-sufficient on the home front may be the enjoyment that comes from rolling up your sleeves and giving a project your own personal touch.

In today's highly mechanized world, many of us rush to work and shoulder a seemingly endless stack of conceptual tasks. Instant feelings of accomplishment are often few and far between. And, unless we are lucky enough to work with our hands at something we enjoy, the gratification our ancestors got from building a cabin, plowing a field, or fixing the carburetor on the Model T is missing from our everyday experience.

Learning to do more with our own hands helps restore this lost sense of accomplishment. This not only helps to satisfy a very real human need within, but in an indirect way helps us cope with what so many of us call the "rat race." As we become more self-sufficient, we also gain a new appreciation for technology, and realize that it contributes significantly to our quality of life.

There's no doubt that in learning to become more self-sufficient homeowners most of us end up making a few mistakes along the way. But chances are good we will overcome most obstacles and learn from our experiences. Meanwhile, within ourselves, we often discover creativity, imagination, and other hidden capabilities we didn't even know we had. And it's hard to put a dollar value on that.

WHAT YOU COULD SAVE ON A ONE-DAY PROJECT

If you would pay a professional this much per hour . . . Hourly Wage	You would pay this much per 8-hour day . . . Daily Wage	And would need to earn this much before taxes* Pre-Tax $
$16	$128	$202
$18	$144	$227
$20	$160	$253
$22	$176	$278
$24	$192	$303
$26	$208	$329
$28	$224	$354

*Approximate, based on 1991 tax rates for married couple with taxable income of $64,000. Includes FICA, Medicare, and state tax rate of 8%. Chart assumes equal proficiency and does not consider flat-rate service call charges or markups on either labor or materials.

The
NEW YANKEE WORKSHOP

How Norm Abram Designed And Set Up
The Most Famous Workshop In America

After appearing for 13 years on *This Old House,* friendly, down-to-earth Norm Abram has graciously accepted the spotlight as the country's best-known carpenter on a new television series of his own. Over the past three years, the *New Yankee Workshop* has become a household word, not only as a TV series, but also as a place — a workshop nestled in the outskirts of Boston where craftsmanship reigns as raw materials are transformed into finished projects that are worthwhile making.

Like fishermen staring at tackle-boxes, millions of viewers watching Norm's programs find themselves comparing his television workplace with their own. Thousands have asked for more information on how it is set up, organized, and equipped.

The truth is that the shop didn't evolve overnight. Throughout his years as a contractor, and continuing after he became the voice of carpenter wisdom on *This Old House,* Norm had always hoped to some day set up a dream workshop, one packed with all the tools and space he would ever need to take on even the most challenging of projects.

Just a little over five years ago, Norm's dream came true with the planned launch of his new PBS show. He designed the workshop from the ground up, and even did most of the construction himself, including the workshop's handcrafted door. Talk to him about how it all worked out and you might be surprised at what Norm likes most about the shop: the high ceiling.

"So many homeowners have their shops in a basement or garage," he explains, "and their ceilings are typically very low. In the *New Yankee Workshop,* we have the luxury of a very high cathedral ceiling. There is actually 16 feet between the floor and the steel I-beam that supports the rafters. The I-beam runs right under the ridge, spanning the entire 36-foot length of the shop. There aren't any posts to break up open space, so I never have a problem moving things

around or bumping into obstructions. And there's always plenty of natural light during the day, because of the skylights in the roof and the bank of windows built into the south wall."

The shop's ample overhead clearance and 936 sq. ft. of floor area, however, still present a space challenge when a television program must be taped. "When we're shooting, I might have enough room to move around, but that is not always true for our main cameraman, Dick Holden. To gain space quickly, I have mobile bases under the larger shop tools, including the jointer, shaper, and band saw. You can buy mobile bases for different tools, or make your own, with heavy-duty, locking casters. Either way, this kind of mobility would also be great in a small shop, where you often need to move one tool out of the way to be able to use another."

Norm concedes that being able to design a workshop from scratch gave him a tremendous advantage; his only restriction was that the shop be connected to an existing garage. "I actually determined the workbench and machine locations as I designed the space," he says. "First

Norm planned an abundance of electrical outlets in his shop. Unlike the wall outlets in a home, typically close to the floor, most of his shop outlets are high on the wall, several inches above workbench height.

INSIDE THE NEW YANKEE WORKSHOP

This artist's rendering depicts the layout and components of the *New Yankee Workshop*, the setting for Norm Abram's PBS series of the same name. Norm considers this workshop, with just a few future modifications, to be his dream shop, a fantasy come true that has gestated for years in the thinking stage. The television series, produced by Morash Associates and WGBH Boston, began its first season in 1989.

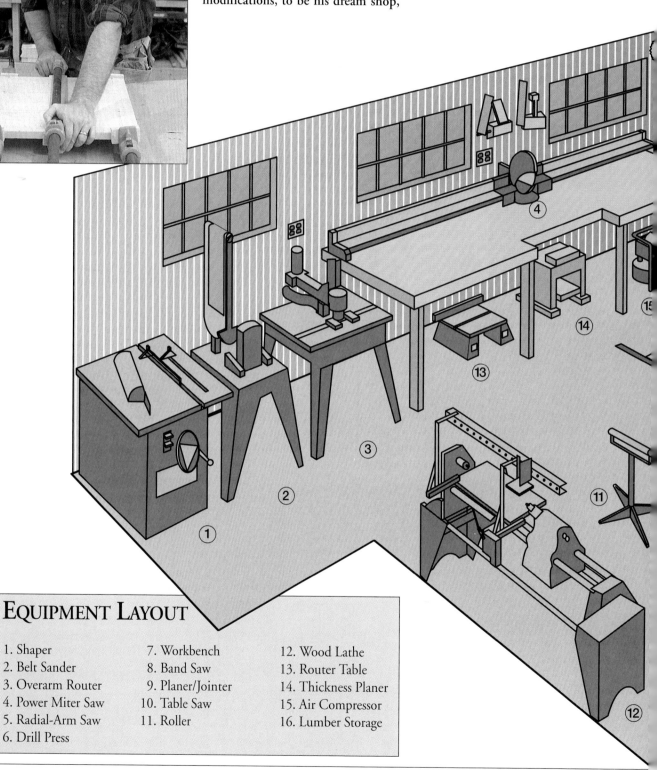

EQUIPMENT LAYOUT

1. Shaper
2. Belt Sander
3. Overarm Router
4. Power Miter Saw
5. Radial-Arm Saw
6. Drill Press
7. Workbench
8. Band Saw
9. Planer/Jointer
10. Table Saw
11. Roller
12. Wood Lathe
13. Router Table
14. Thickness Planer
15. Air Compressor
16. Lumber Storage

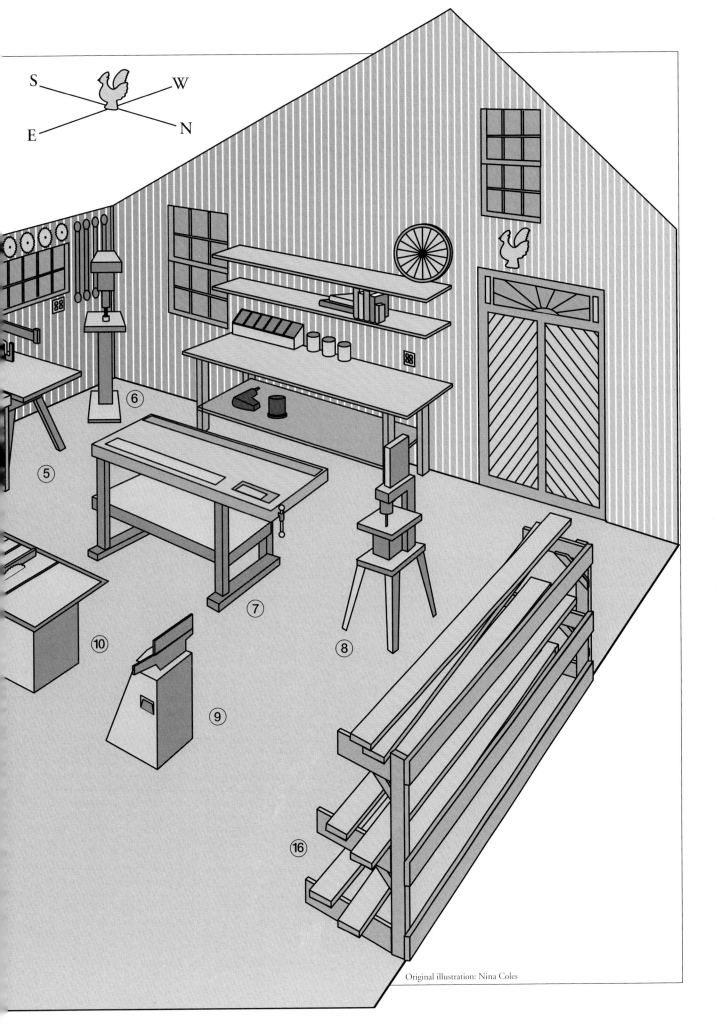

S W
E N

⑤ ⑥ ⑦ ⑧ ⑨ ⑩ ⑯

Original illustration: Nina Coles

and foremost was where to put the table saw. Because it is the workhorse of the shop, I gave it a good, central position. For power, I ran electrical conduit before pouring the concrete slab so I would have a floor outlet right where the saw would set."

His table saw is not a cheap one, and he didn't stop with what came from the factory. By adding extension tables and an auxiliary fence, Norm increased both the saw's capacity and accuracy. "With the saw's extended table surface," he says, "it is a lot easier and safer to rip or cross-cut large pieces, especially plywood panels."

Another challenge in laying out the *New Yankee Workshop* was to make sure there wasn't a shortage of benchtop space. There is a large workbench against the west-facing gable wall, with a pair of wide, long shelves above it. The shelves are home to books, screws, drill bits, and hardware, while the lower part of the bench stores a full complement of portable power tools.

The largest expanse of bench space stretches 16' along the south wall, and incorporates work stations for the power miter saw (also called a chop saw or motorized miter box) and the radial-arm saw. When the sawdust begins to fly here, it signals the beginning of a new creation. "I first like to lay out a selection of boards and choose the best ones to make certain pieces," Norm says. "Then I usually cut pieces to rough size on the radial-arm saw or chop saw. This procedure lets me group the pieces according to the section or subassembly where they will be used. It's an important first step because it eliminates the aggravation of discovering, in the middle of a project, that I'm missing a crucial piece."

Just above his main workbench, Norm uses a retractable, coil-type extension cord that comes down from the ceiling. "I really like the overhead cord," he says. "It lets me move easily around the bench while using a portable power tool, without tripping over any conventional-type extension cord. You can find the coiled cord at most hardware stores now, and mail-order tool suppliers also stock them."

Probably the most unique feature designed into the *New Yankee Workshop* is the heating system. The shop has a radiant floor system, heated by a solution of water and antifreeze that circulates through tubing embedded in the concrete slab. Perimeter and underslab insulation helps retain the heat transferred to the slab from the heating solution. "This particular system has been used in Europe with great success," notes Norm. "We've tried it in several houses and it has always worked out well. I like it in the shop because the heat is even, and because there are no ducts, baseboards, or radiators to collect dust or get in the way."

Too many woodworkers lose enthusiasm for a project once the final assembly is completed. But, Norm observes, any project worth making is worth sanding and finishing well. Tip: It is much easier to give parts, such as shelves and interior faces of cabinet sides, a final sanding before they are joined to other parts.

Norm has a separate finishing room near the *New Yankee Workshop* that is safe from workshop sawdust and well-ventilated for personal safety. Tip: When you need to apply finishes in your shop, thoroughly clean up the night before and set out your project. The next morning, most of the remaining dust will have settled.

A good shop, though it may resemble a miniature hardware store, wages war against wasted time searching for what is needed. Tip: Make it a continuing goal to experiment with various systems of storing portable tools, hardware, and materials to keep project work from bogging down or becoming frustrating.

Norm notes that the new generation of environmentally friendly, water-based finishes require different application techniques than old solvent-based finishes. Tip: Most of the clear water-based varnishes need to be applied in very thin layers. To get the best results, review the directions on the can.

With Norm's full lineup of stationary power tools, it is easy to overlook the many portable power tools that see action on *New Yankee Workshop* programs. Some, like drills and belt sanders, are old standbys that Norm has used for years. But there are a few newer tools that draw great praise from the carpenter everyone knows. One is the cordless drill. There are several in the workshop, and one is always chucked with a No. 2 Phillips-head bit for driving bugle-head screws. Similar to drywall screws, these handy fasteners come in various lengths for all kinds of assembly work.

The biscuit (or plate) joiner is another relatively new tool that Norm has taken a shine to. This tool is designed to mill shallow slots in joining pieces of wood. Football-shaped wood "biscuits" fit into the slots to align, as well as strengthen, a joint. "Laying out and cutting slots is so easy with this tool," Norm observes. "I use it when making panels and assembling face frames, and it is also great for reinforcing miter joints."

Last, but not least, on Norm's list of favorite portable power tools is his random-orbit sander. "What's unusual about this tool," he says, "is that it not only is great for fast, coarse stock removal, but also does excellent work as a fine finish sander. It's just a matter of switching grits and varying the pressure you apply. And, because of the random orbit, you don't have swirl marks showing up on the surface. This is the kind of sander to buy if you can only afford one."

Sanding leads to sawdust, and herein lies the only remaining challenge in this dream workshop. There is no centralized sawdust collection system, but for a reason. "I'd really like to put one in," Norm says. "Sawdust and shavings from stationary tools would be drawn into a central collection point, such as a large bag, through ductwork that runs to each machine. Most of the sawdust would be drawn into the system before it could get into the air or fall on the floor. Our problem is that the ductwork would interfere with our cameraman's mobility when we are taping a show."

But Norm hasn't given up on this one last final touch to come. He thinks there is a way he can overcome these problems and design a quiet, unobtrusive sawdust collection system that will do the job. Just how he's not ready to say, but smiles and quips, "You'll just have to keep watching the *New Yankee Workshop*." ❧

IDEAS FROM THE NEW YANKEE WORKSHOP

- **Collect Shop Clamps**. It is just about impossible to have too many clamps in a woodworking shop. At the *New Yankee Workshop* Norm has pipe clamps, bar clamps, spring clamps, C-clamps, picture-frame clamps, and straight-edged bar clamps that also are useful as cutting guides for portable power tools. Build a clamp rack to centralize your clamps and cut down on search time.

- **Make Sawing Easier**. It can be difficult, even unsafe, to cut large panels and pieces on a table saw if you are not set up for it. Keeping the top of your workbench the same height as the top of your table saw will provide extra support. Norm built extension tables on two sides of his table saw, and also has outfeed rollers, to provide essential outboard support.

- **Mobilize Shop Tools**. Any workshop can seem cramped when a large project is underway. Putting casters under one or more tools, such as a table saw, band saw, or jointer, helps you move them out of the way easily to create open space. Mobile bases are available for many tools, or you can make your own using heavy-duty locking casters.

- **Avoid Pack Ratting.** Unless you have a definite use for small cutoffs, such as kindling or toy making, get rid of wood scraps. A large scrap pile takes up space, and is a dust source as well as a fire hazard. Keep just enough pieces on hand to make shop aids such as cleats, jigs, or clamping blocks.

- **Go With The Carbide**. Whether you are buying blades for the shop saw, router bits, or shaper cutters, carbide surfaces will give you long, reliable service. Carbide-tipped tools can handle hardwoods and high temperatures without dulling like high-speed steel.

- **Consider Shop Networking.** Connecting up with fellow woodworkers can be fun and educational. By joining a local woodworking group, you can make friends who are happy to share ideas and techniques. Many associations also offer attractive benefits: discounts from suppliers; group buying power for shop supplies like wood, glue, sandpaper, and finishes; and seminars in various woodworking specialties.

Project success depends on many factors, says Norm, but one key is learning how to use glue during assembly. When too much glue is used in a wood joint, squeeze-out can easily make later finishing difficult. Trying to wipe excess glue off the wood may do more harm than good by spreading it onto surrounding wood grain. In most cases, it is best to wait until the squeeze-out hardens, then pare it off with a sharp-edged tool like a chisel or scraper.

STORAGE PROJECTS

*Three Great Ways To Overcome
The Home Space Shortage*

At first it seemed you could never fill all of the space in your home. Who could have so much stuff? But over the years, possessions accumulate. If you had inventory listings written down to track how this happened, you would see that when things are bought and carried home, older possessions are not sold, given away, or trashed as regularly as they should be.

The result? Within 10 years the American home is stuffed to the rafters. Not only is there no space left but, because few of us take the time to do the organizing we should, we also begin to forget where things are kept. Even in the home shop, for example, if items are not categorized and kept in open view, we find ourselves running to the hardware store to buy what we need instead of looking for something we know we already have.

Fortunately, help is available. The Western Wood Products Association has set its best minds to the task of helping unclutter the "stuffocated" American home and has developed plans, all summarized in a full-color booklet called *The Breathing Room Book.* Subtitled "Storage Projects That Create Living Space," it provides a dozen great ideas, three of which are presented here: A modular storage system, complete with plans, along with ideas on how to create a storage wall and how to outfit a storage room.

The booklet also provides suggestions on how to seek out storage space opportunities in your home, including built-ins, island spaces, dividers, modular units, and platforms that use space under existing structures or furniture. As the basic building material for its storage projects, the association suggests using solid-sawn, natural board western wood hem-fir, which includes Douglas fir, Englemann spruce, Idaho white pine, lodgepole pine, sugar pine, ponderosa pine, western latch, western cedars, and incense

Short on storage room? One solution is to search out the unused space you already have, suggests this booklet.

cedar. All offer the advantages of being easy to work with, long lasting, and attractive.

The star of the association's storage concepts is the modular utility storage system detailed on pages 22–25. Developed by Czopken & Erdenberger Interior Planning & Design of Portland, Oregon, it's a do-it-yourself project that can solve virtually every storage problem around the house — from bulky, hard-to-store items such as sports equipment and garden supplies, to space eaters like canned goods and out-of-season clothes. And,

because the system features a modular design, all of the shelves, drawers, and open spaces are instantly adjustable to fit your changing storage needs. Shelves and drawers ride in 1" spaces between cleats, so it's easy to add extra shelving or remove it as needed. For easy access to the back of the unit, 1x6 shelves may be staggered or stepped by using one, two, three, or four boards per shelf.

In the plans for the system on pages 24 and 25, you'll see that the design uses standard-size lumber of 1x4s, 1x6s and 2x4s so cutting and waste is kept to a minimum. The system is designed to go together quickly, with no complicated joints or intricate patterns to cut. The only tools you'll need are a hammer, saw, plus a measuring tape, level, and framing square.

Note: If you would like to review more storage ideas, you can order **The Breathing Room Book** *for $2.50 postpaid from Western Wood Products Association, Yeon Building, 522 S.W. Fifth Ave., Portland, OR 97204-2122. You also can order plan sheets for most of the projects shown in the booklet, including Understair Work Center (Plan 52), Mobile Baking Cart (Plan 54), Kitchen Island (Plan 53), Bookcase (Plan 56), Room Divider (Plan 57), Kid-Size Storage Modules (Plan 62), Fort Bunker (Plan 58), and Mobile Workbench (Plan 61). The Understair Work Center and Fort Bunker plans are $1 each; the rest are $.75 each.*

IDEA: STORAGE ROOM

If you're lucky enough to have a basement, garage, or spare room, you have all the makings of first-class storage. If you don't, you might consider the advantages of adding a storage room to your home. Adequate storage can make a significant difference in the future resale value of your home, and meanwhile you get to enjoy the benefits of having things organized and accessible.

A good way to start outfitting a storage room is to daydream a bit. Your first impulses may be sound ideas, and you can afford to idealize a little as you begin to work on paper. Before you finalize your design, get some opinions from others — especially builders or suppliers who can show you how to get the most from your dollar when you know what you're after.

For example, to make the most efficient use of space, you could build several storage modules side by side, as shown here. By adding shelves, pegs, and cupboards, you can accommodate almost anything you have to store, from garden equipment to games and groceries.

For do-it-yourself projects, the workbench shown is big enough for nearly any type of work. Plans available from the Western Wood Products Association show how you can lengthen or shorten the basic bench structure to make it fit the space you have available. And by building the mobile bins that store beneath the bench, you will be able to eliminate much of the strain involved in handling heavy items.

NOTE: BOTH CART & BINS ARE MOBILE

IDEA: STORAGE WALL

Here's an efficient way to utilize an unused wall in your kitchen or elsewhere in your home. It's a combination storage and work area — a roomy countertop surrounded by space for the things you need to work with.

The entire assembly can be built in, as shown, or freestanding. Pull-out pantry "closets" provide instant access from both sides. This is high-density storage at its finest. Everything is right at your fingertips, instead of being down in the base-ment or out in the garage.

You also could add some nice touches inside the cabinets. Consider a wooden rack for hanging stemware, for example, if you decide to use it in a kitchen. Or build in tray dividers to keep precious hand tools within easy reach, instead of scattered around in various places, if you decide to use the unit in your home shop.

Helpful options can include plumbing to a sink in the countertop, for example, a miniature refrigerator in place of one cupboard, or even over-the-counter lighting. However you customize a storage wall, you'll have a handy way to store an abundance of possessions. And you'll have a close working relationship with everything you decide to store here.

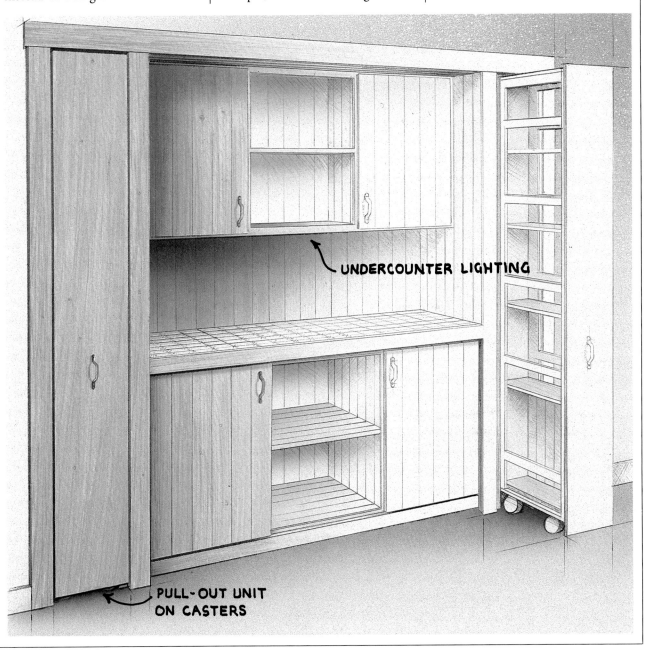

UNDERCOUNTER LIGHTING

PULL-OUT UNIT
ON CASTERS

WAX EDGES OF DRAWERS
TO KEEP THEM OPERATING SMOOTHLY

IDEA: MODULAR STORAGE SYSTEM

This modular storage system epitomizes flexibility, adjusting to your every storage need. It can be revised again and again to accommodate just about anything that comes along and needs a place of its own.

Construction of this modular system couldn't be much simpler. The basic structure is a series of ceiling-high 2x4s sandwiched between 1x6 cleats. And there is no hardware required. A 1" gap between each cleat forms the grooves that support shelving or slide-in drawers.

This sample concept, developed by the Western Wood Products Association, is based on modules with 2' widths and 30" depths. But to keep things as flexible as possible, make the shelves of 1x8 boards. That gives you an easy way to create different shelf depths, so you can store items of varying heights.

The drawers are designed without glides. The long side edges simply project into the grooves and function as runners.

No matter how you structure the system right now, chances are your needs will change over the years. But don't worry; you can adjust it as required.

For detailed instructions on how to make a modular storage system of your own, turn to page 24.

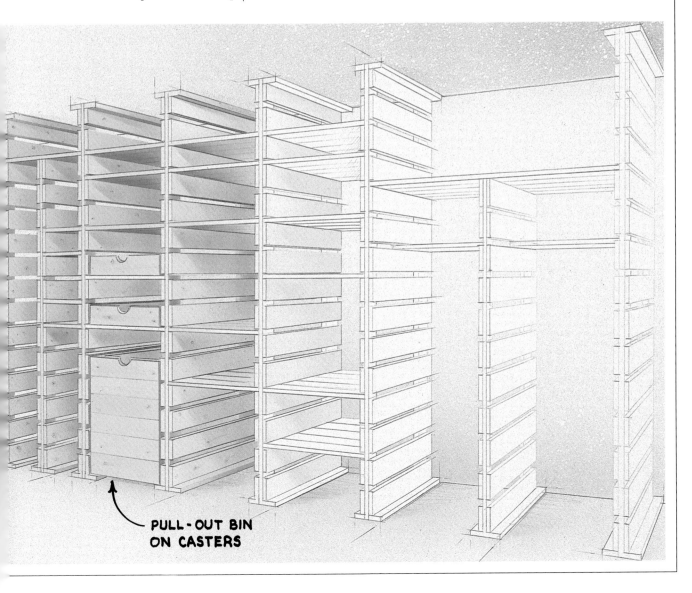

**PULL-OUT BIN
ON CASTERS**

TECH NOTES: BUILDING YOUR OWN MODULAR STORAGE

Fig. 1   27³/₄" wide x 22" deep x 93" high
(or height of ceiling)

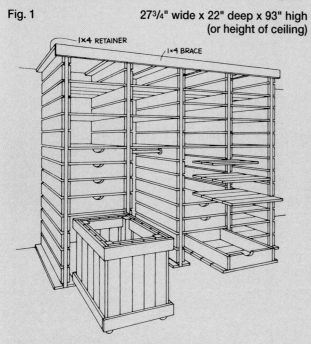

The modular storage unit shown here is easy to adjust to whatever length and height you need. Horizontal 1x6 boards are spaced 1" apart over 2x4 supports. The 1" slots let you insert shelves, drawers, or bins as needed. When additional storage space is required, the units can be expanded by simply adding another upright or two. The entire unit is portable because uprights slip into 1x4 retainers on the ceiling and floor. No nails are required. If you decide to move, just pack up the parts and take them along.

MODULES

Fig. 2

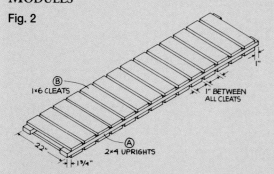

1. Measure height from floor to ceiling and cut 2x4 uprights (A) to length. (For ease of installation, trim ¼" off upright length.) Cut 1x6 cleats (B) to length (22").
2. Lay the 2x4s on the floor (Fig. 2), with outside edges spaced 22" apart. Glue/nail the first 1x6 cleat to the 2x4 uprights, positioning it 1³/₄" from the bottom. Make certain bottom and sides are square and fasten with three 4d (1¹/₂") nails at each end.
3. Glue/nail remaining cleats to one side, allowing a 1" space between cleats, keeping sides and cleats square. Position top cleat so it is 1" down from the top of 2x4 uprights. Turn the unit over and add cleats to other side (Fig. 2). Tip: A 1"-wide board used as a spacer will speed installation and improve accuracy.

Materials List For Modules
(Material required for one shelving module, 27³/₄" wide)
(A) Uprights: Four 2x4, 93" (or wall height)
(B) Cleats: Fifty-six 1x6, 22"
(C) Retainers: Eight 1x4, 22"
(D) Shelves: One to four 1x6 per shelf, 23³/₄".
Front Brace: One 1x4, cut to total width of modules
Nails: 4d, 6d, and 8d
Yellow Glue

4. Nail two 1x4 retainers (C) to ceiling joists (Fig. 3). Toggle bolts may be used if ceiling is drywalled. Space retainers 1¹/₂" apart, making sure they are parallel. Install second set of retainers on the ceiling, parallel to the first, 25¹/₂" on center. Continue to add retainers as needed, 25¹/₂" on center.
5. Slip 2x4 uprights of one module between the retainers. Using a level, make certain module is plumb, then install second set of retainers on floor (Fig. 3). Use 8d nails if floor is wood; use concrete nails and/or adhesive if floor is concrete. Repeat with additional modules.
6. For added stability, nail a continuous 1x4 brace to front of modules, flush with ceiling. (See Fig. 1.) Use glue and two 6d or 8d nails at each upright.
7. Cut 1x6 lumber 23³/₄" long for shelving (D). Slip boards into the slots to form shelf. You can use up to four boards per slot, depending on the depth of shelf you need.

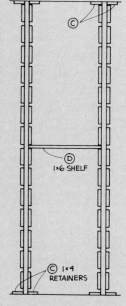

Fig. 3

Illustrations, text: Western Wood Products Association

DRAWERS

Fig. 4

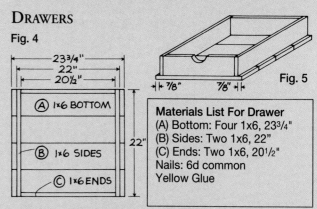

Materials List For Drawer
(A) Bottom: Four 1x6, 23³/₄"
(B) Sides: Two 1x6, 22"
(C) Ends: Two 1x6, 20¹/₂"
Nails: 6d common
Yellow Glue

1. Cut 1x6 sides (B) and ends (C) to length. Glue/nail corners to form a square (Fig. 4). Center four 23³/₄" shelf boards over the square, overhanging drawer frame ⁷/₈" on each side (Fig. 5). Glue/nail in place, using 6d nails. Cut handhold in front, or install drawer pull. Use additional 1x6 lumber to create drawer dividers.
2. Slip drawer into the slots between cleats. Shelf boards act as drawer runners. Waxing runners will help drawers slide easily.
3. For deeper drawers, use 1x8, 1x10, or 1x12 lumber instead of 1x6s for sides.

BIN

Fig. 6

20½" wide x 19" deep x 22" high
(plus casters)

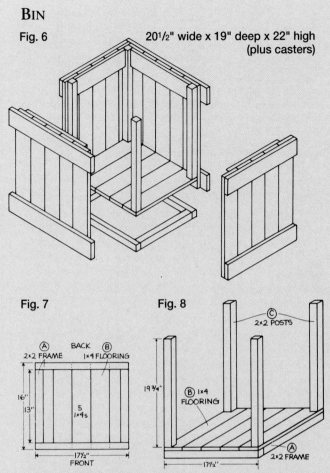

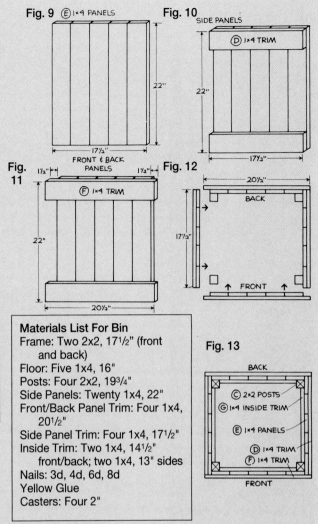

Fig. 9 Ⓔ 1×4 PANELS

Fig. 10 SIDE PANELS

Ⓓ 1×4 TRIM

22"

22"

17½"

FRONT & BACK PANELS

17½"

Fig. 11

1½" 1½"

Fig. 12

Ⓕ 1×4 TRIM

20½"

BACK

22"

17½"

FRONT

20½"

Materials List For Bin
Frame: Two 2x2, 17½" (front and back)
Floor: Five 1x4, 16"
Posts: Four 2x2, 19¾"
Side Panels: Twenty 1x4, 22"
Front/Back Panel Trim: Four 1x4, 20½"
Side Panel Trim: Four 1x4, 17½"
Inside Trim: Two 1x4, 14½" front/back; two 1x4, 13" sides
Nails: 3d, 4d, 6d, 8d
Yellow Glue
Casters: Four 2"

Fig. 13

BACK

Ⓒ 2×2 POSTS
Ⓖ 1×4 INSIDE TRIM
Ⓔ 1×4 PANELS
Ⓓ 1×4 TRIM
Ⓕ 1×4 TRIM

FRONT

Fig. 7

Ⓐ BACK Ⓑ
2×2 FRAME   1×4 FLOORING

16"
13"

5
1×4s

17½"
FRONT

Fig. 8

Ⓒ
2×2 POSTS

19¾"

Ⓑ 1×4
FLOORING

Ⓐ
2×2 FRAME

17½"

1. **Base:** Glue/nail 2x2 frame (A) together, using two 8d (2½") nails per corner (Fig. 7). Cut 1x4 flooring (B) to length and glue/nail to frame, using two 4d nails at each end.
2. **Posts:** Attach posts (C) to base, keeping sides square with base (Fig. 8). Tip: Before applying 1x4 flooring, glue/nail the four 2x2 corner posts to outside corners of two 1x4 bottom boards. Nail from the bottom, using two 6d nails per post. Or, toenail post to base.
3. **Bin Sides:** Cut twenty 1x4 sides (E) to length and assemble the four side panels (Fig. 9). Each side uses five 1x4s, 22" long. (For tighter joints and a more finished appearance, edge-glue and clamp 1x4s until glue sets.)
For Side Panels: Glue/nail 1x4 trim (D) to top and bottom of panel, flush with edges. Use 3d (1¼") nails (Fig. 10).
For Front and Back Panels: Glue/nail 1x4 trim (F) to panel, flush with top and bottom edges (Fig. 11). Trim extends 1½" on either side of panel. Attach with 1¼" nails.
4. **Position front and back panels** on frame so base of panel is flush with bottom of frame, and top is even with top of posts. Outside edges of vertical 1x4 panels are flush with posts (Fig. 12). Turn bin on side and glue/nail posts to panel, using 8d nails. Glue/nail base to frame.
5. **Position side panels** so base is flush with frame and outside edges are covered by front and back panels. Glue/nail to posts and base; nail corners where front and back panels overlap sides (Fig. 12).
6. **Inside Trim (G):** Before cutting boards, check actual measurement between posts to ensure accuracy (Fig. 13). Glue/nail trim to inside, flush with top, using 6d (2") nails. Toenail to posts.
7. **Install** purchased casters on 2x2 frame.

CLOTHES POLE/ WIDE STORAGE AREAS

Omit shelving (Fig. 14). Install clothes pole brackets in center of cleats approximately 40" above floor for shirts, 64" for longer items. Cut pole to length and install.

Build (or cut down) one module to desired height (Fig. 14). Install four 1x6 shelves, 49½" long. Secure short module by nailing down through shelves into cleats and 2x4 uprights with 8d nails.

Fig. 14

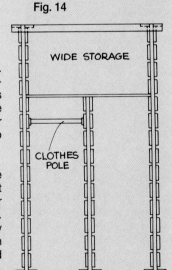

WIDE STORAGE

CLOTHES POLE

Caution: Be certain that you review and understand all steps of construction and verify all dimensions before cutting your material. While every effort has been made to ensure accuracy in the design and drawings, the possibility of error always exists; verify your plans carefully before beginning your project.

The
FUNCTIONAL DECK

*Four Simple Ways A Deck Can
Help Solve Backyard Problems*

Decks can be much more than an attachment to a home that increases its resale value. They also can provide the perfect solution to a unique backyard problem, or allow you to take advantage of a one-of-a-kind opportunity. The ideas here, assembled with the help of the California Redwood Association, show four ways homeowners across the country used a deck as a way to reclaim valuable outdoor space for conversation, dining, sitting, or relaxing.

What can that be worth? Ken and Shawn Demont in California say it was worth more than the $7,000 they spent to create their new outdoor environment. To save money, they built their deck themselves, even though they had no previous carpentry experience. For their three-level deck (see next page) they used construction heart redwood, an economical garden grade. The wood is easy to saw and nail, has no toxic chemicals, and is virtually free of pitch and resins. Its dimensional stability also helps keep boards from twisting, cupping, and checking, while its natural extractives help prevent decay and insect damage.

Here are the basic steps they followed:

• They placed posts in accordance with local code and removed existing concrete only where footings had to be dug. They set precast pier blocks in 18" square holes and poured concrete around them. For the deck, they toenailed 4x4 posts to wood nailing blocks. Three 6x6 posts for the trellis were installed 3½' from the home exterior, positioned according to existing windows.

Want a hot tub outside? Build a lanai with a two-level surround off your deck, as shown opposite, and enclose it with glass on two sides to keep out cool breezes.

• For beams they used 4x6s spaced 8' apart for the main deck, 4x8s for the bedroom-level deck, and 4x10s for the upper level. After attaching the beams to the posts, they nailed 2x6 joists to the beams, 24" on center. Because their deck is freestanding, blocking was used between joists to make it more stable.

• For the deck surface, they nailed 2x6s bark side up to the joists, using a staggered nailing pattern with one nail per bearing surface to prevent splitting that can occur when moisture evaporates from unseasoned wood. To leave gaps between the deck boards for drainage, they used 16d nails as spacers.

• For the trellis, they bolted two 6x6 girts on each side of the posts at 45-degree angles to support two 5'-long 2x8s that flank each post to form a T. Four 2x8s set on edge span the posts and 2x4s were nailed at right angles to the 2x8s. To the 2x4s they nailed 2x2s which run the length of the structure.

• The stairs between the main level and upper deck were built 11'3" long, with 11" treads and 7½" risers. Because of the length of the stairs, five stringers were placed 24" on center for support. The step leading to the bedroom deck was made by building an angled box and facing it with redwood 2x6s.

*Note: The Demonts found the California Redwood Association's booklet **Deck Construction** a helpful guide in sizing the understructure of the deck and in building the benches. You can order a copy by writing the association at 405 Enfrente Dr., Suite 200, Novato, CA 94949 or by calling 415/382-0662.*

IDEA: PROVIDE A LINK TO NATURE

Problem: Shaded by beautiful trees and overlooking a river valley below, the best view in this Milwaukee backyard was a distance away from the house. **Solution:** Homeowners Derrick and Jeanne Procell took advantage of nature by building an 188-sq. ft. asymmetrical redwood deck, with a 10'x14' dining level and a 6'x8' conversation level that is 7" lower. The deck's shape took form around existing trees, with only three feet of it positioned on the slope's edge. The rest extends beyond into the trees to create a special feeling of privacy. Safety railings were added to the valley side, and redwood benches were built to provide seating. Low-voltage lighting, a flagstone path, and colorful plants help keep the deck inviting day or night.

Design: Milt Charno   Photo: George Lyons

IDEA: CREATE MORE OUTDOOR SPACE

Problem: This San Rafael, California, home had no usable outdoor living area. A small front yard sloped straight into the street, while the back was a patchwork of concrete and loose bricks. **Solution:** Shawn and Ken Demont constructed a 1,000-sq. ft. redwood deck in three levels with built-in benches and planter boxes. The third level, two steps above the main deck, provides direct access from the bedroom wing of the house. A freestanding, stacked trellis blocks the afternoon sun and provides privacy from the homes on the hill above. Angled steps and planter boxes in various shapes help define the three levels of the deck, while deck boards installed at right angles to those on adjoining levels help create visual variety.

Design And Photo: Mark Becke

IDEA: RECLAIM A MUDDY YARD

Problem: The shady backyard on this wooded lot in New York State kept the grass from growing and, as a result, the yard was muddy much of the time. **Solution:** A two-level, 800-sq. ft. deck of redwood was built between the greenhouse at the rear of the home and the hill beyond. Two giant oak trees were saved and, to create an adequate deck area, an existing retaining wall was removed to allow for additional excavation. The remaining slope was tiered with 8x8 railroad ties faced with 1x6s. Planter boxes and a bench built of 2x4s set on edge were integrated into the retaining walls. To create visual interest, deck boards were installed diagonally. Redwood was used for the decking, bench, and retaining wall facing lumber.

Design: Edward Assa Photo: Peter Loppacher

IDEA: WRAP AROUND A POOL

Problem: The Dareld Riemers of Colgate, Wisconsin, had a steep slope for a backyard behind their Tudor-style home and they wanted more outdoor living space, as well as an above-ground pool. **Solution:** To accommodate the steep slope, a new redwood deck was stepped down the site in a series of angular levels to reach the new swimming pool. A 3'-wide elevated deck/path leads from the top 14'x14' sun deck level to the lower step-deck levels. A portion of the backyard was excavated for the 24'-diameter pool, then a curved retaining wall of fieldstone was built to contain the area behind the pool. The 2x6s for decking were installed diagonally; a built-in bench provides poolside seating. For details on a similar project, see page 131.

Design: Milt Charno Photo: George Lyons

Photos: Delta International

SHOP SAWYERS

*A Tool Expert's Insider Tips On
How To Buy A New Saw*

You might imagine that assembling a list of tools to outfit a home shop would be very simple. It is to start with. For example, on average, straight sawing makes up about 80% of working wood, curved sawing is about 10%, and sanding is about 5%. Turning, jointing, shaping, and drilling together make up only about another 5%.

So, if you are average, the first tool to consider purchasing for a shop is a good stationary circular saw. It becomes more difficult after that, however, because there is more to it than averages, says Howard Silken, professional tool specialist and inventor. To make more decisions before laying out money for tools, you have to ask yourself some critical questions:

What exactly do you want to do with your saw? Build things to save money? Create useful items or artistic crafts? Satisfy an urge to work with your hands? What experience have you had with power tools, especially saws? Do you study the manuals that come with tools you buy? Are you willing to buy fewer, but better quality, tools to keep within your budget? Do you like owning fine tools, even if you use them only rarely?

Your answers will help you make your first decision: whether to buy a table saw or a radial-arm saw. Next, you need to decide whether it should be a benchtop or a floor saw, and to decide what size you need.

A table saw and a radial-arm saw

For contour cutting, shown opposite, you need a band saw; otherwise, choose between a table saw, right, or a radial-arm saw.

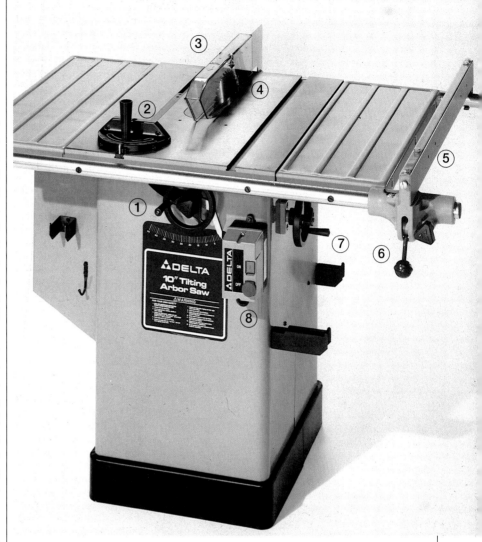

Major parts of the table saw include 1) elevation crank, 2) miter gauge with lock handle, 3) blade guard, 4) saw blade rising through table insert, 5) rip fence, 6) rip fence lock handle, 7) tilt crank, and 8) on-off switch. Switches with locking features help prevent unauthorized and possibly hazardous use by others.

are vastly different. On the radial saw, the blade is suspended over the table. If you have used a table saw much, you might find it difficult to adapt to a radial saw. It may feel like it works upside down or backward. Woodworkers who have both saws usually use the radial saw only for crosscutting. A good radial-arm saw, however, can dado, rip, shape, sand, dovetail, mortise, mold, rout (with adaptor), wire-brush, grind, buff, and perform many other operations.

A quality radial-arm saw is a beautiful, complicated, multipurpose, versatile tool. Even experienced woodworkers utilize only about 20% of its capabilities. The radial saw is a good bet if you are willing to learn as much as you can about using its full potential. It can be very safe to use if you follow all the rules; it can be extremely dangerous if you do not.

BUYING A TABLE SAW

Many excellent professional woodworkers swear by their table saws. If you lean toward the table saw, consider these tips.

Tilt Arbor. Most stationary saws on the market, including radial saws, have a tilt arbor. If you want to cut (crosscut or rip) at a bevel angle, it is the blade that tilts, not the table. One tool that still uses a tilt table is the Shopsmith. The Shopsmith is a multipurpose machine that works best with smaller pieces of material. If you need capacity to cut larger pieces, however, you will want to make sure that your saw has a tilt arbor.

Motor And Drive. One advantage of the radial-arm saw is that it is direct drive. There are a few table saws that are direct drive, but they are rare. Most table saws are belt driven.

Some use standard V belts, while others use rubber-molded timing belts that are flat with teeth on the inner side. The teeth engage slots in the drive pulleys, much like a bicycle chain engages its sprockets.

Most saws using timing belts have universal motors with brushes. These motors are like those in vacuum cleaners; they rev up to speeds as high as 10,000 rpm to develop power. (All portable tools use universal motors.) To bring the rpm down to proper saw blade speed, they must be geared down, pulleyed down, or slowed using a combination of both. To keep the pulley ratio about 2 to 1, the size of the drive pulley on the arbor shaft must be very small, usually less than 1". Timing belts are used because a

V-belt pulley this size does not have much surface to transfer power without slipping.

If you buy a table saw with a standard V belt, you can get replacements at most auto or tool supply stores. Timing belt replacements are difficult to find. If you buy a saw with a timing belt, buy a spare or two to replace the original when it breaks or its teeth wear away. Also be aware that you may have difficulty replacing universal motors in special castings. Almost any 3,450 rpm motor of the right horsepower can be used with V-belt drive saws, however.

Saw Heft. Another consideration when buying a table saw is its construction. The heavier the saw, the better. Heavy saws, for example, will have less vibration, less runout, and usually more accurate fence and miter gauge alignment. So if you see a low price on a 10" benchtop saw, pick it up and see how heavy it is. If the saw feels light, don't buy it.

To keep the weight (and price) of a saw down, marketers like to whittle away at the tabletop. The tops of some saws are made of sheetmetal. Others are plastic that looks like metal but is not. One good whack on a corner and off it will come. Better-made saws have cast-iron tables. Some have solid cast iron or cast aluminum extensions. Both are good.

Saw Features. Examine a saw's motor mount, table mount, and method used for blade tilt and elevation. You may have to turn the tool upside down to check these out. It is easy to do on cheap saws; on better saws, you usually can make an in-

spection from the rear.

If the castings under the table are made of white metal (usually zinc), beware. White metal gears and drives will abrade very quickly, particularly if sawdust gets onto the teeth or threads. Sawdust from plywood, particleboard, and Masonite is very abrasive. If the mechanism underneath is machined cast iron, it will be a better tool.

Saw Blades. The saw blade that comes with the saw can tell you something about its quality. It will likely be a combination (rip or crosscut) chisel-tooth blade. If it has a painted surface, however, chances are good it will be an untensioned blade. Always ask the salesperson if the blade is tensioned. If the answer is "I don't know," ask for another salesperson, or leave and buy your saw elsewhere.

Also be wary if the blade is chromium coated. These blades hold their cutting edge longer than regular blades; the chrome coating is very hard. The first time you have that blade sharpened, however, the file removes the chrome surface and you are left with a sharp but relatively soft metal blade. From then on, the blade

will have to be sharpened after very little use.

Saw Size. If you are convinced that the table saw is right for you, the next decision is whether to buy a small one (an 8") or a large one (a 10"). To make this decision, you need to know what you want to do with it.

Small saws are good for model making, small artistic work, framing, and small woodworking, such as making toys, chairs, and small cabinets. Large saws are better if you will be doing construction, making large furniture, using plywood sheets, or doing work that will need a 3" depth of cut. Just remember that a 10" saw will do everything an 8" saw will do, but an 8" saw will not do what a 10" saw can do.

BUYING A RADIAL SAW

Achieving accuracy on a table saw requires skill. On the radial saw, the accuracy is built into the tool, not the operator. That sounds good, but there are some major challenges to meet before you can get the most out of a radial-arm saw. First, you have to know how to set it up. Here are some additional considerations.

Saw Adjustments. Any radial-arm saw that does not hold its alignment can be frustrating, and its shortcom-

BASIC TABLE SAW TECHNIQUES

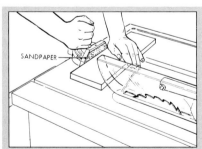

Crosscutting. Cutting across grain at 90 degrees, square with both edge and flat side of wood, using either groove in the table. Miter gauge can be swiveled to compensate for minor inaccuracies. The miter gauge bar is held against one side of groove; sandpaper on gauge head helps steady work.

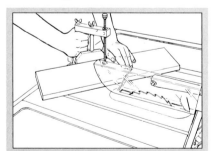

Miter Cutting. Same as crosscutting, except cutting at angle other than 90 degrees with edge of wood. If miter gauge is used in left-hand groove, left hand is held against gauge head, and right hand is on lock handle. In right-hand groove, right hand holds workpiece and left hand holds lock handle. Hold-down clamp increases accuracy.

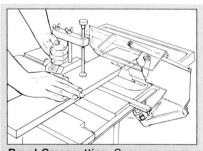

Bevel Crosscutting. Same as crosscutting, except cutting at angle other than 90 degrees with flat side of wood. Compound miter cutting uses a combination of miter cutting and bevel crosscutting, sawing at other than 90 degrees to both edge and flat side of wood. Ripping, resawing, and rabbeting are all done using the rip fence.

Major parts of the radial-arm saw include 1) track arm adjusting screws, 2) miter scale for setting track arm, 3) track arm clamp knob, 4) sawdust chute, 5) blade guard, 6) leaf blade guard, 7) table fence slot, and 8) elevating crank rod. Table fence serves as backstop for crosscutting and as guide edge for ripping.

ings defeat the purpose for your purchase. With a poor quality radial-arm saw you may spend more time trying to get it square than using it. There are at least seven adjustments that need to be made before you make the first cut:

1) eliminate any end play in the arm; 2) align the table so it is parallel to the arm; 3) adjust rollerhead bearings to a snug fit in the arm track; 4) adjust the miter locater to position the arm at a perfect 90 degrees to the fence; 5) adjust the bevel locater so the blade is 90 degrees to the table; 6) adjust the rear support of the motor to eliminate "toe" or "heel," and 7) adjust all locks so they hold any setting firmly.

All this needs to be done before you use the saw. You also need to know how to set it up correctly for operation, as well as how to use certain alignment tricks.

Cutting Action. When comparing a radial-arm saw to a table saw, consider crosscutting. When crosscutting on the radial, the lumber does not move. If the piece is long or heavy, it can be supported by any device the same height as the worktable of the saw. You can square off the end of an 8' 2x4 with ease.

Because the blade of a radial saw engages the lumber on the top side first, you can tell exactly where the cut is going to be made before the blade strikes the wood. On a table saw, the blade has to cut into the lumber before you see the blade on the cutting line. The cutting action of the blade on the radial saw pushes the lumber down and back against the fence. It can't go down because of the table, and it can't go back because of the fence. Only light hand pressure (away from the blade) is needed to hold the material in place.

Crosscut Length. A disadvantage of the radial saw is the length of the crosscut. The average 10" radial saw will cut 18". You can cut 24", but it has to be done in two cuts; the first cut with the blade in back of the fence, and the second cut with the blade in front of the fence. This is done by starting the second cut with the blade in the kerf made by the first cut.

You can cut the full 24" in one shot by making a "feed" cut in the crosscut position. This method is more complicated, and should not be done without proper instruction. To cut a 4' x 8' panel into two 4' x 4' pieces on a radial saw, you need to make four cuts. On a table saw, you can do it in one cut. Making it on a small table saw can be difficult, especially if the panel is a heavy ¾" piece of plywood or particleboard. At least on the radial saw the panel does not move while you are cutting it.

Types Of Cuts. When making compound cuts (with the arm mitered and the blade tilted), the radial saw has it all over the table saw. In truth, there is no angle at which the radial saw cannot be positioned. You can even position the blade horizontally, and many attachments are used this way.

Some of the biggest complaints with the radial-arm saw relate to its ability to rip. The complaints include: 1) the work binds during the rip; 2) sawdust gets thrown into the operator's eyes; 3) the lumber kicks back at the operator; 4) rips are tapered, and 5) the blade is 90 degrees to the table in the crosscut position, but not in rip position. Most often such problems are the result of the operator, not the saw, the saw is out of alignment, or the guard is set incorrectly.

Which to buy? Howard Silken, who has been using, selling, and developing saws and accessories for more than 35 years, sums up his personal opinion this way: If you will take the time to learn how to use it right, go with the radial-arm saw. If not, go with the table saw. He suggests buying your saw (in fact, all of your tools) at a tool store where they offer service, know their tools, and are willing to share their knowledge.

BUYING A BAND SAW

Before you decide on a saw, you may want to consider a band saw. If you decide to buy a band saw, either as a main saw or an auxiliary saw, try to buy a good one the first time around. It will be cheapest over the long haul. As with other saws, there are specific considerations worthy of your attention.

Construction. Silken advises staying away from plastic and/or sheet-metal, except for wheel covers. The entire base of a good band saw, as well as the support section that holds the upper wheel, should be made of cast iron.

One band saw that he owns, a Delta

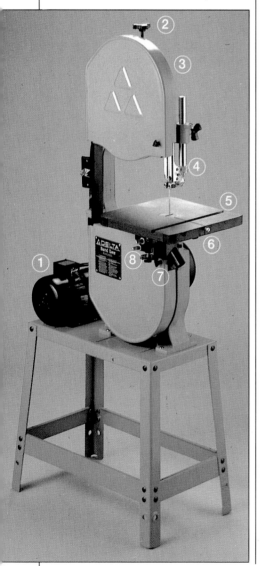

14", has two separate castings for the base and upper support section. They are held together with a large bolt and locating pins on matching machined surfaces. The separate castings offer an advantage. Normally the 14" saw has a 6" depth of cut. By inserting a 6" riser block between the two castings, and using a longer bolt, the depth of cut can be increased to 12". If you need a cut this deep, this feature is worth the price of the saw.

Table Features. The front and the rear of the table should be well supported; the front is more important than the rear because that is where you first place the material before cutting. Notice the slit in the table. Does it go from the front of the table to the center hole? Or, does it come from the right side?

Having the slit start in front seems like a good idea. To change blades, you simply remove the covers and slide the blade in the slit and up onto the wheels. This design allows no supports under the front half of the table, however. If there were supports, you couldn't get the blade back to the wheels. A slit from the right side enables the saw to have two supports, one in front and one in the rear, without interfering with blade mounting.

With this arrangement, once the blade is in the center hole, you can simply turn it 90 degrees to mount it on the wheels. If a band saw has this design, both supports may have independent locks on them to secure the cast-iron table at the desired angle of cut.

Major parts of the band saw include 1) motor, 2) tension handle, 3) upper wheel guard, 4) blade guard and guides, 5) miter gauge groove, 6) blade slot, 7) dust spout, and 8) blade guide adjusting screw (left) and table clamp (right). Band saws can be used for contour cutting, straight cutting, or resawing.

Blade Guides. The blade guides on any band saw can be a weak link. The problem is having a thin, flexible piece of metal moving at a high rate of speed and being forced back and sideways as you are cutting. The guides have to keep the blade traveling straight, and keep it from wandering left or right, or forward or back. If the saw is not properly constructed or adjusted, constant friction can cause the guides, as well as the blade, to wear away in a short time.

The guide system on the Delta 14" in Silken's shop works well. If the blade is tracked correctly and the guides are adjusted properly, cutting is easy, quiet, vibration-free, and accurate. Delta uses two fairly large rear bearings to keep the blade from being pushed off the wheels. (They are adjusted so they do not revolve except when cutting.) The sideways motion of the blade is controlled by hardened blocks of steel adjusted so they do not touch the blade except when cutting.

Wheel Crowning. What keeps the blade on a band saw running on the center of the wheels and tracking correctly is not the blade guides, but the crown on the center of the wheels. There are a few band saws on the market that do not have crowned wheels. They depend on minute adjustment of the upper wheel, as well as the guides, to keep the blade on center. Nevertheless, saws of this type constantly need repair or replacement of the blade guides.

Some manufacturers machine the crown on the wheel as the wheel is made. The crown is transferred through the rubber tire as it is stretched and glued to the wheel. Other manufacturers use tires that have the crown in the rubber. There are disadvantages to both methods.

Glued-on tires can be difficult and messy to remove. When replacing, the wheel must be clean of any excess glue;

a slight bump can make the blade bounce. The blade also may bounce if the tire is not stretched on evenly. Most tires are affixed with shellac or a special preparation. Once you mount the tire, it is best not to run the band saw for at least 24 hours. If the glue or shellac is not dry, the tire can come off and cause big problems. **Band Saw Rubber.** When replacing tires, keep in mind that shellac has a limited shelf life, and if it is too old it will not dry. Check any older shellac first by applying it to a piece of scrap wood. If it doesn't dry hard by the next day, don't use it.

One major problem with tire replacement is locating new ones. In fact, you may find it impossible to get tires for band saws more than five years old. Made of rubber, or some combination thereof, in time tires will get hard, cracked, or glazed, and the blade will slip when cutting under a heavy load. For this reason, it's a good idea to get extras when you buy your new band saw. ❧

EYEBALLING RADIAL-ARM SAWS

Howard Silken, a Florida tool inventor who has developed his own improved version of the radial-arm saw, emphasizes that the accuracy of a radial saw is built into the tool, not the operator. This is true, if 1) the saw can be aligned and will hold its alignment; 2) you know how to align it, and 3) you know how to set up the saw properly. He offers these tips when you go to buy a radial-arm saw for your own home projects:

• A rigid cast-iron arm with ground-in track of precise width its entire length is best. Roller head bearings are adjusted to a snug fit in the track, which puts a slight drag on the saw as it is pulled forward during crosscuts. The drag should be equal and opposite to the climbing action of the blade. If the track is not parallel, bearings can be snug in one section, but loose in another. This can be dangerous, as well as inaccurate.

• If two rods are used for a track, those that are set into a ground-in groove in the cast-iron arm are preferred. The rods should be well fixed to the arm. The rods on some saws can be rotated 180 degrees to renew accuracy; when completely worn, they can be replaced at much less cost than regrinding the arm.

• The arm should lock to the post so it will not move under pressure once a miter angle is selected. This is done either by squeezing the wrap-around casting of the arm that engages the post, or by forcing a plug or rod against the post. The wrap-around method provides much more metal-to-metal grab.

• It's best if the miter locator lever is held in place on the arm by two opposing heavy-duty adjusting screws that are threaded into cast protrusions on the arm. The slot on the post that accepts the miter locator should be hardened and tapered.

• When changing depth of cut, the post should only move up and down and not turn even ⅒th of a degree in the base. If it does, the end play in the arm will destroy precision. The best design to prevent rotation is using a key in a keyway.

• The large hole in the base that accepts the post should be milled in the casting, with a milled slot in the back. By slotting the back, wrap-around bolts can squeeze the base snug around the post to eliminate any end play of the arm, due either to wear or misadjustment of the base to the post.

• The pin for the yoke locator that sets the saw for rip or crosscut should fall into a cast-iron hole. Or, if it falls into cast aluminum, the hole should have a hardened bushing. The bevel lock should be the wrap-around type, not the pinch type, and the kerf adjustment at the rear of the motor should be a three-point suspension type.

• Motors should be all metal and not the clamshell type. Don't be overwhelmed by gimmicks, including electronic readouts. If the saw is not sturdy, can't be adjusted, or will not hold its adjustment, you will have wasted your money.

CHALLENGES

Photo:

PAINTED SURFACES

Techniques To Make Your Home Painting Projects
Easier And More Successful

As experienced painters know, it often takes longer to get ready to paint than it does to apply the paint. In their eagerness to get the job finished, many homeowners are tempted to skimp on preparation. But, when they do, those shortcuts almost always come back to haunt their work sooner or later.

While there is no substitute for proper preparation, more new products are becoming available to make all phases of painting and clean-up easier. Combined with procedures outlined here, they can help take the drudgery out of home painting and help give a professional look to your final results.

THE HOME EXTERIOR

Traffic and air pollution can deposit an oily film on your home's exterior. If not removed, these deposits can cause new paint to fail prematurely. Even if the air in your area is relatively clean, existing paint still must be washed to remove cobwebs, soot, and dirt. Use a detergent in water, and rinse surfaces thoroughly.

Keep in mind that many exterior house paints are designed to be "self-cleaning." They contain a chalky ingredient that is meant to wash off in rainfall, taking dirt and grime along with it. In dry climates and in protected areas, such as under eaves, however, the chalk doesn't wash off naturally. To avoid problems when you repaint, scrub off the chalk with soapy water and a brush. Another alternative is to use a "bonding primer" which is designed to penetrate the chalk and adhere to the paint base underneath. In any case, dirt must be washed off.

A power washer is an excellent tool for cleaning exterior surfaces. If you have a large area to cover, you might consider buying your own washer; otherwise heavy-duty units are available for rent.

PREPARING SURFACES

Old enamel or any glossy paint needs to be roughed up by sanding or by using a "liquid sander" so new paint will stick. Old paint of any kind that does not tightly adhere to the surface must be removed before you repaint. Defects in the old coating can signify a number of problems, and painting over defective coatings usually results in the problems resurfacing in the future.

If the old paint is clean and tightly bonded to the surface, you don't need to remove it. If old paint surfaces need work, however, you can use scrapers, sanders, heat, chemicals, power washers, or combinations of these methods.

To find a washer with enough pressure to peel paint, you will probably have to go to a rental yard. (Units sold for the consumer market are lower in pressure.) For a high-powered rental unit, you also will need a high-volume water supply because some of these spray water faster than a typical garden hose can supply.

Hint: To reduce water supply problems, run the hose into a barrel, tank, or large tub, then draw water out of that reservoir for the washer. That way the water supply is regenerating whenever you are not washing — while you stop to move a ladder, for example.

FIXING AND SEALING

Any opening in the siding or trim invites moisture penetration, which in turn leads to paint problems, as well as rot. Don't expect paint to seal cracks or splits in the wood. Repair or replace all damaged siding or trim, then prime the new wood before painting.

Thoroughly caulk and seal all joints where the siding meets windows or door trim. If the windows need reglazing, follow label directions on the putty for drying time before painting. Metal flashing or drip caps above doors and windows should be free of rust and leaks, and tightly sealed around the edges. If the galvanized coating is damaged, rust streaks can develop and bleed through new paint.

If knots in the wood are oozing sap or pitch, seal the affected areas with a knot sealer, or a stain killer such as B-I-N, Bulls-Eye, or KILZ. Apply primer over the sealer as soon as it dries, to protect it from the elements.

PREPARING INTERIORS

Inside the house, all surfaces must be clean and in good repair as well. Enamel, common in kitchens and bathrooms, must be washed thoroughly, then roughed up by sanding or with a "liquid sander" or deglosser. Otherwise, new paint will not stick. Also take care of problem areas.

If nail pops are a problem, drive new nails or screws about 1½" above and below the loose nail. Drive nailheads in to form a dimple on the panel's surface. Fill the dimple with patching compound, then sand it smooth.

Repair cracks, nail holes, and other damaged areas with spackle and patching plaster. Stains or marks from crayons, ink markers, lipstick, rust, or water damage should be sealed with a stain-killer, so they do not bleed through the new paint.

Use masking tape to tape edges of woodwork, windows, light fixtures, or any other area you want to protect. Tape plastic drop cloths to baseboards to protect floors. If you are painting the ceiling and walls different colors, tape around the walls until the ceiling is painted, then tape around the ceiling before you paint the walls. Be sure the tape adheres tightly, so paint won't leak under it, and remove the tape as soon as the paint dries.

Cover furniture and carpets with plastic sheets. For floors, the thicker plastic costs slightly more, but it won't tear as easily. Cover hanging light fixtures with plastic bags. Even the most careful painter creates some drips and spatters, so protect all surfaces you don't intend to paint. Remove electri-

FIVE WAYS TO REMOVE PAINT

1 Using Scrapers. Scraping is the most basic method of removing old paint, and a variety of scraping tools are available to accomplish the task. Be prepared to use plenty of elbow grease, and exercise care to avoid gouging the siding. Some sanding may be necessary as a final step.

2 Using Sanders. Sanding is used more often as a final preparation step than as a removal method. Weathered bare wood should be sanded to brighten it up before painting. Careful use of power reciprocal or belt sanders works; disk sanders are used less often on wood siding because the circular motion cannot follow the grain.

3 Using Heat. Heat softens and blisters paint so it can be scraped off easily. Some devices utilize an electrically-heated pad, others use a gas flame. A third type, a heat gun, uses a stream of air heated to several hundred degrees by an electric heating element.

4 Using Chemicals. Chemical removers are used more for woodwork and furniture than for siding. If you prefer this method, however, new products are available which are safer and easier to use than older, traditional materials.

For example, a new 3M product, Safest Stripper, can be applied without gloves, contains no methylene chloride, is noncaustic and nonflammable, and cleans up easily with water. It also remains effective for several hours after application, which is helpful when doing large-scale jobs.

5 Using Power Washers. High-pressure washers work fast, but they must be used with caution. A stream of water ejected under enough pressure to peel paint can be dangerous. Also, you'll need good rain gear, especially if it is cool outside when you are running the unit. Good eye protection is a must, and children and observers should be kept away from the area.

cal covers, heat registers, and other easily removable hardware or fixtures you don't intend to paint. Take down drapes or curtains and store them in another room.

After surfaces are washed, scraped, and taped, you are ready to start edging. Various edging tools are available, from small rollers to flat pads. The old standby brush is still the most popular. However, good brushes are expensive and hard to clean thoroughly enough to make them last very long. One new alternative is to use inexpensive, disposable brushes, such as 3M's Newstroke Snap-Off Paint Brush. The brushes are inexpensive enough so you can just throw them away instead of cleaning them, yet they provide a smooth, even coating with all types of paints, stains, and varnishes. Available in various sizes, they can be used for any type of paint job.

APPLICATION METHODS

Should you spray or brush exteriors? Much depends on the nature of your siding. Spraying will cover about any surface. If you prefer not to spray, you can brush paint on clapboards, board-and-batten, tongue-and-groove, and other wood sidings. Shakes can be painted or stained using brushes or painting pads.

1. REMOVING OLD PAINT

A prime example of how home paint prep work is becoming both easier and safer, Safest Stripper from 3M emits no toxic fumes and doesn't even require gloves. The remover goes on easily with a brush, stays active for hours, and cleans up with just water.

After old paint softens, it can be removed with a scraper or with 3M's Heavy-Duty Stripping Tool, which uses replaceable stripping pads. Flexible stripping pads also are available for curved surfaces. When using a scraper, guard against gouging the wood.

In this project, the final residue of the old finish and the stripper were removed using final stripping pads. Designed to replace 0-Grade steel wool, the 3M pads offer the advantages of not rusting, shredding, or leaving metal fragments in the wood.

Photos: 3M

2. SANDING FOR NEW PAINT

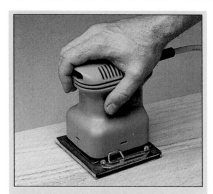

Reciprocating or finishing sanders can be used in final prep stages or to brighten up weathered wood. Use progressively finer sandpaper. Rotary sanders, commonly used on metal surfaces, should be avoided on wood because they won't follow the wood grain.

Newer sanding aids, such as 3M's Hand-Ease Sander and Flexible Sanding Sponge, help make short work of prepaint preparation. Especially useful on smaller projects, the Hand-Ease Sander comes with easily replaced refills that are adhesive-backed.

This Flexible Sanding Pad from 3M also conforms to curved surfaces, and is made with a premium abrasive that lasts longer than ordinary sandpaper. Available in three grades, it can be used dry on indoor or outdoor projects or, to reduce dust, for wet sanding.

Rolling paint on is a preferred method inside the home. It is fast, easy, and less messy than spraying. Spattering still can occur if you roll too fast; that's why you need drop cloths. Apply the paint evenly and smoothly, avoiding thin spots or sags due to over-application.

Try to set up good lighting so you can monitor coverage. Even so-called "one-coat" paints may leave spots where the old color shows through. If you are planning a drastic color change, two coats will probably be necessary anyway, especially if you want to cover up a dark color with a lighter one. (In this case, you may save money using a primer as the first coat, rather than applying two coats of finish paint.)

After the paint dries, inspect the job before removing tape and other protective coverings. If you're satisfied that another coat is not necessary, remove the masking tape, drop cloths, and/or newspapers. If you want to use rollers or other equipment again, clean them thoroughly. Use water for latex paint, paint thinner or mineral spirits for oil-based materials. ❧

3. SAVING TIME WITH TAPE

Using masking tape saves time and produces a neater job. Use around moldings, baseboards, windows, and fixtures. Also tape drop cloths or newspapers to baseboards to fix them in place. Try to remove the tape as soon as you are finished painting.

When you don't want to remove tape right away (between coats, for example), you can use special blue Long-Mask masking tape available from 3M. The special tape is sunlight stable and will come off cleanly even if left on surfaces for up to seven days.

If you need to mask for major painting jobs, you might benefit from a tool developed for professionals. The Hand Masker tape applicator marketed by 3M has a cutoff blade for straight cuts and handles tapes in a variety of widths. It costs about $35.

4. SELECTING PAINTING TOOLS

Select the right brush by asking for help at the store, if necessary. A new concept in brushes is a low-cost brush from 3M that is discarded after use. It was developed after research showed that most home painters use a brush only once before discarding it.

The Newstroke Snap-Off brush has handles of recycled paper that do not contain plastic or wood or metal ferrules. Available in five sizes, the brushes not only save on clean-up time, but allow you to avoid using chemical paint solvents or large volumes of water.

If cleaned after every use, paint rollers can be reused many times. Use warm, soapy water for latex paint and rinse thoroughly. For oil- or solvent-based paint, use paint thinner or mineral spirits. Always allow rollers to dry thoroughly before storing them.

READING OLD PAINT

Reading the old paint on your home's siding can often tell you a great deal about the condition of your home. Any sign of peeling, cracking, or blistering in the existing paint will not only mean more work in getting ready to re-paint, but also can reveal structural problems that need to be corrected before you paint.

Alligatoring. Cracks and scales that make the paint look like alligator hide can be caused by paint applied over dirty or oily surfaces; too many coats of paint; finish coats applied over wet undercoats; too much oil added to an oil-based paint; latex paint applied over an old glossy oil-based paint, or an incompatible pigment or vehicle in the paint. Regardless of cause, alligatored paint should be removed.

Bleeding. Pitch and sap can continue to ooze out of knots in natural wood siding for years. Remove any paint left on these spots, then seal knots with clear or white-pigmented shellac or other knot-sealer preparations, such as B-I-N or KILZ. As soon as the sealer dries, follow up with your regular exterior primer.

Blistering. Usually caused by painting over a damp or wet surface, it can also can be the result of painting in direct, hot sunlight. Remove the loose paint, and repaint only when the surface is dry if you are using oil-based paint. (Latex paint can be applied to damp wood when necessary.)

Checking. Similar to alligatoring, but with smaller, less prominent cracks, checking may simply mean the coating is old. Paint loses flexibility over time and is less able to withstand the normal shrinking and swelling of wood which occurs with changes in moisture and heat. In any case, all loose paint should be removed.

Mildew. A fungus which grows on dirty, moist, shaded surfaces, mildew looks like spots of dirt, but won't wash off with a detergent. To remove and kill mildew, wash with a solution of 1 part household bleach to 3 parts water, or with a commercial mildew-removal product. When repainting, use mildew-resistant paint. Mildew means excessive moisture, which may lead to rotting siding, sills, or studs. Cut back any shrubs that may be keeping air and light away from the siding. If the moisture is coming from condensation inside the house, take steps to reduce this problem.

Peeling. The cause of peeling paint is usually moisture under the coating. Peeling around windows, doors, or corners may indicate poor flashing or caulking. Eventually this also can lead to rotting trim, siding, studs, or sills. To remedy the problem, be sure that all cracks and joints are caulked and that flashing is properly installed over doors and windows, or anyplace where rainwater can enter.

If peeling is more general and on larger areas, moisture is likely migrating through the walls from inside the house. This can be caused by high interior humidity levels and lack of effective vapor barriers. Working from the exterior, three methods can reduce the problem: 1) installing siding vents or wedges to let moisture escape without being absorbed by the siding, 2) using latex paint, which can breathe and let moisture out, or 3) making sure soffit and attic vents are adequate.

If the problem is severe, more drastic measures may be needed. Interior vapor barriers are the best solution. Normally these are installed between studding and interior wallboard or panels, and may be part of the insulation facing material or a separate plastic sheet. If you are tearing out walls to add insulation or put in new wall paneling, be sure to install a tight vapor barrier. If you are not remodeling, you may gain some vapor protection by using vinyl or aluminum foil-type wall coverings.

The best way to keep interior moisture levels down is with adequate venting and dehumidification. If interior humidity can be kept under 40%, moisture migration problems are greatly reduced or eliminated.

Rust Stains. If rust streaks show below siding nails, the siding was not put on with galvanized or aluminum nails. Streaks will show up again if the problem is not corrected. One way to correct the problem is to remove the old paint, then seal the cleaned nailheads with a stain killer before repainting. Another solution is to countersink the nails and fill in the holes with wood putty. For repair or replacement, use only aluminum or galvanized nails.

Rust running down the walls under flashings indicates that the galvanized material has lost its zinc coating. In this case, the flashing will have to be replaced or sealed so it won't rust further. Use a rust-treatment product as a primer under regular paint.

MECHANIZED PAINTING

*New Technology Can Help Take The
Drudgery Out Of Home Painting*

Recently the home painter has been able to reap the benefits of mechanization with what some call "power painting." Applying the paint still requires human hands, but mechanical devices speed the task by keeping a steady supply of paint pumped to the painter. Painting can be mechanized a number of ways, but the most common is airless spraying for exterior work and power rolling for interiors.

Many types and sizes of airless units are available to suit a particular job, and offer several advantages over compressor units. First, they cost less. Airless units don't require a compressor, air tank, or pressure regulator. Motors or gasoline engines are smaller for airless units than for compressor-type sprayers of similar capacity.

Second, airless sprayers produce less overspray and less air pollution. Their tighter spray patterns give you more control, so you can keep the paint directed onto intended surfaces instead of into the air or on other surfaces. Because airless sprayers spray only paint, not air, delivery is faster.

On the other hand, power rollers are preferred for interior work because even airless sprayers will produce some spattering and drift inside the house. (The exception is in workshops, where the smaller sprayers are often used, and where shielding and spatter problems are no worse for sprayers than for aerosol spray paints.)

CHOOSING EQUIPMENT

Here are some factors to consider when looking for power sprayers or rollers, depending on the types of jobs you plan to tackle.

Odd Jobs And Projects. For smaller exterior jobs and workshop projects, consider a "cup gun." These electric units are self-contained and carry a small quantity of paint, varnish, or stain in their own reusable canister. They rely on a small piston to atomize paint under very high pressure, so safety considerations are important.

Cup guns are made in various sizes and grades, depending on the thickness of material to be sprayed. Read the label descriptions carefully before you buy one. A unit designed to apply thin stains and varnishes may not handle thick latex paint. The size of the nozzle also is important, depending on the kind of material you plan to spray. Careful cleaning after each use prolongs the unit's life.

Fences, Decks, And Floors. To step up from the basic cup gun, consider a larger unit which offers a suction tube as well as a cup. These can draw paint directly out of a can or backpack reservoir, eliminating the problem of frequent cup refills on larger projects. Also, the cup gun head (without the cup full of paint) is much lighter and easier on the arms.

HVLP: A SPRAY EQUIPMENT BREAKTHROUGH

An important consideration on finishing projects inside the home is air quality. Many finish materials emit fumes that can be troublesome, not only for the applicator and members of the household, but for the environment as a whole.

As a result of these concerns, a new type of sprayer has been developed — the HVLP (high-volume, low-pressure) system. This revolutionary new painting technology employs high air volume instead of high air pressure to propel the spray. The Wagner Finecoat System equipment shown at left, for example, operates at only 4 pounds per square inch (psi), yet generates enough volume to handle most finishing tasks around the home and shop. The equipment can help you apply stain, varnish, urethane, lacquer, or enamel paint more safely, especially indoors.

Because the turbine-driven unit offers an 86% transfer efficiency, it results in a minimum of overspray, waste, mess, and air pollution. Getting set up with an HVLP unit costs $180 to $190.

Cup guns generally handle both exterior latex and oil-based paints, but thicker materials may have to be thinned. The guns can be somewhat noisy, sounding very much like a large buzzer.

Exterior Painting. For larger jobs, a diaphragm (or hydraulic) unit is best. These combine an electric motor and hydraulic pump with a reservoir of a gallon or more of paint, plus a hose and spray gun. Usually you also can add a suction tube which allows you to pull paint directly out of a gallon can or 5-gallon bucket.

More costly than cup guns, these units offer higher capacity, quiet operation, and the versatility of power rolling inside, as well as airless spraying outside. Roller handles, various extension tubes, and other accessories also are available. With extension tubes, many home painting jobs can be done without using ladders, a definite safety factor.

Interior Walls. If you are only interested in painting interior walls, you also have a number of alternatives for mechanizing rolling. Besides the heavy-duty sprayer/roller combinations, there are several lower-powered units designed just for rolling. Some are even cordless.

These devices push a steady supply of paint to the inside of a special perforated roller. Controlled by a trigger or thumb button, you call for more paint whenever you need it, and just keep rolling. The job goes fast, because there is no need to keep dipping your roller into the tray. Also, you avoid the mess and spills that trays can cause.

With accessory extension tubes, you can roll paint onto ceilings without using scaffolding or ladders. Accessory painting pads also are available for nonstop edging.

This self-contained cup spray gun is designed for thin materials, such as stains, sealers, and light-bodied paints. A tiny carbide piston pump operating at high speed draws paint into a cylinder, then atomizes it by expelling it at very high pressure through a nozzle. This Wagner 120 Power Painter costs about $60.

A heavier-duty cup gun from Wagner, the 355E, offers a suction tube option, as well as a 1-quart paint container. Used with a 1-gallon backpack reservoir, it offers easy spray pattern control and more convenient and safer use on ladders. It can be used with latex paints, as well as thinner materials, and sells in a kit with accessories for around $170.

If you plan a heavy painting schedule, high-performance hydraulic diaphragm pumps offer quiet operation and the option of either airless spraying or power rolling. This equipment can handle a wide variety of latex and solvent-based applications both inside and out. The cost of this 425 system is around $360; you also may find it available for rent.

SAFETY AND MAINTENANCE

Any sprayer can be dangerous. Paint from either cup spray guns or diaphragm pumps comes out of the spray tips under enough pressure to be injected through the skin, potentially creating a serious injury.

Power painting equipment is increasingly designed to be as safe as possible and still get the job done. Follow safety precautions for each machine, and use the built-in safety features for the equipment. Never remove nozzle guards or allow children or irresponsible persons to operate the equipment, and always follow the safety procedures necessary with any electric tool.

Thorough cleaning is essential to assure proper operation and to prolong the life of power painting equipment. Pistons and pumps are made of finely machined, close-tolerance parts. They will last a long time if cleaned properly and completely after each use. Incomplete cleaning of sprayer hoses can lead to frequent nozzle plugging. ❧

This cordless paint roller system may offer the ultimate in interior painting convenience. The battery-operated unit is designed to apply up to 30 gallons of paint on one set of four D-cell batteries, and can help you apply a gallon of paint in as little as 20 minutes. The cost of this Power Roller from Wagner runs around $60.

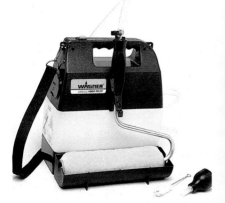

Note: The painting equipment shown here is from Wagner Spray Tech, an innovator in developing painting equipment for both homeowners and contractors. To get more information on how to mechanize painting projects, check your local hardware or home center store, or contact Wagner directly by writing 1770 Fernbrook Lane, Minneapolis, MN 55447, or calling 800/328-8251 (612/553-7000 in Minnesota).

KITCHEN ENGINEERING

*Once You Know What To Do, Kitchen
Remodeling Can Become A Matter Of Details*

Kitchen remodeling can present a dilemma. It's the planning stage that can gridlock a project, especially when your kitchen appears to have insurmountable problems that need to be solved—challenges that no one else seems to have to deal with. But, once you have figured out what you can do, the battle is more than half won. The rest of the project becomes a matter of detail and following the plan step by step.

So if you have a box full of rough sketches or have been moving cutouts around on grid paper like a chess game, take heart from Jim Krengel, owner of Kitchens By Krengel in Minnesota's Twin Cities. His entire life has been devoted to planning and executing kitchen projects. He will tell you that there is a solution for every kitchen in every home, no matter how unique yours appears to be.

Once you have a master plan, says Jim, remodeling your kitchen can be a rewarding experience that will add substantially to the value of your

GETTING TO A MASTER PLAN

How do you get started? Here are some pointers Jim Krengel has gathered from his years of thinking about what can be done to improve kitchen spaces:

• Any kitchen remodeling project starts with you. So start by making lists to find the path that will lead to what you want, and keep them handy. Make a list of everything you dislike about your present kitchen. Then make another list of everything that you like. Make still another list of everything you think you would like in your new kitchen. Next consider how much you can spend, and how long you intend to stay in the home. Decide whether you are remodeling for the long term and for yourself, or for resale.

• Realize that the kitchen of the '90s is an entirely different place than it was even a generation ago. No longer does Mom spend the whole day there preparing three meals. Instead, it might be Dad working in the kitchen, or one of the teenagers. Today's kitchen is a room that must cater well to several members of the family, and often at the same time.

• Don't expect it to be easy. The kitchen is the most challenging space in the home to design and equip properly. One reason is that, because there are so many products available, many kitchen dealers must limit themselves to only certain products. For example, it is estimated that there are more than 660 different cooktop units available. To help narrow your choices, the services of a certified kitchen designer are especially valuable.

• To get qualified help, consider contacting a member of the National Kitchen & Bath Association (NKBA). These dealer members have established spotless reputations. Or, look for a Certified Kitchen Designer (CKD). To get this title, a designer must have firsthand experience in designing, planning, and supervising kitchen installations, and must pass a rigorous exam.

• One advantage of using certified kitchen designers is that they can look at your kitchen with fresh eyes. Designers are trained to find creative approaches to using space. To avoid being obligated to buy the products they handle, you can ask them to prepare plans for you for a fee. You can ask them to help you as much, or as little, as you need.

• Avoid "new kitchen fever" the same way you would try to avoid "new car fever." Too often prospective kitchen remodelers get so caught up in a look, style, or finish that they forget to ask if their plan will solve their current kitchen's problems. Double-check your lists. Also, don't simply accept a kitchen plan that a designer offers; make sure it is the plan you really need.

• Try to avoid equipping your kitchen with components that may be trendy and quickly go out of date. Time goes by fast, and the hottest-selling look today may be out of fashion tomorrow. Make selections according to lasting qualities. If you want, add a little trendiness in expendable items, such as curtains and accessories, that can be changed easily to bring your kitchen back into style.

home. Investments in kitchen remodeling will almost always generate more payback than any other home improvement project when it comes time to sell.

Experienced designers agree that any kitchen project boils down to challenges, creativity, and compromises. To get a glimpse of what the professionals go by, see **The 31 Rules Of Kitchen Design** at the end of this section. One good way to get ideas is to ask to review a designer's portfolio of before and after floor plans. You'll get an idea of what others have done to overcome design challenges. While none may look exactly like yours,

they will confirm that you don't have to settle for remodeling in an uninspired way. They also will show that, no matter how bad you think your kitchen is, and no matter how tight the space might be, there is always hope.

Redoing a kitchen can be expensive. National averages run from $15,000 to $25,000. But, rather than give up on a kitchen you want, or lower the quality of cabinets and equipment, here are some ways you can stay within a limited budget.

1. Tear out the old kitchen counters and cabinets yourself.

2. Remove plaster and lath from the

walls, if the project calls for it.

3. Serve as a carpenter's helper during installation, working under the direction of the installer.

4. Install your own cabinets by having an installer work with you the first day to get you started.

5. Take over the decorating, painting, wallpapering, or staining of new unfinished wood trim. (You must, however, finish your part on time or you may hold up the job.)

6. Design your kitchen to be remodeled in stages, finishing the primary work area first, then adding cabinets and other features later as you can afford them.

CLOSE-UP: THE GLOBAL KITCHEN

As one example of what can be done, here is a close-up look at a very smart kitchen remodel originally inspired by the Paul Simon album *Graceland*. The singer-songwriter collaborated with a South African group to create a fresh new sound that kicked off a trend known as "world music." This led the folks at Ralph Wilson Plastics Company to launch what they called The Global Design Challenge, an effort to apply the same kind of international teamwork to kitchen and bath design.

They assembled designers from around the globe and challenged them to demonstrate how outdated home spaces could become models of up-to-the-minute design. Each space, an actual kitchen or bath, was assigned to a team of two designers. Jim Krengel teamed up with Australian Rina Cohen on one tired, older kitchen. Armed with a fresh new line of Wilsonart laminates, they redesigned it into one with true personality, functionality, and international style. The results are brimming with fresh ideas.

THE CHALLENGE

The owners of this small home are a married couple in their mid-thirties, with no children. Both are employed, and enjoy working together in the kitchen, especially when throwing dinner parties on weekends.

The couple's wish list for their new kitchen included better space planning, with particular emphasis on making the room functional for two cooks working simultaneously; a large main sink with an additional preparation sink; expansive countertop space at varied heights; accessible storage for small appliances, dishes, and glassware; an eat-in breakfast nook; and a large pantry.

THE SOLUTION

In creating a more spacious kitchen, designers Jim Krengel and Rina Cohen had two factors in their favor. They could move the washer and dryer out of the kitchen area, and could extend the kitchen slightly into an adjoining room, and onto the adjacent patio slab.

Visually, they used a sophisticated but colorful approach. The kitchen has always been the center of activity in the house, and the new environment is one its occupants will enjoy spending time in.

Rina Cohen, a member of the Design Institute of Australia (MDIA), has extensive interior design experience. She worked for several prominent architectural and interior design companies before opening Rina Cohen Interiors, Melbourne, in 1987.

Jim Krengel, a certified kitchen and bath designer (CKD and CBD), is the president and owner of Kitchens By Krengel, Inc., St. Paul and Minneapolis. He is a renowned design lecturer and a past president of the National Kitchen & Bath Association.

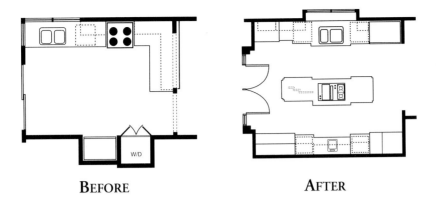

BEFORE   **AFTER**

This typical L-shaped kitchen was somewhat drab and ill-suited to the lifestyle of its owners. After remodeling, vastly increased countertop space surrounds the central island. The two cooks can work in separate areas, or meet at the island.

*NOTE: The booklet **An Adventurer's Guide To Kitchen and Bath Design**, The Global Design Challenge, contains examples of another kitchen and two baths that represent a synthesis of ideas from different cultures. For a copy, write to Ralph Wilson Plastics, 600 South General Bruce Dr., Temple, TX 76504. For complete plans of the Global Kitchen shown, send check or money order for $15 to Working Drawings, 1900 Westridge, Irving, TX 75038.*

Repeated staggering of cabinet and countertop height adds interest and function to the two work areas. This side features a small preparation sink, a convection microwave, a dishwasher, and expansive countertop space. All plumbing fixtures and fittings are American Standard, and the appliances are GE Monogram.

The separate work areas are divided by the central island. The island top is Gibraltar Solid Surfacing in Silverpine, with inlays of Wilsonart Decorative Laminate in Metalwork. This end of the kitchen looks into the dining room. Cooktop controls are accessible from either side of the island.

The far end of the island forms a breakfast nook, opening to the patio area. The second work area includes a large sink, a microwave and a conventional oven, and a second dishwasher, handy after large dinner parties.

CRAFTWOOD Two-Tint Veneer in Pepperdust

CRAFTWOOD Two-Tint Veneer in Clear Teal

WILSONART Decorative Laminate in Pebble

WILSONART Decorative Laminate in Metalwork

GIBRALTAR Solid Surfacing in Silverpine

Florida Tile Natura® Terra Series in Desert Beige

Florida Tile Natura Terra Series in Ocean Green

Hartco Burnside Plank Flooring in Light Oak

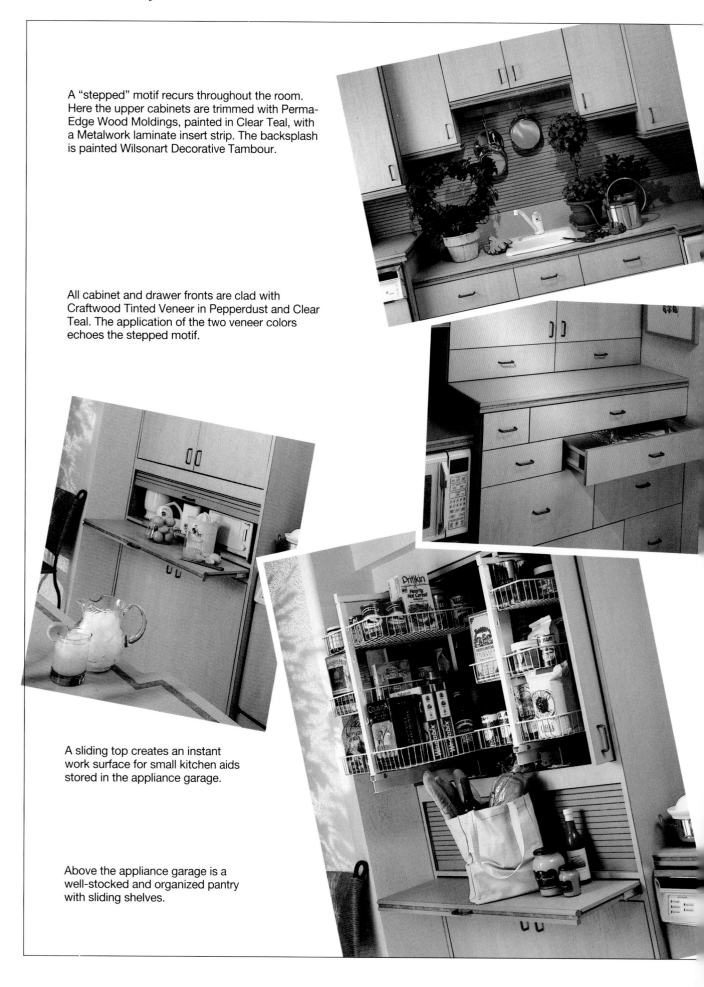

A "stepped" motif recurs throughout the room. Here the upper cabinets are trimmed with Perma-Edge Wood Moldings, painted in Clear Teal, with a Metalwork laminate insert strip. The backsplash is painted Wilsonart Decorative Tambour.

All cabinet and drawer fronts are clad with Craftwood Tinted Veneer in Pepperdust and Clear Teal. The application of the two veneer colors echoes the stepped motif.

A sliding top creates an instant work surface for small kitchen aids stored in the appliance garage.

Above the appliance garage is a well-stocked and organized pantry with sliding shelves.

The raised counter above the oven is ideal for food just out of the oven or nearby microwave. This area steps down to a lower counter, used mainly for food preparation.

Countertops are clad with Wilsonart laminate in Pebble. The edge treatment is painted Perma-Edge Wood Molding, with an insert strip of Metalwork laminate.

The kitchen floor is the Natura Terra Series, in Desert Beige with an Ocean Green accent, from Florida Tile. The dining room floor is Hartco Burnside Plank in Light Oak.

Corners of the island top reflect the recurring stepped motif. The island pedestal, like the top insert, is Metalwork laminate.

TIPS ON GETTING STARTED

Jim Krengel advises that the best way to start a kitchen project is to think through the factors that can help get you on the right path. Ask yourself the questions below before you start, not after that new kitchen is in and you begin to have second thoughts:

1. Who does most of the cooking, and what are their special needs?

2. Do other members of the family help in food preparation, serving, or cleanup?

3. Do you use your kitchen to cook from scratch or mostly heat up food?

4. If you want to use the kitchen for socializing, what adjustments will you need to make?

5. If you open up your kitchen to other rooms, what about noise, odor, and lighting?

6. If you often eat in the kitchen, can you incorporate existing formal dining space to gain a bigger kitchen and larger eating area?

7. Do you entertain often, and what other secondary activities will the kitchen be used for?

8. Do you want it designed only for yourself, or do you want it to appeal to future buyers of your home?

STICKING TO THE BUDGET

A creative plan can help you save money and still get you a super kitchen. Example: One couple's original plan was a U-shaped kitchen with generous storage and counter space, but the price estimate was more than the budget would allow. Jim Krengel found that the couple didn't need three entire walls of storage, and that a garden window seemed more important. He changed the U to an L-shape, with the cooktop installed in an island. This created a tighter "work triangle" that saves steps. The sink and window were moved into a corner, while a new pair of double windows added a southern exposure, overlooking a garden. The area behind the sink provided a generous ledge for plants. The changes not only improved the

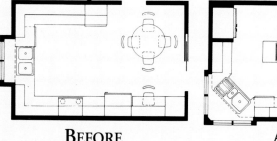

BEFORE

AFTER

The original plan above was designed as a U-shape, with three walls of cabinets. The revised L-shaped plan features an island cooktop with a command-post view of the front hall. The sky windows over the island helped augment the light from corner windows, giving the kitchen an open, airy feeling.

kitchen's look, but brought the costs down well within the budget.

Note: An excellent idea resource is the booklet *Smart Solutions For Problem Kitchens: A Professional's Portfolio*, produced by Maytag in cooperation with Jim Krengel. The step-by-step guide covers kitchen appliances, cabinets and materials, and provides tips on costs, references, payment schedules, and how to live through a kitchen remodeling experience. For a copy, send $2 to Maytag, Consumer Information Center, Newton, IA 50208.

THE 31 RULES OF KITCHEN DESIGN

These rules are adapted from guidelines established by the National Kitchen & Bath Association. Though in abbreviated form, you can use them as a handy checklist for evaluating your own kitchen remodeling plans.

1 At least a 32" walkway at all entrances.

2 No doors that interfere with work centers, appliances, or counters.

3 At least 42"-wide work aisles; at least 36"-wide passageways for one cook or at least 48"-wide passageways for two cooks.

4 At least 144" wall cabinet frontage for kitchen under 150 sq. ft; at least 186" for larger kitchen.

5 At least 60" wall cabinet frontage within 72" of primary sink centerline.

6 At least 156" base cabinet frontage for kitchen under 150 sq. ft.; at least 192" for larger kitchen.

7 At least 120" drawer frontage for kitchen under 150 sq. ft.; at least 165" for larger kitchen.

8 At least five storage areas to improve accessibility and functionality.

9 At least one functional corner storage unit unless no corners are planned.

10 At least 15" to 18" clearance between countertop and bottom of wall cabinets.

11 At least 32" countertop frontage for kitchen under 150 sq. ft.; at least 198" for larger kitchen.

12 No two primary work centers separated by full-height, full-depth tall tower.

13 At least 24" countertop frontage on one side of sink, 18" on other side. If second sink, at least 3" counter space on one side and 18" on other side.

14 At least 3" counter space from edge of sink to inside corner of countertop. Or, at least 18" counter space from edge of sink to inside corner of countertop if return counter space is blocked.

15 At least two waste receptacles planned.

16 Edge of dishwasher positioned within 36" of edge of one sink. At least 21" of standing room next to dishwasher.

17 At least 36" continuous countertop provided for preparation center.

18 At least 15" counter space on latch side of refrigerator, or on either side of side-by-side refrigerator. Or at least 15" landing space no more than 48" across from refrigerator.

19 At least 9" counter space on one side of cooking surface, and 15" on the other, for open-ended kitchen. At least 3" clearance at an end wall for enclosed configuration.

20 No cooking surface below an operable window unless window is 3" or more behind appliance and more than 24" above it.

21 At least 15" landing space next to, or above, oven if appliance door opens into primary traffic pattern. A 15" landing space no more than 48" across from oven acceptable if appliance does not open into traffic area.

22 At least 15" landing space above, below, or next to microwave.

23 Bottom of microwave between counter and user eye level (36" to 54" off floor).

24 All major appliances used for surface cooking have ventilation system, with fan rated at 150 CFM.

25 At least 24" clearance between cooking surface and a protected surface above. Or at least 30" clearance between cooking surface and an unprotected surface above. Microwave hood combination appliance may be lower than 24" at back wall.

26 Work triangle between stove, refrigerator, and sink totals 26' or less.

27 No major traffic patterns cross the work triangle connecting primary centers.

28 Minimum 24" wide x 12" deep counter/table space for each seated diner.

29 At least 36" walkway space from counter/table to any wall or obstacle behind it if area is to be used to pass behind seated diner. Or at least 24" space from counter/table to any wall or obstacle behind it, if area is not to be used as walk space.

30 Window/skylight area equal to at least 10% of total square footage of separate kitchen, or of a total living space which includes kitchen.

31 Ground-fault circuit interrupter protection for all receptacles within 6' of water source. Smoke alarms installed.

The —
LOG CABIN

*A Beginner's Guide To Techniques,
Shortcuts, And Hands-On Schools*

A log cabin in the wilderness, constructed by hand in the traditional American pioneering spirit, has long been the dream of many of us trapped in urban areas. Granted, very little true wilderness is left, and much more is involved than simply cutting down a few trees and stacking the logs together. But, yes, you can build your own log cabin, and there are many ways to do it, depending on the amount of work, time, and money you wish to invest.

Today, log homes are built in a wide variety of styles, shapes, sizes, and materials, and can range from a simple log cabin in the woods to an ultra-sophisticated log mansion, complete with multiple-car garage and basement. Log homes offer a welcome break from 2x4s and sheetrock. They also provide more than an aesthetic beauty; these energy-efficient structures are cooler in the summer and warmer in the winter than "stick-built" homes because of the bulk of the wood used in their construction.

Another major advantage is that they are owner friendly. Scraping, painting, and other general maintenance required for standard houses aren't necessary in the upkeep of a log home. But the biggest advantage for most people, regardless of the size of the log home being built, is the cost. Even log homes custom-built by a log crafter sometimes cost less than homes built with standard construction.

This northern Minnesota log cabin was built by a graduate of the Great Lakes School of Log Building near Ely. Students, opposite, learn the basics in ten days.

Log homes also help conserve natural resources. Fewer trees must be cut for the construction of some log homes than for standard houses of similar size because the wood doesn't have to be milled. The energy needed to mill the wood also is saved. And the logs used are often the "thinning" trees normally removed to allow better-grade trees to grow to saw-log size.

BUY OR DO IT YOURSELF?

There are several routes to acquiring a log home. The simplest, but most expensive, approach is to purchase a manufactured log home and have it erected by the manufacturer. Of the more than 500 log home producers in the industry, manufacturers make up more than 90%. The logs in these homes are normally milled to precise shapes to ensure tight, secure homes.

Log home manufacturers and/or their representatives can be found in the advertisements of many magazines, and even in the Yellow Pages (also see page 61).

Or, if you prefer, you can have a log crafter build the home of your dreams. These are usually custom homes built to the purchaser's designs. If you would like a small hunting or naturalist's cabin in the woods, but don't have the time or inclination to build it yourself, this might be the best choice.

Another option, involving more work but a great deal less cost, is to purchase a "kit" log home, which is essentially a package of precut logs. Kit homes are available in a variety of types. You can buy only the milled logs if you want to cut your own notches and window/door openings. You can purchase the walls only, along with the spikes, gaskets, and other items needed. Or, you can purchase the "shell," which includes the walls, roofing, doors, and windows. The last

First-timers can learn the various skills required to assemble a log structure by attending a hands-on construction course. Such training prepares them to tackle their own log cabin project, from stripping to cutting joints, photo directly above, to stacking and fastening, photo bottom right. Students at Ron Brodigan's school actually assemble a log home during the course, learning the special building methods and the proper use of the tools required to perform them. Teamwork is an essential aspect of the construction process, photo center right, and students live and work together as a crew.

is the complete package — everything mentioned above, plus flooring and all the other materials needed to finish the log structure. Before you buy a manufactured home kit, however, be absolutely sure you understand exactly what will be furnished.

In most instances, you select a home from a drawing and floor plan. Shells and complete kits come with numbered logs and a set of instructions. These do take quite a bit of effort in construction, but with patience and a little skill, you can build your own log home fairly easily.

You can, of course, create a log home from "scratch." This does offer a number of advantages. The first is the financial savings. This also may be the only practical method if you wish to build a hunting camp in an isolated area where construction materials can't easily be trucked to the site. Even if you don't have access to logging timber, you can usually purchase logs. If you're in an area that is commercially logged, you can contract with the company. Some builders living near national forests have bought "thinning logs" quite economically from the Forest Service.

If you have no logging or log-cabin-building experience (very few first-time builders do), books and magazines are available which illustrate the building tactics used across the country. Many of these discuss construction techniques for various log homes and offer photos of the finished product.

LESSONS FROM THE PROS

To get a head start on log building, you also can attend a school that teaches those very skills, such as Ron Brodigan's Great Lakes School of Log Building. Located in Isabella, Minnesota — in the heart of the Superior National Forest, 30 miles from Ely, and just a few miles from the Boundary Water Wilderness Area — the school offers a series of 10-day

The mystique of building with logs draws students from all walks of life to special schools (see page 60 for listings). Participants at the Great Lakes school near Ely, Minnesota, top two photos, learn the scribe-fit, round-log technique. Log cabins built by previous graduates, photo left, vary in styles and interior finishing, above. They provide the housing for succeeding log-building classes.

LOG-BUILDING SCHOOLS

Great Lakes School of Log Building. Discussed in text. Contact office (at 3544½ Grand Ave., Minneapolis, MN 55408; 612/822-5955) or the school (at 570 C.R. 2, Isabella, MN 55607; 218/365-2126) evenings during courses.

Palmquists' "The Farm." A weekend workshop with emphasis on blending new tools and technology with old Scandinavian methods. Taught by Jim Palmquist, experienced woodsman and former University of Wisconsin extension agricultural agent.

Housing available. Contact Palmquist's "The Farm," Box 134, River Rd., Brantwood, WI 54513; 715/564-2558.

Sun Country School of Log Building. A two-day introductory seminar and two-, three-, and four-week sessions available on log and timber frame construction. No housing is available, but camping arrangements can be made. Contact the Sun Country School of Log Building, HCR 71, Box 1960, Timber, OR 97144; 503/324-0922.

courses: six weekdays and two full weekends. Courses start in late February and run through late July.

Students participate in a hands-on log-building experience, learning all the techniques needed to erect their own log homes. These skills include log felling and handling, site preparation, and chain saw maintenance and safety. Students also gain a thorough knowledge of how to use all the necessary hand tools. The first blisters on soft hands often appear while peeling logs with drawknives, shovels, and spuds.

All the homes constructed by the Great Lakes School are built using the scribe-fit, round-log technique, a traditional north country log-building style. Done properly, it provides one of the tightest fits possible, plus a beautiful appearance. The log structures at the school, all built by former students during courses, reveal Ron's excellent craftsmanship and the skills he passes along to his students.

The exciting, yet exacting, part of the course is the actual scribing and fitting of the logs for a structure. Students learn how to create a perfect "chinkless" fit using adzes, axes, chain saws, chisels, and gouges.

Other skills acquired include installation of doors and windows, square-notching tie beams and the second-floor structure, and the construction of trusses and other roof systems. Lone log-lifting systems, log-building history and techniques, wood characteristics, and proper and safe use of preservatives and coatings are also subjects of discussion. The skills taught on chain saw use alone are worth the price of the course.

A diverse group of students sign up for the log-building courses. Attending one recent course were Fred, a general business manager, and Diane, a social worker from Minneapolis, who were typical of the couples studying log building with a desire to create their own home "for one of these days when we want to get away from it all." Jonathan, a college graduate from Minnesota with a small-business degree, saw the possibility of starting his own company. Mark, a surveyor from New York, wanted to learn how to build his own hunting cabin. Other students included a veterinarian from Texas, a youth group coordinator, a college student, and a computer design operator.

Women and men over the age of 18 are welcome to attend the course; younger students must be accompanied by an adult. No construction or carpentry background is needed, nor any unusual strength — just a strong desire to learn log building. The students stay in rustic wood-heated bunkhouses with fireplaces. Freshwater wells, privies, and an old-fashioned Finnish sauna are available. RV spaces (without hookups) are also available.

Regardless of whether you're looking to build a small cabin in the woods, a second home on your favorite lake, or perhaps even a first home, consider logs. And if you really want the enjoyment of owning a traditional-style American home, consider building your own. The drawings on the pages 62 and 63 will give you an idea how one type of log cabin goes together. ❧

Note: **The Complete Guide To Building Log Homes**, *a 400-page book by Monte Burch, provides an overview of the entire log construction process, from buying land and drawing floor plans to choosing log styles and joinery. Autographed copies are available from Outdoor World Press Inc., Dept. D, P.O. Box 278, Humansville, MO 65674-0278. The hardcover edition is $31.45 postpaid; paperback copies are $18.45 postpaid.*

LOG CABIN CONTACTS

To help make a survey of what is available, you can contact the log home companies listed below. They are all members of the Log Homes Council; many of them grade logs under an approved grading system.

Air-Lock-Log Company, P.O. Box 2506, Las Vegas, NM 87701 (505/425-8888).

Alta Industries, Route 30, Box 88, Halcottsville, NY 12438 (914/586-3336).

Amerlink, P.O. Box 669, Battleboro, NC 27809 (919/977-2545).

Appalachian Log Homes, 11312 Station West Dr., Knoxville, TN 37922 (615/966-6440).

Appalachian Log Structures, P.O. Box 614, Ripley, WV 25271 (800/458-9990).

Asperline, RD 1, Box 240, Route 150, Lock Haven, PA 17745 (717/748-1880).

Authentic Homes Corporation, Box 1288, Laramie, WY 82070 (307/742-3786).

Beaver Mountain Log Homes, RD 1, Box 32, Hancock, NY 13783 (800/233-2770).

Brentwood Log Homes, 427 River Rock Blvd., Murfreesboro, TN 37129 (615/895-0720).

Cedar Forest Products Company, 107 W. Colden St., Polo, IL 61064 (800/552-9594).

Cedarlog Homes, P.O. Box 232, Hubbard, OH 44425 (216/534-0182).

Century Cedar Homes, P.O. Box 24013-306, Winston-Salem, NC 27114 (919/922-2914).

Colonial Structures, 7817 National Service Rd., Suite 502, Greensboro, NC 27409 (919/668-0111).

Eastern Log And Timber Homes, P.O. Drawer 948, Summersville, WV 26651 (304/872-5300).

Garland Homes By Bitterroot Precut, 2172 Hwy. 93 N., P.O. Box 12, Victor, MT 59875 (800/642-3837).

Gastineau Log Homes, Old Hwy. 54, Route 2, Box 248, New Bloomfield, MO 65063 (800/654-9253).

Greatwood Log Homes, Hwy 57, P.O. Box 707, Elkhart Lake, WI 53020 (715/876-3378).

Hearthstone, Route 2, Box 434, Dandridge, TN 37725 (800/247-4442).

Heritage Log Homes, P.O. Box 610, Gatlinburg, TN 37738 (800/456-4663).

Hiawatha Log Homes, P.O. Box 8, Munising, MI 49862 (906/387-3239).

Honest Abe Log Homes, Route 1, Box 84, Moss, TN 38575 (615/258-3648).

Kuhns Bros. Log Homes, RD 2, Box 406A, Lewisburg, PA 17837 (717/568-1422).

Lincoln Logs, Riverside Drive, Chestertown, NY 12817 (800/833-2461).

Lindal Cedar Homes, Justus Div., Box 24426, Seattle, WA 98124 (206/725-0900).

New England Log Homes, 2301 State St., P.O. Box 5427, Hamden, CT 06518. (800/243-3551).

North American Log Homes Systems & Country Kitchens, S. 8680 State Rd., Route 240, Colden, NY 14033 (800/346-1512).

Northeastern Log Homes, P.O. Box 46, Kenduskeag, ME 04450 (800/624-2797).

Northern Products Log Homes, P.O. Box 616, Bomarc Rd., Bangor, ME 04401 (207/945-6413).

Precision Craft Log Structures, 711 S. Broadway, Meridian, ID 83642 (208/887-1020).

R&L Log Buildings, RD 1, Shumway Hill Rd., Guilford, NY 13780 (607/764-8275).

Rapid River Rustic, P.O. Box 8, Rapid River, MI 49878 (906/474-6427).

Real Log Homes, P.O. Box 202, Hartland, VT 05048 (603/643-6200).

Rocky Mountain Log Homes, 1883 Hwy. 93 S., Hamilton, MT 59840 (406/363-5680).

Satterwhite Log Homes, Route 2, Box 256A, Longview, TX 75605 (800/777-7288).

Shawnee Log Homes, Route 1, Box 123, Eilliston, VA 24153 (703/268-2243).

Southland Log Homes, P.O. Box 1668, Irmo, SC 29063 (800/845-3555).

Stonemill Log Homes, 7015 Stonemill Rd., Knoxville, TN 37919 (615/693-4833).

Tennessee Log Buildings, P.O. Box 865, Athens, TN 37303 (800/251-9218).

Timber Log Homes, 639 Old Hartford Rd., Colchester, CT 06415 (800/533-5906).

Town & Country Cedar Homes, 4772 US 131 S., Petoskey, MI 49770 (616/347-7255).

Ward Log Homes, 39 Bangor St., P.O. Box 72, Houlton, ME 04730 (800/341-1566).

Wholesale Log Homes, P.O. Box 177, Hillsborough, NC 27278 (919/731-9286).

Wilderness Log Homes, Route 2, Plymouth, WI 53073 (800/237-8564).

Wisconsin Log Homes, P.O. Box 11005, 2390 Panaperin Rd., Green Bay, WI 54307 (800/678-9107).

Woodland Homes, P.O. Box 202, Lee, MA 02138 (413/623-5739).

Yellowstone Log Homes, 280 N. Yellowstone Rd., Rigby, ID 83442 (208/745-8108).

TECH NOTES: BUILDING A LOG HOME

The illustrations here show the approach one builder, Whispering Pines Log Homes of Verndale, Minnesota, uses to assemble a log home. The large cutaway shows a typical log home section built over block foundation walls, using conventional 2x8 sill plates (anchored to block with 8" anchor bolts), 2x10 rim joists, and 2x10 floor joists. The half-log starter course goes over 1/2" CDX plywood subflooring around the perimeter. Tongue-and-groove logs are fastened together with 10" spikes, and with 3/4" caulked dowels at joints. Acrylic caulk is used for "chinking." The final course is also half logs, over which a conventional rafter system is built and covered with 15-lb. builder's felt or tar paper, and shingles of your choice. The company has built over 200 log homes since 1981 using logs of white spruce, western red cedar, and red pine. For more information on the firm's approach, write Whispering Pines Log Homes, Box 99, Hwy. 10 West, Verndale, MN 56481 or call (218) 631-1974.

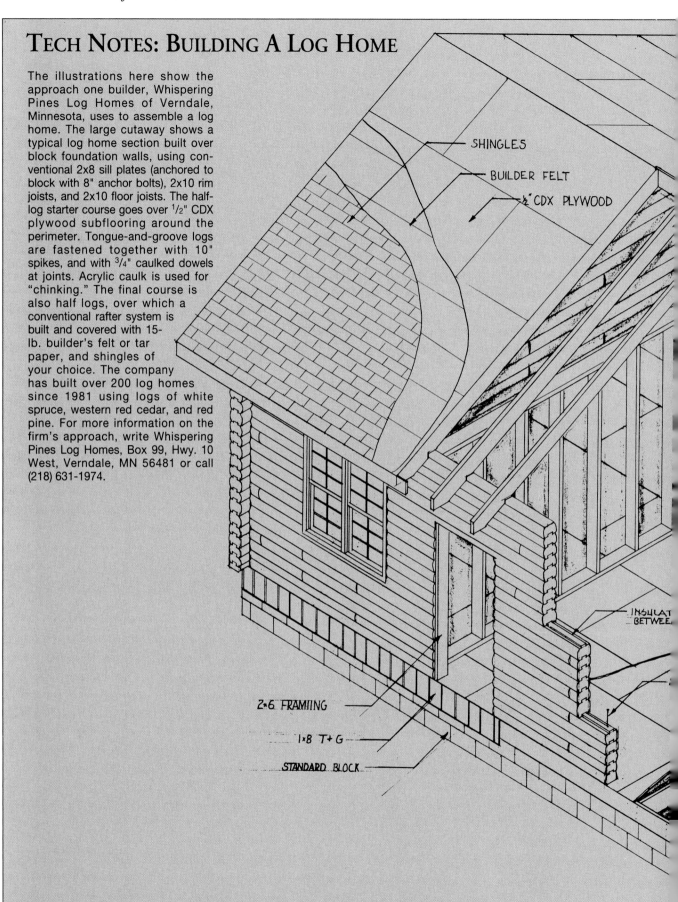

SHINGLES

BUILDER FELT

½" CDX PLYWOOD

INSULAT BETWEE.

2×6 FRAMING

1×8 T+G

STANDARD BLOCK

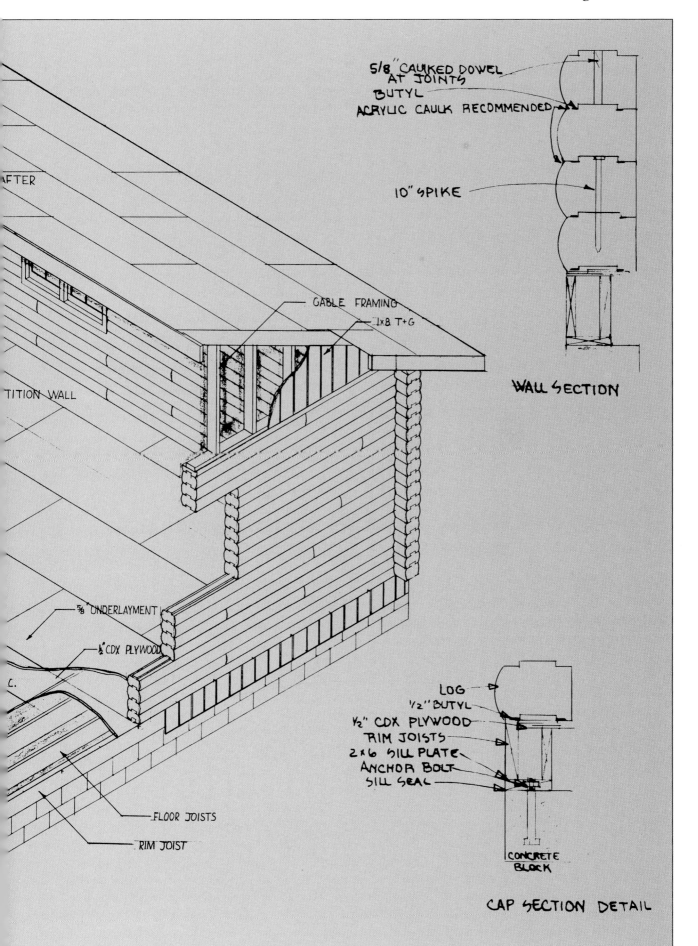

5/8" CAULKED DOWEL AT JOINTS
BUTYL
ACRYLIC CAULK RECOMMENDED

10" SPIKE

WALL SECTION

RAFTER

GABLE FRAMING

1x8 T+G

PARTITION WALL

5/8" UNDERLAYMENT

1/2" CDX PLYWOOD

C.

FLOOR JOISTS

RIM JOIST

LOG
1/2" BUTYL
1/2" CDX PLYWOOD
RIM JOISTS
2x6 SILL PLATE
ANCHOR BOLT
SILL SEAL

CONCRETE BLOCK

CAP SECTION DETAIL

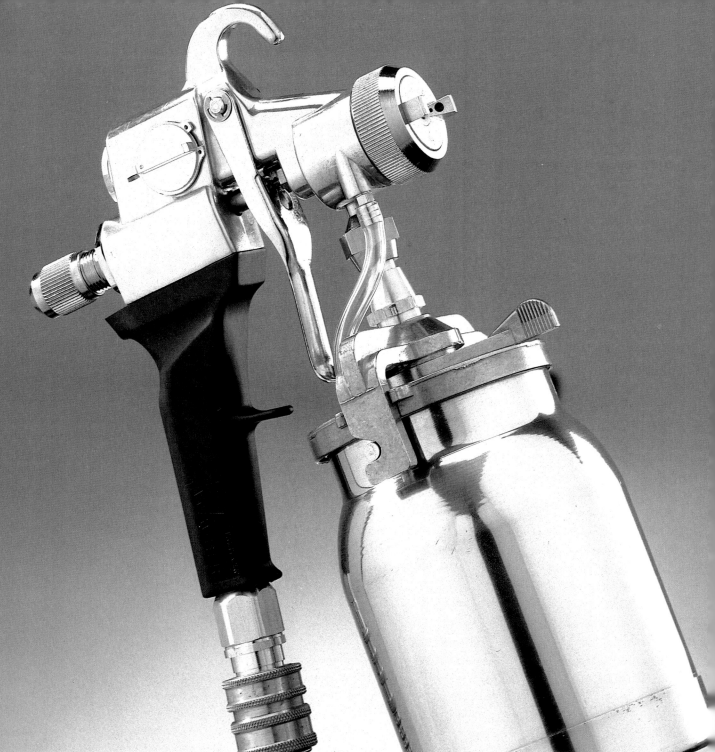

Home
PROJECT OUTFITTERS

*Renting Tools And Equipment Can Offer A Pile Of
Advantages — Even If You Can Afford To Buy*

The homeowner trying to install ⅝"-thick drywall on a ceiling by himself, the one trying to carry squares of shingles up a light-duty ladder, or the one trying to drill ½" holes in concrete block all have something in common.

Each could get the job done faster, better, and most likely safer, if they had the right equipment. A drywall lifter, a shingle conveyor, and a hammerdrill, respectively, would make

10 Reasons To Consider Renting

Why rent? There are a raft of reasons to consider renting tools or equipment, rather than buying, and some of them aren't obvious. Check the following list, and you may heading to the nearest rental store sooner than you think.

1 Preserve Working Capital. While there are some tools almost no one would rent — a ¼" drill you can buy for $12, for example — the most obvious advantage of renting is that you don't have to buy tools or equipment you might need only occasionally. This is an advantage whether you don't have the cash, you need the money for other things, or you simply don't want to tie up cash in equipment.

2 Tackle Impossible Jobs. Often you can take on jobs yourself with rented equipment that would otherwise be out of the question. Instead of hiring the job done, you can sometimes save yourself up to $50 an hour by doing the job yourself — and that's after-tax money you are saving.

3 Maintenance Problems. When you rent, you find equipment ready to go, cleaned, and serviced. While most stores expect you to bring equipment back in good shape, you generally don't have to worry about routine maintenance like greasing, changing oil, and sharpening blades.

4 Get Jobs Done Faster. The fear that rental equipment may not be as good as what you might buy is a myth. Rental equipment, by the nature of its use, must be extra sturdy to stand up. It also must be easily maintained and operated. If a rental store has it, chances are excellent it will be both adequate for the job and reliable.

5 Get Jobs Done Better. Often renting equipment can let you do a better job because the tools you use are either of higher quality than you would otherwise use, or they are capable of producing better results. For example, you could hand-trowel a basement slab, but a power concrete trowel gives you a smooth finish in half the time.

6 Get Jobs Done Safely. This one is so important, it may even be the main reason to rent. The average rental store has been in business 18 years, and has had enough time and experience to identify and remove unsafe equipment. Also, renting industrial-quality equipment, such as jacks, ladders, and scaffolding, can often help make your projects safer.

7 Avoid Packed Garages. If you buy a gas welder for a welding project, you have to store it when you get done. Most of us have too little storage space to start out with,

and a garage crammed to the rafters is the rule, not the exception. By renting, you automatically preserve storage space.

8 Gain Advice And Access. Rental store operators will usually make certain you know how to use a piece of equipment before you leave the store. It's in their own interest to do this, and their advice can be worth money. Stores also will generally have specific accessories you might need for a job readily available, saving you time running around.

9 Check Buying Plans. Even if you think you might want to buy a tool or piece of equipment, renting still can make sense. By renting, you can gain experience with an item you plan to buy, before you make the big purchase. You can increase your own buying savvy by confirming that the item will do the job, and that accessories you are considering are worthwhile buying.

10 Avoid Borrowing Problems. Shakespeare advised hundreds of years ago to "neither a borrower nor lender be." This can be another main reason to rent, even if you know someone who has what you need. More often than not, borrowing tools and equipment from friends, neighbors, or relatives eventually causes hard feelings.

each of their jobs twice as easy.

If you couldn't afford a tool years ago, you had to go out and buy it, hire someone who had the equipment, or simply try to make do. Today, however, the tools of virtually any trade are available for rent— from a simple wrench to a full fleet of machinery for specialized jobs.

The 12,000 rental firms in North America ring up close to $20 billion

in rental fees every year. Some 3,500 of them belong to the American Rental Association, with headquarters in Moline, Illinois. James Irish, executive vice president of the group, reports that tools for home projects have never been more accessible to do-it-yourselfers; each year hundreds of hardware stores, home centers, and other firms are joining the traditional rental store in making labor-saving

devices available by the hour, day, week, or month.

Rental store managers say do-it-yourselfers are continually amazed at what is available in rental stores. They say watching customers make new "discoveries" that open up project

Renting can put cutting-edge tool innovations, such as the advanced HVLP low overspray gun from Wagner, opposite page, to work on your next project.

RENTAL EQUIPMENT YOU CAN HIRE

High-pressure sprayers are ideal for preparing a house for paint or removing mildew. Safer than higher pressure models, this Aqua Storm 1255 delivers 1,250 psi, has a foot switch, a safety trigger lock, a 35' cord, and a 26' high pressure hose.

HVLP (high volume, low pressure) sprayers are catching on fast to reduce overspray in finish work on cabinets, railings, doors, louvers, and shutters. This Wagner Capspray gun hooks to turbine units to boost spray precision and cut masking and clean-up time.

Steamers help remove wallpaper without solvents, detergents, or chemicals. This Power Steamer has an 8" x 11" steamplate which weighs only 8 oz. for less arm fatigue, a 6' power cord, and a 12' steam hose. It works for 1¾ hours on one fill.

Photos: Wagner Spray Tech

possibilities is part of what makes the rental business exciting.

The association keeps a finger on rental items most in demand by homeowners and contractors (see chart opposite). However, the most commonly discovered "wonder machines" make up an entirely different list. These amazing, work-saving devices can turn those occasional nightmarish jobs into a piece of cake. Here's a sampling:

Sandblasters. The smaller versions resemble a hand garden sprayer and hold up to 40 lbs. of sand. Hooked to an air compressor of at least 2 hp, they blast away at just about anything that needs cleaning. You can clean up brick, remove rust from metal, strip away paint and spills from concrete, even get a grained effect on wood, or an etched effect on glass. Usually the sand, which can be recycled, will be available where you rent the sandblaster. They rent for about $20 for a half day, $40 for all day.

Concrete Saws. Picture what a miserable job removing a section of con-

crete could be without one of these units, which are designed to make straight cuts on wall surfaces or floors. Hand-held saws are available with gas and electric power. Portable models are powered by a gas engine, and can cut up to 4½" deep. Hand-held saws rent for about $5 an hour, or $25 a day.

Sod Cutters. These machines save the day if you need to remove old sod or cut your own new sod. You drive these self-propelled machines like a rototiller, and you usually can set them to cut either 12" or 18" widths, depending on the model you rent. The depth of cut is generally adjustable from just under the surface to as deep as 2½". They rent for about $40 a day.

Impact Hammers. Not all jack hammers require big air compressors; electric hammers are available to help back-busting sledge hammer work. Breaker hammers let you dig, demolish, and break, using only regular household current. Rotary hammer drills are ideal for drilling round holes in concrete. They rent

for about $5 an hour, or $30 a day.

Trenchers. Digging a 2' trench in loose sand is one thing; digging one through compacted clay can spell misery. Power trenchers let you dig trenches quickly and easily for electrical, telephone, gas, or water lines. Other uses include making trenches for small footings or underground sprinkler lines. Smaller trenchers dig 4½", 5", or 6" wide, and to 2' depths. The compact, gas-powered machines work well for snaking through areas where bigger machines can't go or would ruin landscaping. They rent for about $12 an hour, or $50 a day.

Power Compactors. These gas-powered machines make compacting surfaces before pouring concrete a one-man operation. Often called "vibra plate" compactors, they can be used to work around foundation walls, footings, curbs, gutters, and streets. Relatives of this machine include the concrete vibrator (used to eliminate air bubbles and get uniform density when pouring concrete walls) and the power tamperer. You can rent them for about

$10 an hour, or $55 a day.

Stump Removers. Stumps are a tough problem, but these machines get rid of them fast. They don't actually remove the entire stump, but chip it down to about a half foot below ground level. Rotating teeth do the work while you make the adjustments with a hand crank. Chips can be thrown away, or saved for mulching. These rent for about $50 a day, less per day for longer periods.

Pressure Washers. Whether you want to wash off the siding on your house, clean up muddy equipment, or tend to other tough cleaning jobs, these devices will amaze you. The portable units deliver pressures from 1,000 to 3,000 pounds per square inch (psi). If the job involves grease and oil, or other chemicals, you may opt for a steam cleaner to blast away the grime. These units rent for about $8 an hour, or $50 a day.

Floor Strippers. If you need to take up an old tile floor in a large room, this machine can save you hours of tedious work. An electric motor vibrates a sharp blade at the front end to loosen asphalt tile, linoleum, adhesive, paint accumulations, or other buildups. With some models you can remove covering from as much as 2,000 square feet of floor in one day. The strippers rent for about $7 or $8 an hour.

Wallpaper Steamers. Most models hold 2½ gallons of water, and deliver steam at 14 psi to loosen layers of old wallpaper of any kind. A pan-shaped steamplate, connected to a boiler, is held against the wall. The escaping steam loosens the paper in about 5 seconds. These machines operate with household current, and many have both low-water and high-pressure safety shutoffs. They rent for about $15 a day.

There are literally dozens of specialty tools that you may not know you can rent. Tools that are lifesavers, if you need them, include log splitters, brush chipper-shredders, floor nailers, tile cutters, posthole diggers, engine hoists, power drain augers, concrete mixers, power sprayers (including ceiling texture sprayers), floor sanders, fence stretchers, lead melting pots, pipe cutter-threaders, hydrostatic testers, welders, water pumps, fork lifts, and even parking lot strippers to put lines on your driveway.

Sometimes simple convenience can make renting a worthwhile option. In one trip to a rental store you can get all the small, specialized tools you need for jobs like drywalling, carpeting, tiling, roofing, or even taking an engine out of a car. Some stores now will even mix up a yard of concrete and put it in a special trailer for your small jobs, like pouring sidewalks or steps. It might cost you about $70 if you can get the trailer back in a couple of hours or so.

James Irish also points out that rentals can add to life's pleasures after the work is done. Rentals of party supplies, such as tables and chairs, canopies, even pig roasters, are booming. The same is true with rentals of recreational equipment, such as RVs, camper trailers, canoes, tents, and camping and exercise gear.

Need a dance floor? They're available, as are mini-donut machines, should you need them. Some stores even specialize in everything you might need to put on a carnival at your church or school, and will supply you with games, rides, dunk tanks, as well as sno-cone, cotton candy, and popcorn machines.

What are reasons not to rent? You might think twice about renting an item that is either very low in cost, or something that you need to use every couple of weeks. Accessiblity

is a major rent-or-buy factor. One of the challenges is to try to accurately estimate just how often you will eventually use something if you buy it. Then you have to balance that against what your money could be earning elsewhere. ❧

Note: The rental rates listed are approximate and may vary for specific types of equipment by store, city, or state. For exact rates, call rental stores in your area; they usually are listed in the phone book under Rental Service Stores and Yards. Also check listings for home centers, as well as paint, wallpaper, tile, and hardware stores.

THE RENTAL STORE TOP TEN

The listing below shows the top-volume rental equipment, as reported by member firms of the American Rental Association.

Homeowners
1. Floor, Carpet Equipment
2. Lawn Mowers and Edgers
3. Trailers and Trucks
4. Garden Tillers
5. Painting Equipment
6. Sewer Augers
7. Chainsaws
8. Ladders
9. Automotive Tools
10. Tables and Chairs

Contractors
1. Air Compressors
2. Trucks
3. Tractors and Backhoes
4. Electric Hammers and Drills
5. Trenchers
6. Power Augers
7. Generators
8. Pumps
9. Concrete Equipment
10. Electrical Tools

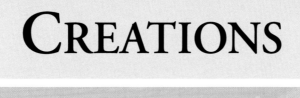

CREATIONS

AN ARTIST'S TOUCH

Continuing Adventures In Uncovering
The Creative Potential Of Wood

Tom Rauschke sees wood differently than most of us. To him, that chunk of tree limb you just threw into your fireplace, or the piece of 4x4 that you just tossed in the trash, may have contained an unlimited number of hidden treasures.

While the rest of us may stop occasionally to admire an especially nice piece of wood, or even feel guilty about using it for a project, we may be hard-pressed to explain what the possibilities might be. But Tom knows. He has been uncovering the beauty hidden inside wood for nearly 17 years.

His approach is to take chunks of wood into his Wisconsin workshop, select one, and create something from it that the world has never seen before. He then sells what he makes for anywhere from $50 to $3,000, though he says one of his creations will generally fetch a price somewhere between $400 and $800.

Tom started creating with wood in 1976, soon after he received a degree in fine arts from the University of Wisconsin, Milwaukee. During college he found he enjoyed the trimming of ceramic pots after he finished throwing them, an act of creating by removing materials instead of adding them. "A subtractive process," he calls it. Later, he and his wife rented their first house, which coincidentally had a small workshop attached to it. The tools inside the shop were an invitation to Tom to begin experimenting with the subtractive process using wood.

"My workshop is probably much simpler than many people would expect," he says. "I don't have fancy equipment, just some pretty conventional tools, such as a band saw, drill press, belt sander, and a Forties-era Delta-Rockwell lathe." He has a workbench where most of his cutting work is done, but he does most of the more intricate carving and sanding

Most works by Tom contain a contribution by his wife Kaaren. **Wood Stork Rookery,** *above, is 15" high, with a large egg turned from spalted elm and birds from hickory and ebony. An embroidered pin set in ebony fits inside a smaller egg (foreground) that fits inside larger egg. Opposite,* **Cutting Garden** *is made of black walnut, done for a theme exhibit titled "Artists Examine The Backyard." It has a working garden gate, boardwalk, and pond in the center with glass that shows off embroidery of ornamental goldfish, which can be taken out and worn as a pin. Miniature tulips and daffodils can be "picked" to create floral bouquets in tiny turned vases. The center flips over to reveal a snow-covered winter garden. The piece sold for $2,000.*

sitting in a comfortable chair.

To make his delicate creations, Tom relies mostly on "found" local hardwoods, using the patterns and colors of the wood like a painter uses a palette. In a good year he will create about 40 finished pieces; he estimates he has turned out some 700 pieces, like those shown in the photos, during his unique career. Some take just a day, some a week, others a month or more. His wife, Kaaren Wiken, contributes by adding finishing touches using the medium of embroidery.

Since he began, Tom has picked up a few tricks that help him in his projects. For example, he says good hardwoods, such as hickory, oak, and black walnut, work the best. "Hickory is used for axe handles and it's a very sturdy wood. Elm works well, too. But cherry and apple, the way I use them, have a tendency to crack." He has learned to first begin his cutting on the thicker bottom part of his shapes, then work up the increasingly thinner walls that have more of a tendency to break near the top.

His source of wood is as close as his own woodpile. "Because we heat our home with wood, I order unsplit firewood from local suppliers. Usually every truckload brings dozens of possibilities. I keep selected chunks in separate piles by species in my barn or three-car garage. The idea is to keep them out of the elements, but not let them dry out too fast. I try to let the wood cure for at least a year after the tree has been cut, but I still have chunks from about six years ago. Sometimes I paint the ends of a piece to slow down the drying process. But the chunks are about two feet long,

Tom Rauschke describes himself as an artist who uses wood as a medium. His 11½"-high **Pond In Forest,** left, is of black walnut with inner bowl of turned ash. A pair of swans of ebony and holly sit on a glass pond which displays embroidery of turtles. The cattails are also black walnut. The foot-high **Anasazi Bowl,** top on opposite page, was turned out of hickory. Its nesting bowls, three separate turnings from the same piece of wood, rest inside on special keys that center them. The center bowl has a cover supporting a ladder of padouk wood. The miniature pots were turned inside and out on Tom's Delta lathe using miniature lathe gouging tools. **Cattail Vase,** above, is 11" high and is also of hickory, with cattails of black walnut. The embroidered butterfly, set in ebony, can be worn as a pin.

so if the ends do crack six inches or so in, there is still a good piece of wood between."

Tom doesn't have any half-completed projects laying around; he almost always focuses on one piece from start to finish. He doesn't start with the wood, either. He starts with a vision in his head of what he wants, then finds the piece of wood that will work just right. He mounts the chosen wood on a lathe faceplate, rough-shapes the outside, then turns out the inner part of his bowl-like pieces. Often a knot or other characteristic of the wood will suggest an alteration to his original idea. "You have to keep flexible," he says.

If you would like to try your hand at this kind of woodworking, Tom suggests experimenting to see how you can combine your imagination with the qualities of wood. "Wood is so wonderful; you can make it into any shape you find inside the tree. You just have to figure out a fast and reasonable way to remove the parts you don't want. That's why I like turning on the lathe; removing excess wood for me is like a painter preparing a canvas. I start with a heavy log and when I'm done I have a delicate

thin-walled shape, along with a big bag of wood chips."

When completed, Tom's projects demonstrate what can be done using lathe turning, cutting, carving, marquetry, and inlay. "To me," he says, "lathe turning brings order out of chaos. My major goal is to showcase the character and color of wood grain. My shop work is not a mechanical process; it's an adventure of exploring, inventing, and evolving."

His philosophy toward wood may be why he refers to his shop-studio as XN-TRIX, which is pronounced literally as "eccentrics." While most of Tom's and Kaaren's work is spontaneous, they create commissioned works, too. You can write them about their unique creations at XN-TRIX, W. 625 Little Prairie Rd., Palmyra, WI 53156-9621. ⁊

CREATIVE CARVING TECHNIQUES

Nest Goblet began life in an elm tree. Tom first shapes the piece on the lathe. The base, still joined to the original wood chunk, is clamped into a vise. After tracing a pattern, cutting is done with a fine-bladed jeweler's saw.

Tom smooths and slightly bevels the cut edges with a pair of chip carving blades that are sharpened so one is used to push, the other to pull. The piece is sawed from the original chunk and work is completed on the base.

After all work is done, the final step is to smooth the wood with 220-grit sandpaper, then apply a finish coating of 100% tung oil. The tung oil brings out the grain and color, and also helps preserve the wood.

SENSATIONAL SUN ROOMS

America Is Discovering Some Brand-New Ways
To Brighten Up Life At Home

Sun room fantasies come in different forms for different people. For some, the dream comes as a vision of a sun-filled breakfast nook. For others, it is a wide, open room off the kitchen used for chatty entertaining. Still others envision a sun-drenched greenhouse area where vegetables or orchids flourish in spite of raging blizzards or ice storms outside.

Fortunately, new technology and construction techniques are converging to help make sunnier home spaces a reality for more homeowners than ever before. Sun rooms, in addition to skylights and bay windows, are fast becoming a favorite way to brighten home interiors at any latitude. A sun room can be incorporated into virtually any home, either existing or new construction, in nearly any size or configuration. The options are nearly endless.

For example, you can inset a sun room into your roof line, or project it from a side of your home. You can use one to enclose a ground-level deck, whether it is at the back, front, side, or corner of your home. You can use one

to cover a cantilevered balcony. It can be all glass — ceiling and walls — or glass walls only. Depending on its orientation, you can use existing walls of your home or end walls of either glass or wood. Where floor to ceiling walls are not a good option, you can use a partial base wall.

SUN ROOM OPTIONS

The demand for more inside sun has led marketers of premium franchise home building packages, such as Lindal Cedar SunRooms, Seattle, Washington, to develop special sun room packages for installation by contractors or do-it-yourselfers. The company reports that the demand for sun rooms is just beginning to be tapped. One reason for the appeal is that the attractive structures blend in well with any home exterior, including wood siding, shakes, stucco, stone, or brick. Another is that a south-facing sun room, with built-in solar heat storage, can help earn its "energy keep" in cold weather.

To take advantage of passive solar heating, a sun room needs thermal mass of some sort for heat storage and an automatic or manual method of

transferring heat. If the room is not open to the inside of the home, heat transfer can be managed manually, simply by opening and closing doors or windows between the sun room and the rest of the home. A fan-assisted transfer system also can be used to automatically move collected heat into the home and cold air out to the sun room. A back-draft damper can be installed to automatically close and seal out cold drafts at night.

On the other hand, if heat gain in summer is more of a concern, a number of options are available to reduce unwanted solar heat, including Low-E and Heat Mirror glazing options. These newer glass panels recognize different solar wave lengths and allow light to enter while blocking out heat. Low-E glazing improves energy efficiency by 50% and Heat Mirror by 150%. Both also screen out the ultraviolet rays that fade carpeting and furniture.

Fans also can be used in sun rooms to circulate fresh air and vent excess hot air. For the best cross ventilation, they are set in end walls, opposite an opening window or door. In addition,

One couple converted this little-used and neglected second-story deck into a luxurious glass and cedar sun room.
The space, shown opposite, is now a favorite family gathering place.

BEFORE

AFTER

a shading system on the exterior can be used to block out as much as 75% of the sun's heat before it reaches the interior. The exterior shades offered by Lindal, for example, can be manually lowered to cover the roof, or both the roof and sidewalls, of a sun room. In high-heat areas, cedar shade panels can be substituted for part of the overhead glass, or the room can be built without roof glass, or with skylights instead of large glass panels.

SUN ROOM DECISIONS

The cost of a sun room can vary from about $45 to $100 per square foot, while the total cost for one 12' x 16' might range from about $13,000 to $15,000 or more.

The first consideration is what type of structural material you want: metal or wood. Your choice may depend on your budget. The framework system that holds the glass in Lindal sun rooms is more expensive than metal, but it is of premium-grade, clear-grain Western red cedar from the company's own sawmill in Canada. The company emphasizes the wood's natural beauty, as well as its superior insulation value, which is rated at 2,000 times greater than aluminum.

To begin mapping out what you need, you can pick from a good half-dozen basic sun room designs, then mix and match an almost endless array of options. The two basic architectural styles are curved eave or straight eave. In curved-eave designs, 3'-wide glass bays wrap gracefully from roof to sidewall without any seams or beams. The absence of cross-bars provides an expansive view from anywhere inside, standing or sitting, and reduces interior shadows.

Straight-eave designs, on the other hand, present tall, angular lines and can be matched to a wide range of roof pitches. With this style, the overhead

CHOOSING A SUN ROOM DESIGN

One of two basic architectural styles, Lindal's curved-eave version, above, is called The SunCurve. It adds striking, graceful lines to a home's appearance. A sun room that takes advantage of existing exterior walls, like Lindal's SkyWall, upper right, is a natural for brightening a kitchen. Second-story sun rooms, like the Lindal SunDormer, right, provide a stylish way to bring extra light and warmth into upstairs rooms.

glass is joined to the straight vertical sides using the bird's-mouth joint (a carpenter favorite) to achieve joints that are both watertight and airtight. Beyond choosing either a curved or straight-eave design, you have your choice of several more options, as follows:

Using Existing End Walls. If you have a deck off one side of your home, with existing walls on three sides, you could install a sun room without end walls of its own. This style is often used to brighten a kitchen, and it can sit on its own base to the exterior side of the kitchen counters. Such sun room designs can be inset into your home to a depth of 3' to 6', and built to conform to the existing pitch of your roof.

Using Glass Walls Only. In some situations glass roof panels may not be appropriate or desirable — in high snow-load areas, or in extremely hot climates, for example. In these cases, you can opt for a conventional roof and use glass wall panels to open up a wide-vista view. Generally you will be able to choose from glass walls that are either 4' or 6' high.

Using All-Glass Corners. If you have an open corner outside your home, using a glass-paneled hip roof is an excellent way to brighten your home's interior from two sides. This option offers a creative solution for the many situations where a straight roof will not fill the bill. A corner between the house and garage, for example, can be turned into an enjoyable, sundrenched space for year-around use.

Using Second Levels. When thinking of where you could put a sun room, don't ignore second stories. They can help open up upstairs spaces and can be virtually any size, with or without end walls, depending on the opportunities your home pre-

SunWalls, upper left, is the name Lindal gives its sun rooms that use glass walls but a traditional roof. They are a good choice in extremely warm or cold climates. Taking advantage of an open corner on a home, Lindal's SunCorner, left, opens up the interior from two sides. If you don't go with the basic curved-eave design (see SunCurve, opposite page), you can choose the flat glass design, such as Lindal's Straight Eave model, above.

Tech Notes: Installing A Sun Room

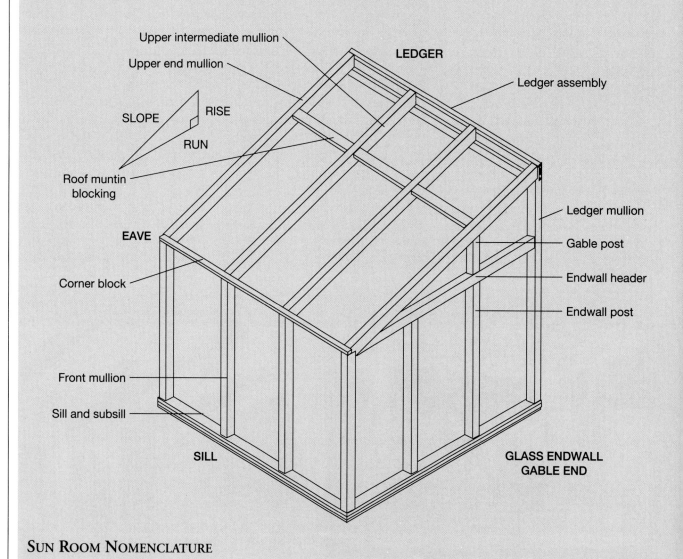

Upper intermediate mullion

Upper end mullion

LEDGER

Ledger assembly

SLOPE · RISE · RUN

Roof muntin blocking

EAVE

Corner block

Ledger mullion

Gable post

Endwall header

Endwall post

Front mullion

Sill and subsill

SILL

GLASS ENDWALL
GABLE END

Sun Room Nomenclature

sents. A second-story sun room can replace existing dormers, or be projected out from the roof. End walls, if needed, can be of wood or glass.

To decide how to incorporate a sun room in your home, first study literature available from manufacturers like Lindal. An excellent publication providing an overview of current offerings is Sun Spaces, available for $3.95 from Home Buyer Publications, 4451 Brookfield Corporate Dr., Suite 101, Chantilly, VA 22022 (800/826-3893). Stanley Tools also has a home plan-

ning kit with a grid board that can be ordered by calling 800/648-7654. Computerized home planning kits also are available from Abracadata, P.O. Box 2440, Eugene, OR 97402 (503/342-3030).

Once you decide where your sun room can go and how you want it to look, there are several other options to consider. For example, besides the Low-E and Heat Mirror glazing options mentioned, you also have a choice of tempered thermal glass, bronze- or gray-tinted glass, or lami-

nated overhead safety glass. Window choices abound. For ventilation, you can use vertically opening casement windows in the glass walls, or horizontally opening awning windows. Or you can choose the three-dimensional, bay-window-like garden window that has become a favorite for use in front of a kitchen sink.

If your sun room will have a traditional roof, you also may want to consider skylights with thermal glass and continuous weatherstripping to bring in more light and allow excess heat

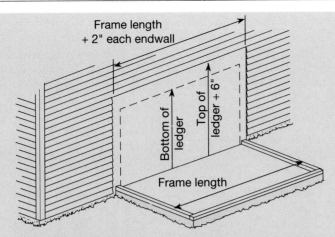

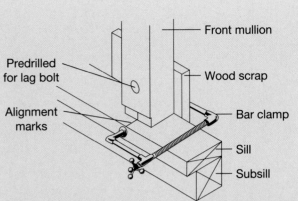

Site Prep. To attach a sun room to a home, the siding must be cut away and a proper foundation prepared. The vertical surfaces and the floor or foundation of the home must be plumb, level, and square. Some doors may require special sill preparation. Installation manuals give exact dimensions needed, depending on the size and style of the sun room.

Mullion Assembly. When attaching mullions, precision work is important. The inside face of the mullion must be flush with the inside of the sill. A C-clamp and block of wood can be used to keep the mullion from drifting while you drill pilot holes and install the lag bolts.

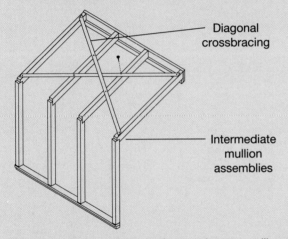

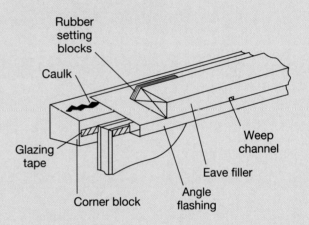

Temporary Bracing. After the front and upper mullions are installed, they can be kept in alignment with temporary diagonal bracing. Because the panels that go between the mullions are glass, exact spacing must be maintained at all points. It takes two or three workers to assemble the unit.

Roof Glazing. After the front wall glass panels are in place, the glass roof panels are installed. Careful attention is required to maintain a tight water seal between the components that join roof and walls together. Both caulking and glazing tape are used, along with metal flashing and a cedar eave filler.

to escape. Your choice of doors can include swinging, sliding, hinged, or French-style.

THE D-I-Y OPTION

If you are an experienced do-it-yourselfer, installing a sun room is fair game. Lindal, in fact, offers a special 60-page how-to manual that outlines the procedure step by step. More complex designs may call for at least some professional help, but you still may be able to save money by doing some of the work yourself.

Ground-level installations require a foundation that meets local codes. In some areas slab-on-grade foundations are allowed, while in others frost-depth footings are required under a crawl space foundation. With Lindal sun rooms, the components can be delivered as a knocked-down kit, ready for assembly by you or a professional crew. Parts are precut, predrilled, and prenotched for flashing, and all pieces are labeled, including the cedar framing and trim. Most kits can be assembled in a few days by a skilled worker and a helper or two. 🌢

Note: For more information about sun rooms in the U.S., contact Lindal Cedar SunRooms at 4300 South 104th Pl., P.O. Box 24426, Seattle, WA 98124 (206/725-0900). A 28-page SunRoom plan book is available for $2. In Canada, contact the company at 10880 Dyke Rd., Surrey, British Columbia V3V7P4 (604/580-1191).

FURNITURE MOSER-STYLE

Measured Drawings For An Elegant Trio Of Tables

If you are a woodworker, a would-be woodworker, or simply a homeowner who wants to furnish your home in good taste, here's a tip.

If you want something to stare at and drool over for a few months, send for Thos. Moser Cabinetmakers' colorful and inspiring 80-page catalog. The seventh since Tom and Mary Moser set up a custom furniture shop some 20 years ago, it's guaranteed to elevate your thinking about furniture to new heights of excellence.

Some of the 84 pieces of furniture inside will tend to remind you of early American Chippendale, Hepplewhite, and Sheridan. Other pieces will recall the simple furniture of the Shakers. Still others appear to offer a hint of Danish, or the Mission Style of the Arts and Crafts movement at the turn of the century. Any one individual work of art would be a gracious addition to any home on your block.

If there is a fly in the ointment, it is the price list in the back, which begins at $250 for a 18" x 24" framed small wall mirror and progresses on up to $5,400 for a 48" wide by 134" long reader's table. Chairs and benches range from about $600 to $2,800; sofas, from $4,000 to $5,250;

Besides rectangular and square tables (see drawings), Thos. Moser Cabinetmakers produces round and oval extension tables. The table opposite provides comfortable seating for four to eight diners.

and beds from $900 to $2,800. Other pieces, like tables, desks, and cases, generally range from $2,000 to $4,000. Study the offerings awhile, however, and you'll agree that the price tags likely reflect fair market value.

Moser furniture mostly is made of solid wood, principally cherry, white

Thomas Moser, cabinetmaker.

ash, and black walnut. No plywood, particleboard, or veneered surfaces are used. Completed pieces are finished with hand-rubbed linseed oil and wax; no stain is applied. The furniture is designed to last for generations, and is built to become the heirloom antiques of future centuries.

To give you a firsthand look at the Thos. Moser approach, the following pages present samples of three of his tables, along with measured drawings and building notes. These require mostly simple, straightforward construction and, if you are a woodworker with some experience, you should have no problem reproducing one in your

own workshop.

Even if you are a beginning woodworker and need to seek advice along the way, creating one would be a worthwhile challenge. The only caution is that these are Thos. Moser copyrighted designs; you may duplicate them for your own use, or as gifts to others, but you may not use the designs if you plan to go into business and sell them to the public.

The story of Thos. Moser Cabinetmakers starts with Tom's childhood in Chicago, where he excelled in manual arts, an adeptness he believes he inherited from his father, who was a stereotyper for the *Chicago Tribune*. After his parents died while he was still in high school, he joined the Air Force, serving during the Korean War. He later went back to high school and continued on to eventually earn a doctorate degree in speech communication.

While teaching at state colleges in Michigan and New York, he and Mary supplemented their income by buying old furniture, refinishing it in their home workshop, and then reselling it. "We had great fun," Tom recalls. "At one point we had 27 grandfather clocks. That's when I first began to look closely at furniture and to really think about the designs and intentions of 19th-century craftsmen."

Tom left a tenured professorship in linguistics at Bates College in 1973 to follow his interest in woodworking. He and Mary bought the old Grange Hall in New Gloucester, Maine, hung a shingle outside, and were in business with 6,500 sq. ft. of space. Working day and night, Tom designed and built furniture while Mary kept the books and sold most of the work. "At first," recalls Tom, "we had no business plan, no sense of marketing, and, to our banker's horror, no cash or cash flow."

However, the demand for furniture built with uncompromising design and utility required them to move to larger facilities in Auburn, Maine, then eventually to their current 40,000-sq. ft. headquarters there. From a shoestring, Thos. Moser Cabinetmakers has grown to reach annual sales in excess of $5 million. Of their 100-some employees, about 50 now work directly in making the furniture. Tom and Mary's four sons are involved in design, construction, and sales.

How the Mosers achieved this success has roots in their attitude towards furniture design. "A good design," says Tom, "is one to which nothing can be added, nothing can be taken away. Wooden structures, whether houses or chairs, gain strength in one of two ways: through mass and weight, or though economy of material. Here we believe that less is more. When you think about it, nature abounds with examples of economical engineering, such as a tree that bends with the wind, a bird, a butterfly, a spider's web."

Moser furniture itself leans toward nature. Made of solid, premium grade wood, it expands and contracts with changes in temperature and humidity. This movement is taken into account in both design and construction. Doors and backs have framed floating panels, moldings are fitted with hidden slotted dovetails, even screw holes are oval to allow for seasonal motion.

Because natural oil finishes are used instead of stain, urethane, or lacquer, the furniture develops a beautiful patina over time. Air and sunlight color the wood naturally with a subtlety not possible with anything that comes from a can.

Tom's basic belief about furniture is that it must combine utility with artistry. The first requirement is that it must be used, he says. "That is why we build tables, chairs, cases, cupboards, clocks, and other pieces that people will actually use in their daily lives. And, while our furniture is not cheap, it is affordable. People of ordinary means should have the same opportunity to enjoy the beauty of wood and fine craftsmanship as the mega-wealthy."

The company has shipped furniture to all 50 states, Germany, Japan, England, and Canada. The typical buyer is 35 to 44 years old, in a professional, technical, or upper management occupation, has 17 years of education, buys collectibles, likes to read and cook, and takes a hands-on approach to home projects. The buyers tend toward practical, conservative lifestyles.

Almost half of those who buy one piece, Tom says, will end up buying another. Many buy one or two items a year; not just to get an object to sit, eat, or sleep on, but also to acquire an investment that will appreciate. "They like to mix and match, and play styles against one another. For many of them, each object in their home has a story; it was a gift, something found in an antique shop one summer long ago, the result of a trade, an inheritance, or some other remembrance of the past."

The success of the company also has a lot to do with the attitudes of those who work there. "Our shop is not an art studio," Tom says, "it is a working shop. It's a friendly and relaxed

The trestle table, opposite, suggests Shaker-style simplicity. Says Tom: "The Shakers did not create revolutionary forms, but rather refined and simplified the forms that were all about them."

place, but there is always a preoccupation with detail. Our company's priorities are: 1) safety — in the total work environment; 2) quality — mistakes are burned, not hidden or sold; 3) efficiency — measure twice, cut once, and 4) profit — money is necessary, but no substitute for creativity.

How long does it take to make fine furniture? Building time at Thos. Moser varies from piece to piece. Including time for making parts, a chair may take from eight to 10 hours. A dining table may take about 30 hours, while a large chest might average 50 to 60 hours.

"By and large," Tom observes, "it's still a pretty labor-intensive process, but worth it. The objects we live with are proof that we make aesthetic judgments in our nest building. A house filled with art and memories and objects you have personally chosen is more rewarding than a place professionally assembled, perfectly matching, and all quite clinical."

From his experience in making and selling furniture, Tom has assembled some general dimensional guidelines that may help you in your own workshop. For example:

• **Seating Widths.** The standard width of side chairs is 18 to 20 inches. The width must be increased to 21 inches for an armchair to allow those with wider proportions to fit between the posts of the arms.

• **Table Sizing.** The standard height for tables and desks is 30 inches from the floor to the top, and 25 inches from the floor to the apron. For dining tables, an absolute minimum is 24 inches of perimeter space per place setting, while 30 inches provides a more gracious setting.

• **Table Selection.** A fully extended dining table should have a minimum of three feet of floor space between the table and the wall. Any table measuring six feet in length or less can always be brought into a room tipped on end; larger tables can present problems.

• **Bed Sizes.** Beds are made to fit standard mattress sizes, and they will accommodate 99% of the mattresses available: twin, 39 x 75 inches; full, 54 x 75 inches; and queen, 60 x 80 inches.

Over the years Tom Moser also has written three books. His first was *How To Build Shaker Furniture,* published in 1977. Next came *Thos. Moser's Windsor Chairmaking* in 1982, then *Measured Shop Drawings For American Furniture* in 1985. All three were published by Sterling Publishing Co. You can contact the publisher for current prices and availability by writing to 387 Park Ave. So., New York, NY 10016-8810. To get a copy of the Thos. Moser catalog, send $9 to 72 Wright's Landing, P.O. Box 1237, Auburn, ME 04211-1237, or call 207/784-3332. For a first-hand look, you can visit showrooms in San Francisco; Philadelphia; Alexandria, Virginia; and Portland, Maine. ❧

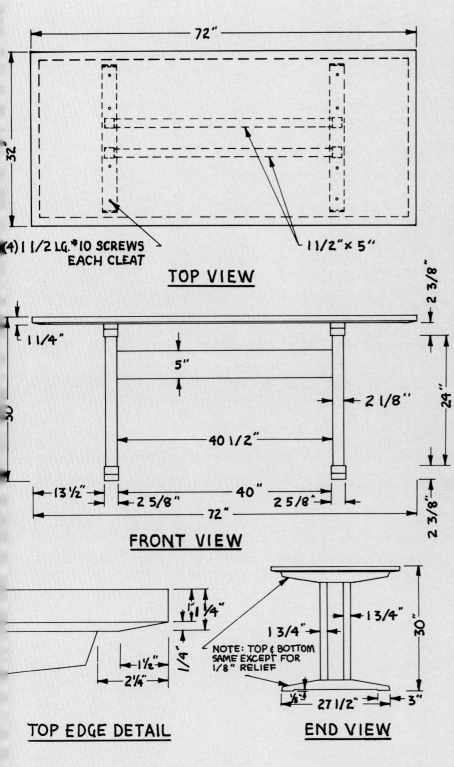

TOP VIEW

(4) 1 1/2 LG. #10 SCREWS EACH CLEAT

1 1/2" x 5"

72"

32"

FRONT VIEW

1 1/4"

5"

2 1/8"

40 1/2"

13 1/2"

2 5/8"

40"

2 5/8"

72"

2 3/8"

24"

2 3/8"

30

TOP EDGE DETAIL

1 1/4"

1/4"

1 1/2"

2 1/4"

NOTE: TOP & BOTTOM SAME EXCEPT FOR 1/8" RELIEF

END VIEW

1 3/4"

1 3/4"

27 1/2"

3"

30

BUILDING NOTES:

To make the top for this contemporary version of a Shaker dining table requires 24 board feet of 6/4" hardwood stock, although clear pine also will work. The underside bevels can be cut with a plane or on a table saw. The entire base consists of only three components:

• four double-tenoned posts with an overall length of 26" and shoulder-to-shoulder length of 24", using a 1" tenon ½" thick, centered, with ⅜" shoulders;

• two feet and two arms finished to 2⅜" x 2⅝" x 27½", with a taper starting at 1" thickness and running to 2⅜" at 11⅜" to end up with an 8¼" flat on top;

• two double-tenoned cross stretchers 1½" x 5", with an overall length of 42½" and shoulder-to-shoulder length of 40½".

The feet are relieved ⅛", resulting in the creation of pads for stable floor contact. All mortise and tenon joints must be dry-fitted very tightly before gluing. The ³⁄₁₆"-diameter dowel pins are set after the joint has been glued and clamped under pressure; the glue should set before drilling and gluing the pins (these need not pass all the way through the legs or the posts). The eight No. 10 x 1½"-long screws used to attach the top should be plugged and sanded flush.

The whole table should be polished using 400-grit wet/dry sandpaper before applying hot linseed oil or "Danish Oil." All oil residue must be wiped off and the rags should be burned or buried. Finally, the table should be waxed and buffed to an even, dull sheen using 0000 steel wool.

THE RECTANGULAR DINING TABLE
30"H x 36"W x 60"L

This elegant piece of furniture celebrates purity of form. As shown, it will seat six comfortably. One built 36" wide and 80" long would seat eight, or one built 42" wide and 104" long would seat 10. The light, yet rugged, table is constructed with a full 1"-thick solid cherry top, and is equally suited for the dining room, kitchen, conference room, or library.

TENON 3/8" THICK × 1" LG.× 2 1/4" LG.

MORTISE & TENON DETAIL

SKIRT

LEG 2 1/8" SQUARE

MORTISE 3/8" WIDE × 2 1/4" LG. × 1 1/16" DP. (2) ADJACENT FACES

THOS.MOSER
CABINETMAKERS

72 WRIGHTS LANDING
AUBURN MAINE 04211
207-784-3332

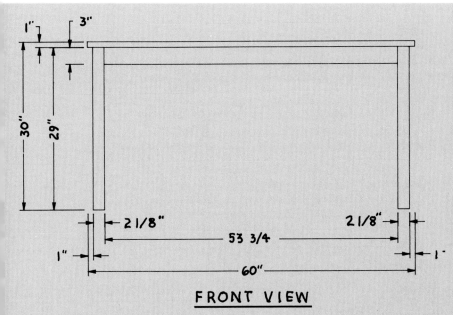

FRONT VIEW

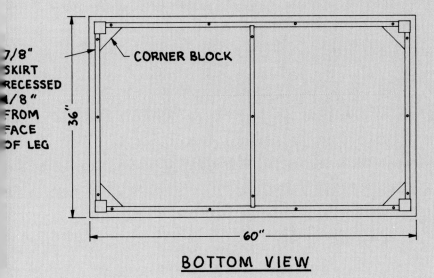

CORNER BLOCK

7/8"
SKIRT
RECESSED
1/8"
FROM
FACE
OF LEG

BOTTOM VIEW

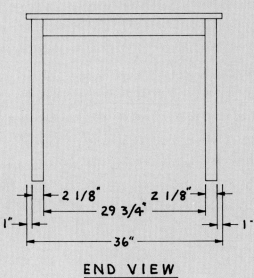

END VIEW

BUILDING NOTES:

To build this rectangular dining table, you will need approximately seven board feet of 1" stock, thirty board feet of 1½" stock, and seven board feet of 2½" stock.

To make the side skirts, first cut them to a rough length of 57", then plane to ⅞" thickness. Joint one edge, then rip to 3" and cut to a finished length of 55¾". The tenon size is 1" long, ⅜" thick, 2¼" overall, centered. The shoulder-to-shoulder length is 53¾". Run a ⅞" dado, centered, ¼" deep, and drill four skirt holes for No. 10 x 2½" wood screws, protruding ½".

For the end skirts, cut lumber to a rough length of 33". Plane to ⅞" thickness, joint one edge, then rip to 3". Cut to a finished length of 31¾". The tenon size is the same as for the side skirt, and the shoulder-to-shoulder length is 29¾". Drill three skirt holes for No. 10 x 2½" wood screws, protruding ½".

To make the divider, also cut stock to a rough length of 33", plane to ⅞" thickness, joint one edge, then rip to 3". Cut to a finished length of 32½". Drill skirt holes for No. 10 x 2½" wood screws protruding ½". For the legs, cut stock to a 30" rough length, plane to 2⅛" square, then mortise two adjacent faces 1¹/₁₆" deep, 2¼" long, ⅜" from the top, ⅜" in from the front face, ⅜" wide. Chamfer the bottom edges.

For the top, glue up a panel to be finished at 1" x 36" x 60". Sand all parts and dry-fit the complete table, checking that the tenons fit, the skirt is flush with the leg tops, and the base is square. Apply glue to mortises and clamp. After the glue has dried, fit divider to dado and toe screw. Then attach corner blocks and top. Sand and apply finish.

THE SQUARE END TABLE

26"H x 20"W x 20"D

This multipurpose piece of furniture can function as a bedside table, be used next to a reading chair as a support for a telephone or a lamp, or brought to wherever it is needed to serve its owners. With crisp, elegant styling, it can be constructed with a drawer, or without one as shown.

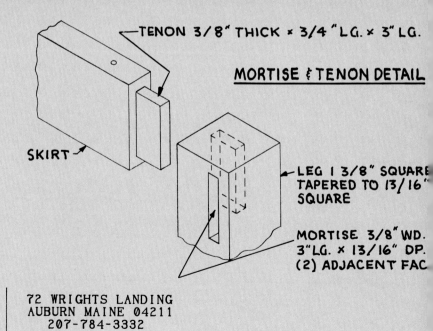

TENON 3/8" THICK × 3/4" LG. × 3" LG.

MORTISE & TENON DETAIL

SKIRT

LEG 1 3/8" SQUARE TAPERED TO 13/16" SQUARE

MORTISE 3/8" WD. 3" LG. × 13/16" DP. (2) ADJACENT FAC

THOS . MOSER
CABINETMAKERS

72 WRIGHTS LANDING
AUBURN MAINE 04211
207-784-3332

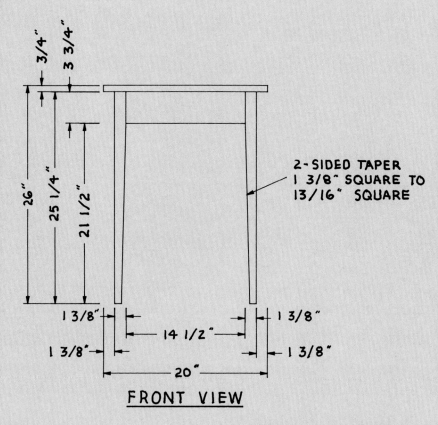

3/4"
3 3/4"
26"
25 1/4"
21 1/2"

2-SIDED TAPER
1 3/8" SQUARE TO
13/16" SQUARE

1 3/8"   1 3/8"
14 1/2"
1 3/8"   1 3/8"
20"

FRONT VIEW

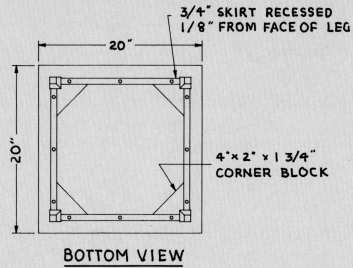

3/4" SKIRT RECESSED
1/8" FROM FACE OF LEG

20"

20"

4" x 2" x 1 3/4"
CORNER BLOCK

BOTTOM VIEW

BUILDING NOTES:

To build this square end table you will need approximately seven board feet of 1" stock and four pieces of 2" x 2" x 27" stock. To make the skirts, first cut stock to a rough dimension of 1" x 4" x 17", then plane to ¾". Joint one edge, rip to 3¾", and cut to a finished length of 16". The tenon size is ⅜" thick, centered, with a ⅜" shoulder top and bottom, ¾" long. Drill three skirt holes for No. 10 x 2½" wood screws protruding ½". (The tenons need to be beveled on the inside.)

To make the legs, plane stock to 1⅜" square and cut to a finished length of 25¼". Mortise two adjacent corners using mortises ⅜" wide, 3" long, starting ⅜" from the top and ⁵⁄₁₆" from the outside edge. Taper the mortised faces of the legs to finish at ¹³⁄₁₆" at the bottom, starting 5" from the top. Chamfer the bottom of the legs.

For the top, glue up a panel to finish at ¾" x 20" x 20". Sand all parts but, to keep a tight shoulder fit, do not sand over the mortises on the legs. Dry-fit all parts, and check that the tenons fit, the skirt is flush with the leg tops, and the base is square. Apply glue to mortises and clamp. After the glue has dried, attach corner blocks and top. Sand all surfaces and apply finish.

CABIN CARPENTERS

Tips On How To Build A Dream Home
Hundreds Of Miles Away

Picture all of the challenges of building any home, even if it were in your own backyard. Then try to picture the extra challenges when you set that project on the shores of a lake 200 miles away. Unless you plan to take years to build, wear out a set of tires on weekends, take a sabbatical from work, or hang on the phone for days at a time, you need to proceed with an extra measure of caution.

Still, that distance between you and your building project doesn't have to mean misery, say experienced contractors whose main business is to help city dwellers achieve their dreams. They say there's no reason why an outsider can't build in a distant vacation area and have it be a pleasurable experience. The trick, they say, is to use the right approach, keep a careful eye on details, and put more effort into planning the project up front.

"When building in an area miles from where you live, success may depend more on the contractor you select than anything else," says Jerry Mueller at Kuepers Construction, Brainerd, Minnesota. The town, about 160 miles north of Minneapolis, lies in the heart of a booming summer vacation area dotted with lakeshore homes owned by residents from nearly all 50 states.

Building vacation homes, such as the Lindal Summit chalet at left on Castle Rock Mountain near Purgatory Ski Resort in Colorado, can be a pleasurable experience if you pay attention to details.

Many of those homes built over the past 10 years are projects completed by a half-dozen local contracting firms accustomed to working with absentee owners whose main residence is outside the area. Contractors headquartered here, some with as many as 40 carpenters

on the payroll, have completed homes that set the owners back as much as $375,000.

They agree on one thing: The days of building an unfinished fishing cabin are over. Most people who consider building a vacation home today view it as a genuine real estate investment. Many of the owners plan to move into the home they build once they retire. Because such homes are substantial projects, the contractor they hire also takes on the role of local consultant.

If, for example, a do-it-yourselfer wants only part of the job done, the contractor will point out that coordinating subcontractors can be quite a challenge if you don't live in the area. They don't blame anyone for wanting to save money, get involved, and learn some things. But they've seen many projects get out of hand when an owner living outside of the area tries to be his own general contractor.

As an absentee supervisor, it becomes tougher to site the home properly, coordinate the work, and keep a handle on the quality of the work being done. The project can end up too low or high in the ground, set too close to lot lines, or too close to the lake. Area contractors know the local regulations and how local zoning and planning committees think. Many say that half of their job is keeping people out of trouble.

Contractors here also point out that trying to coordinate the whole show, when building from a distance, may not save an owner-builder much money overall. It also may mean serious scheduling problems. Absentee owners who try to take on the whole project themselves may find themselves with an awful lot of running around to do.

Local contractors know which subcontractors are good and who's available. By not knowing the workmanship of subcontractors, someone from outside the area also can end up working with less qualified persons.

THE NEW-AGE REC HOME

Recreation-area contractors say today's vacation homes, more often than not, are substantial projects viewed as genuine real estate investments. This Sunburst design from Lindal Cedar Homes was built on Vashon Island, within commuting distance of Seattle. The spacious interior, including three bedrooms and two baths, glows with the warmth of cedar.

The owners had a design they thought was special. And, working with Lindal, they were able to incorporate many of their most-wanted features, such as the garden windows, sun room, and skylight. It's now their dream home.

Photos: Lindal Cedar Homes, Seatt

THE SUNBURST FLOOR PLAN
Overall Size: 60' x 37' 2,525 sq. ft.

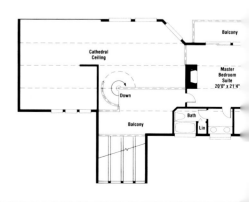

The owners opted for a fresh, bright look using cedar trim in contrast to sleek white drywall, top. The high clerestory windows, above, bathe the dining room with an abundance of natural light. Left, the open baluster balcony leads to the master bedroom upstairs, and adds to the sense of spaciousness in the living room, which boasts a maple hardwood floor.

And keeping subcontractors in line is the key to having things run smoothly. "The subcontractors we use know what side their bread is buttered on," says Mueller. "They have to treat us right and give us good work at a fair price."

If you don't plan on being around the project much, Mueller advises searching for a firm that can make the building process as easy for you as possible. "Our first order of business with prosective customers," he says, "is to show them that we are a legitimate contractor. Then, when we get the job, we pin down as many details as possible to eliminate questions later. We know there will always be some problems, but the goal is to minimize them so that the project can proceed at a good clip."

A critical step at Kuepers is what is called the "blueprint meeting" with the owners, which takes two or three hours. "Along with the blueprint, we have a matching spec book 20 pages long which spells out everything to be used in the home. We go through the blueprint, page by page. Colors selected room by room, as well as such details as door, window, and cabinet specs, are listed right on the blueprint."

The owner initials each page, and the blueprint is kept on file. "Then if changes are made later," says Mueller, "we don't alter the original blueprint, but use change-order addendums which are fully priced out. This way you will know what the changes are going to cost you ahead of time, and exactly where you are at money-wise."

Mueller says they've learned the hard way not to make assumptions on such details as window cladding or shingle texture. "It pays us to take the time to go over the smallest details. Even though we've listed a color as rustic, you may not realize how it will look until you see it already done. And once things are done, they are expensive to change."

His company makes up a complete work schedule for each project, which shows when each stage of construction will be done and when decisions must be made so that materials are delivered on time and there aren't any holdups.

Appointments between the owners and subcontractors, such as floor covering installers, lighting suppliers, and electricians are then carefully coordinated and often scheduled on

> " If you are pressed on budget and you are thinking of erecting a low-cost home without insulation, for example, a good contractor here will advise you to reconsider. "

weekends for the convenience of the owner.

The work schedule also maps out specific checkpoints along the way. "For example," says Mueller, "when we have all the interior walls framed, we do a walk-through inspection with the owner and electrician. If the owner comes up with additional special needs, like spotlights or additional weatherproof receptacles, we take care of it at that time."

The firm normally bills on a monthly basis. In their billing they show the owners the percentage of each major construction element that is completed. "That's what we base our monthly draws on," says Mueller. "At the same time the owner is kept informed of the progress on the build-ing project."

Successful contractors in this resort area emphasize that, whatever else, you should feel comfortable with the contractor you choose. If the building process is a pleasant one, they say, then $2,000 one way or the other won't make that much difference in your monthly payment.

One of the biggest services these contractors offer is just good solid building advice. If you are pressed on budget and you are thinking of building a low-cost home without insulation, for example, a good contractor here will advise you to reconsider. You may be talking under $2,000 more to insulate well. It will double the time you can use your investment, and you're likely to get that money back whenever you sell.

"If you are pressed for money," Mueller adds, "we would advise not skimping in important areas, but to examine other things you may be able to do without, such as that custom cathedral ceiling, extensive brickwork, extra bedroom, or that finished basement. We would try to show you where it's possible to cut back, or even help you decide whether you might be better off putting that money in the bank."

What if you want to provide your own materials? Many contractors will tell you that if you allow the contractor to handle the materials you might come out about the same, especially if you figure time and transporation. Area contractors know the best sources of supplies, and they generally can get a better price. They also will get materials they like to work with, and won't have as many problems if they run out and need to get more. ❧

SELECTING A LONG-DISTANCE CONTRACTOR

Here are checkpoints to consider if you are selecting a contractor to help you build a vacation home miles away from where you live.

References. Check out each contractor's past customers. Go see the homes a contractor has built and ask the owners what they thought of working with the firm. Look at three or four homes, and don't be bashful about quizzing the owners on how the project went.

Service. Should you go with a one-man operation, or look for a larger firm? A bigger firm may be able to spend more time with you than a smaller firm where the owner also is pounding nails. You don't have to write off an aggressive young contractor trying to get established; just make sure you will get the service and workmanship you expect.

Thoroughness. Need help in deciding what to build? If so, you may need a larger firm that has an in-house architect. Even smaller contractors, however, may be able to help you, especially if you want something similar to what they already have built. It may depend on what ideas and how much time you have.

Because most problems stem from poor communication or misunderstandings, try to have everything documented before you start.

Flexibility. If you want to do some of the work yourself, look for a contractor willing to be flexible. Many contractors will take a project to any stage. They can just put up the shell and get it under lock and key. Or they can put up the shell and finish off critical areas like a couple of bedrooms, a bath, and a kitchen. That way the structure is livable and you will be able to work on the rest of it in comfort, at your convenience.

Credit. Be sure to check out credit references, reputation, and years in business. You don't want to find a lien on your property after the job is done. It's possible to pay a general contractor in good faith and find that he's left town and the subcontractors who didn't get paid are on your doorstep. The law varies by state. In some states, for example, suppliers who can file a lien must notify the owner of that fact within 10 days after supplying the material or doing the work.

Pricing. Interpret all bids cautiously. Make sure everyone is bidding on the same thing, and try to consider how the workmanship, materials, and service may vary. Don't automatically accept a low bid, especially if there is a chance that you may end up fighting with the contractor throughout the project. Look for a solid price that covers everything. Any add-ons allowed at the end of the project should be spelled out, and any changes made during the project should be made by specific written agreement.

Insurance. Make sure the contractor carries workers' compensation and liability insurance to protect you from personal injury lawsuits and disasters on the job. If a contractor is backfilling your basement and it caves in, you might be stuck if he doesn't have insurance. Be especially cautious when hiring low-price subcontractors. You might think you'll save $50, but if something happens and the subcontractor doesn't have insurance, it can cost you big money.

Workmanship. If hiring a general contractor, who will actually be doing the work? Workmanship can vary greatly, depending on which subcontractors are used. It's a good idea to ask the contractor about guarantees. Even if laws in your state make a contractor stand by a structure for a period of years, you may be left holding the bag if the contractor goes out of business.

The WHIRLPOOL BATH

Engineered Bliss For Mind, Body, And Soul

Those who have them would say it's simply smart living: Just twenty minutes in a whirlpool bath is all that it takes to rejuvenate both body and spirit after a hard day's work or a strenuous workout. As a bonus, outfitting your master bath with a whirlpool adds to the resale value of your home.

Not long ago the whirlpool bath was an anomaly in the home, with choices restricted to customized versions of traditional bathtubs. Today almost unending permutations of choices are available, in an array of sizes, styles, materials, and options. You can find traditional or contemporary styles of cast iron, acrylic, or fiberglass in a full palette of colors. You can select the pump size you want, either solid-state Piezo or air switches, and other add-ons such as in-line water heaters, low-water-level sensors, or even preprogrammed automatic fill systems.

You will find most of the good whirlpools priced $1,500 to $2,500,

Whirlpools can be raised, as Kohler's Fleur model, opposite; sunken, as the Super Bath model, above, or installed in a recess. Prices range from about $1,000 on the low end, on up to $5,000 or more, depending on size, style, and special built-in features.

with any hired installation work and upgrade features extra. The least expensive are the simply designed fiberglass versions, while those of cast iron may be double that. The more exotic styles of more modern materials can run triple the low-end price.

Shapes range from models resembling conventional bathtubs to ovals, rectangles, triangles, and even figure-eights, to fit from one to four bathers. Tip: Take along measurements if you plan to replace an older tub of unconventional dimensions; you still may need to do some remodeling to accommodate the whirlpool you want.

What to look for? The illustration on pages 98 and 99, provided by the Kohler Co., presents a quick checklist of advanced features to look for in the whirlpool itself. Unless you are already familiar with high-tech bathing, however, you no doubt will

have questions. Some of the most frequently asked:

• Are more or bigger water jets better? The water jet is one of the most misunderstood components of the whirlpool bath. Actually it's not the size or number of jets used that determines their effectiveness. Instead, it's the ratio of air to water coming out, the adjustability of the air-water mixture, and the position of the jets within the whirlpool. Better whirlpools have jets that rotate easily and allow the ratio of air to water to be adjusted for a "custom" massage.

• What's the best configuration? Once you have narrowed your choice to a few models, don't be bashful about climbing into showroom display models (ask permission first). Jump in for a "dry run" and try sitting in it, stretching out, and lying back. An amazing variety of designs are available to accommodate different-size people, and many have special features such as lumbar supports, armrests and headrests. You might as well aim for the best fit possible.

• What should it be made of? Highly durable enameled cast iron remains a premium material for whirlpool construction. Newer materials, such as cast acrylic and some of the new advanced composite materi-

SELECTING A WHIRLPOOL

With all the options to consider, choosing a whirlpool can be a challenge. The illustration below features a Kohler whirlpool, and highlights those features considered important by Kohler Co., the country's leading whirlpool manufacturer. Its cast-iron whirlpools have a slip-resistant bottom and, for entry and exit safety, many of the models incorporate convenient grip rails. For more comfort, an in-line heater maintains a consistent water temperature, even during long periods of bathing. Another high-tech option allows you to program the whirlpool to automatically fill to a desired level and temperature any time within a 24-hour period.

Switch Choices. Kohler offers two types of whirlpool switches positioned for easy access. Solid-state Piezo switches have LED indicators and start the motor electronically. Air switches use a pulse of air to start up the system.

Pump and Motor.
High performance, self-draining pumps are powered by $3/4$-, $1/2$-, or 1-hp motors, depending on whirlpool size and number of jets. High-end whirlpools have two-speed motors and a low-water-level sensor to keep the pump from running dry.

Ergonomic Design. Updated designs offer smooth body-contoured shapes, curved lumbar back supports, plus headrests, armrests, and footrests to support the body and relieve muscle tension.

Recirculating Harness. Better assemblies, of high strength PVC, are fully self-draining to eliminate water residue in the system after bathing; rounded curves reduce noise and boost pump efficiency.

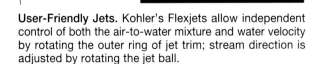

User-Friendly Jets. Kohler's Flexjets allow independent control of both the air-to-water mixture and water velocity by rotating the outer ring of jet trim; stream direction is adjusted by rotating the jet ball.

WHIRLPOOL SHAPES

Whirlpool designs number in the hundreds, varying from traditional to exotic. The shapes here are a minor sampling: Top, Kohler's Tea-For-Two of enameled cast iron in Heron Blue measures 60" x 32" x 18"; center, the Allegra in Wild Rose is of high-gloss acrylic and measures 60½" x 60½" x 24"; and, popular acrylic Infinity in Tender Grey comes in 72" x 42" x 21" and 60" x 42" x 21" models.

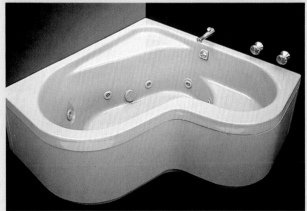

TECH NOTES: INSTALLING A WHIRLPOOL

The specifications here are representative of Kohler SuperBath whirlpools that weigh 260 lbs., have a 170-gal. capacity, and use either a 120- or 230-volt pump. Basic installation includes shimming beneath the pump bracket, if a subfloor is not level, using a 5" x 7" piece of plywood.

When the bath is positioned, the drain is connected to the trap, then the pump bracket is secured to the subfloor with lag screws. Piping or the pump cannot be used to support or position the unit, and an access must be provided to the pump assembly.

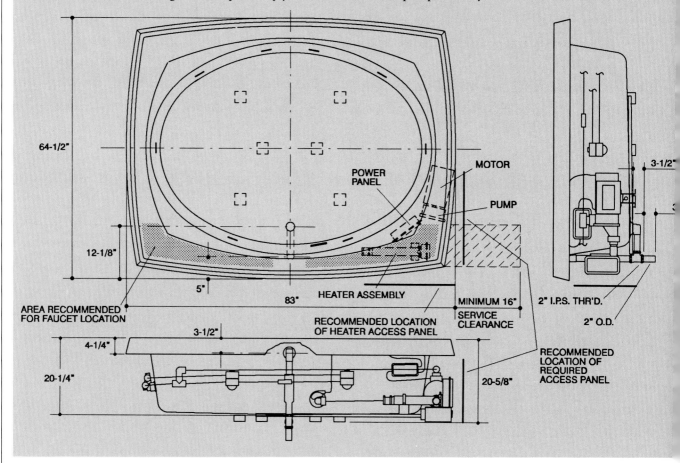

als, also wear well and allow more flexibility in design. Less expensive and less durable are gel-coated fiberglass, other plastics, and enameled steel.

• Will it stand up over time? To assure the highest quality, it's safest to buy one built by a reputable manufacturer. Beyond that, check the tubing used on the underside. It should be rigid or fully supported for complete drainage to avoid water collection and possible bacteria growth. (Non-supported flexible PVC piping can age and eventually create water pockets even after the bathtub has been drained.) UL and IAPMO approval of the entire whirlpool, not just individual components, is also a sign of a safe and reliable product.

Even if you are an advanced do-it-yourselfer remodeling a master bath, you should consider getting help with whirlpool installation or, at the very least, having all electrical connections done by a professional, licensed electrician. You want to make sure that the whirlpool is installed correctly, for the same reasons you would opt for airbags and anti-lock brakes in your next new car — to protect yourself and your family. The pumps on some whirlpools require 120-volt power, while others need 230. Either way, a separate 15-amp, ground-fault protected circuit is required. If your main breaker box is full, this may mean adding an additional load center.

There may be other ways, however, that you can help reduce installation costs. Depending on who you work with, removing your old bathtub and hauling it away, clearing the area for installation, or finishing the surround or wall surfaces yourself all may be ways to reduce the bill. Talk it over with plumbers and contractors. Whirlpool distributors may go out of their way to avoid making recommendations, but they may have bulletin boards or other listings of

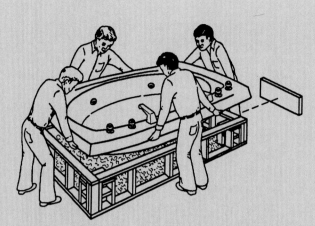

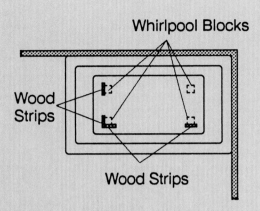

One installation option is to provide a bed of 2"-thick gypsum cement on the floor where the bath will be set. Because the pump bracket must sit flat on the floor, excess cement must be cleared from the vicinity of the pump.

Another method of installing uses 1x2 wood strips around blocks under the whirlpool to hold it in postion. The strips are needed only on the support blocks on the open sides of the whirlpool.

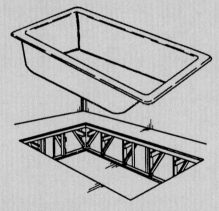

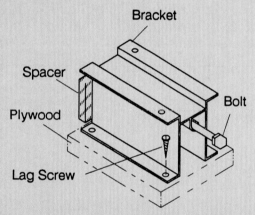

For sunken installations, the whirlpool tub is set into a specially built opening, using a bead of RTV caulking at the rim/wood interface. The whirlpool must be level and resting on all support blocks, not hanging by the rim.

Plywood is used, if needed, to support the bracket under the pump. Factory spacer between bracket and unit is removed, electrical connections are made, walls are finished, and the joint between bath rim and wall is sealed with silicone sealant.

professionals who install whirlpool baths. Compare prices, get more than one bid, and check out their references.

Whirlpools can be installed in either new or existing construction. If you decide to take out your old tub yourself, the procedure is to disconnect the drain at the trap, then remove the old wall material. To protect the floor, slip boards under the old bath while moving it out of the recess. Be sure to check the flooring under the bath area and repair it if necessary.

The whirlpool can be installed three different ways — in an existing or newly built recess, in an island-like peninsula, or partially sunken into the floor (see TECH NOTES). In recesses or corners, two methods exist to help secure, level, and support the bath: 1) using a 2"-thick layer of gypsum cement on the floor, or 2) using 1x2 wood strips around blocks under the whirlpool. In all cases, even in sunken installations, the whirlpool must be level, resting on all supporting blocks and not hung by the rim.

If the subfloor is not level, some shimming of the bath and pump may be necessary. If gypsum cement is used, excess cement must be cleared from the pump area so that the pump bracket rests flat on the floor. If the whirlpool pump and piping are factory assembled, they should be left intact and not relocated. In all installations, access to the mechanical components must be provided for any future maintenance. ❧

Note: To make the whirlpool selection process easier, Kohler has a three-system approach that helps you quickly pinpoint those models that best fit your needs. For more information, write the company at Kohler, WI 53044, or call 414/457-4441 for information on the dealer nearest to you.

WILD PROJECTS

*Building Code Plans
For Five Hospitable Bird Structures*

If you enjoy being a friend to wildlife, building houses for cavity nesting birds can be a rewarding experience — and more than just a hobby. Cavity nesting birds need all the help they can get as intensified forest management and firewood cutting reduce natural cavities.

The following plans and instructions come from the Minnesota Department of Natural Resources, and were compiled by Carrol L. Henderson, the state's DNR non-game wildlife supervisor. He emphasizes that the keys to success include building houses according to specs, and placing and maintaining them properly. "If they aren't built or maintained right," he says, "they can become sparrow slums, remain unused, or actually become a death trap to nesting birds and mammals."

Here are other tips to consider before starting these small-scale construction projects:

• Build for specific birds, because different species have different house-size and entrance-hole requirements. Provide a hinged side or roof so the house can be checked easily and cleaned each year.

• Use at least four ¼"-diameter drain holes in the bottom of houses, except for the Peterson bluebird house, which has a sloping floor and swing-door front to allow drainage.

• Though wren houses can be suspended from eaves or tree limbs, firmly attach all other houses to a support post, building, or tree. On trees, use lag screws and washers that can be unscrewed to allow for tree growth.

• Don't put perches on houses because only house sparrows and European starlings prefer them. A wood slab with bark can be placed horizontally under the entrance of a wood duck or common merganser hole to make it easier for landing at the entrance.

• Allow the top-front edge to over-hang at least 2" to help protect entrance holes from wind-driven

*The Wood Duck (see plans, page 104)
prefers wooded swamps
and river bottoms.*

rain and to keep cats from reaching in from above.

• Drill at least two ¼" holes near the top of the right and left sides, except in duck boxes, to provide ventilation. Recess the floor ¼" up from the bottom of the sides to help prevent deterioration from moisture.

• Softwood, such as pine, is fine for smaller nests. Cedar, redwood, or cypress may be used for larger boxes. Pine or plywood can be used for duck

boxes if it is treated on the outside with wood preservative or painted. Don't use creosote or green preservative.

• Use galvanized nails, if necessary, but remember that they loosen as wood expands and contracts. Cement-coated or ring-shanked nails are best with cedar and redwood houses; they won't allow the boards to loosen.

• Unwanteds — including mice, squirrels, bees, and wasps — may take up residence in houses. If wasps take over, remove the nest and spray the interior with a disinfectant like Lysol, being careful not to get stung. If ants invade, place a commercial ant killer like Terro in an upside-down pop bottle cap under the nest.

• When nesting season is over, open the front or side of songbird houses and leave them open during winter to keep deer mice from nesting. The mice may try to defend the house against returning songbirds the next spring.

• Try to be precise about entrance hole sizes. Any hole that is 1¼" in diameter or larger will admit house sparrows, and any larger than 1½" will admit European starlings. ❧

*Note: For more detailed information on these and other wildlife projects, you can order a 112-page book titled **Woodworking For Wildlife** for $9.95 plus $2 shipping from Minnesota's Book Store, 117 University Ave., St. Paul, MN 55155. (State residents, add sales tax.) This helpful book includes several other nest boxes and platforms for use in forests, lakes, rivers, marshes, ponds, and adjacent uplands.*

PETERSON BLUEBIRD HOUSE

NOTES: For Eastern Bluebird, mount houses 4' to 6' above ground, about 100 yards apart, facing north, east, or northeast. • A bluebird trail consists of five or more houses along a road or fenceline. • Remove nest as soon as first brood leaves the house to allow a second brood to be raised.

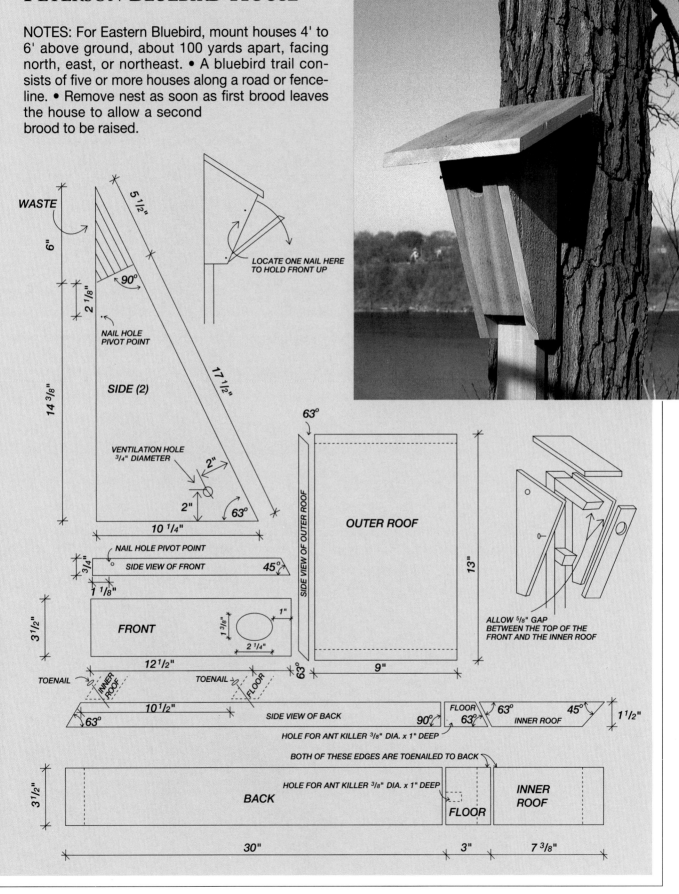

WASTE

6"

5 1/2"

90°

2 1/8"

NAIL HOLE
PIVOT POINT

LOCATE ONE NAIL HERE
TO HOLD FRONT UP

14 3/8"

SIDE (2)

17 1/2"

VENTILATION HOLE
3/4" DIAMETER

2"

2"

63°

10 1/4"

NAIL HOLE PIVOT POINT

3/4"   SIDE VIEW OF FRONT   45°

1 1/8"

3 1/2"   FRONT   1 3/8"   1"

2 1/4"

12 1/2"

63°   SIDE VIEW OF OUTER ROOF   63°

OUTER ROOF

13"

9"

ALLOW 5/8" GAP
BETWEEN THE TOP OF THE
FRONT AND THE INNER ROOF

TOENAIL   INNER ROOF   TOENAIL   FLOOR

10 1/2"   SIDE VIEW OF BACK   90°   FLOOR   63°   45°   1 1/2"

63°   63°   INNER ROOF

HOLE FOR ANT KILLER 3/8" DIA. x 1" DEEP

BOTH OF THESE EDGES ARE TOENAILED TO BACK

HOLE FOR ANT KILLER 3/8" DIA. x 1" DEEP

3 1/2"   BACK   INNER
ROOF

FLOOR

30"   3"   7 3/8"

WOOD DUCK BOX

(Can also be used for Hooded and Common Merganser, Common Goldeneye, and Pileated Woodpecker)

NOTES: For Wood Ducks, use oval hole 3" high and 4" wide, and attach 3" x 18" strip of ¹/₄" hardware cloth (with cut edges folded back) inside under entrance as ladder for newly hatched. • Place 3" or more mixed sawdust and chainsaw wood chips inside for nesting material. • Mount house on 16' 4x4 post with aluminum or tin sheet nailed around it to keep squirrels and racoons out. On water, keep house 6' to 8' above surface. In trees, mount above 20' if possible. Face house toward water or toward south or west. On land, place 30' to 100' from water's edge. • For Common Merganser, use oval hole 5" high and 9" wide and place 15' to 17' high facing water. For Hooded Merganser, use oval hole 3" high and 4" wide, and place 20' to 25' high. For Common Goldeneye, use oval hole 3¹/₂" high and 4¹/₂" wide, and place on predator-proof posts or poles in woods next to wetlands.

¹/₄" HOLES

FLOOR

9³/₄"

BACK

32"

SIDE (2)

24"

5"

HINGE OR CLEAT
ROOF FOR CLEANING

FOR PILEATED WOODPECKER,
FILL BOX TO TOP WITH SAWDUST

ROOF

16"

FRONT

19"
24"

11¹/₄"

11¹/₄"

LUMBER
ONE 1 x 12 (³/₄"x 11¹/₄") x12'
NOTE: PILEATED WOODPECKER BOX SHOULD BE CONSTRUCTED FROM ONE 2 x 12 (1¹/₂"x 11¹/₄") x 12'
CEDAR AND FLOOR MUST BE 8¹/₄" WIDE INSTEAD OF 9 ³/₄" FOR USE OF 1¹/₂"-THICK LUMBER.

11¹/₄"

BACK	SIDE	SIDE	FRONT	FLOOR	ROOF	← WASTE
32"	24"	24"	24"	9³/₄"	16"	

HOUSE WREN HOUSE

(Can also be used for Black-Capped Chickadee, White-Breasted Nuthatch, and Prothonotary Warbler)

NOTES: For House Wren, make hole 1⅛" dia. Locate boxes 5' to 10' above ground in tree or under building eave. • For Black-Capped Chickadee, make hole 1⅛" dia., put 1" of saw-dust in box, and mount 5' to 15' high in area with 40% to 60% sunlight. • For White-Breasted Nuthatch, make hole 1¼" and locate 12' to 20' above ground. • For Prothonotary Warbler, use 1¼" hole and place 3' to 5' above water level on snag or post in shallow woodland pools, or on sides of home or out-buildings near water.

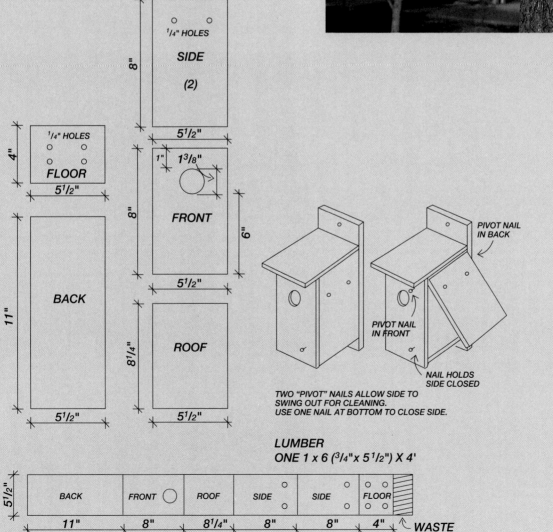

TWO "PIVOT" NAILS ALLOW SIDE TO SWING OUT FOR CLEANING. USE ONE NAIL AT BOTTOM TO CLOSE SIDE.

LUMBER
ONE 1 x 6 (¾"x 5½") X 4'

TREE SWALLOW HOUSE

(Can also be used for Eastern Bluebird and Great Crested Flycatcher)

NOTES: For Tree Swallows, mount 4' above ground near water; space boxes 25 yards apart, facing east. • For Eastern Bluebird, place 4' to 6' above ground, about 100 yards apart, facing north, east, or northeast. • For Great Crested Flycatcher, use $1^{3}/_{4}$" hole and place house 10' to 20' high.

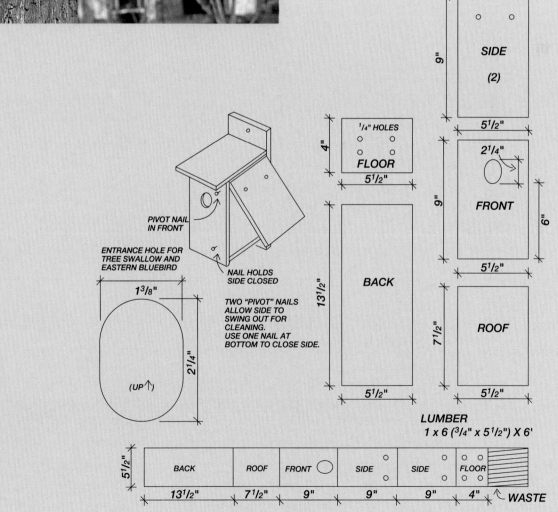

PIVOT NAIL IN FRONT

ENTRANCE HOLE FOR TREE SWALLOW AND EASTERN BLUEBIRD

NAIL HOLDS SIDE CLOSED

TWO "PIVOT" NAILS ALLOW SIDE TO SWING OUT FOR CLEANING. USE ONE NAIL AT BOTTOM TO CLOSE SIDE.

$1^{3}/_{8}$"

$2^{1}/_{4}$"

(UP↑)

$^{1}/_{4}$" HOLES

FLOOR

4"

$5^{1}/_{2}$"

BACK

$13^{1}/_{2}$"

$5^{1}/_{2}$"

SIDE (2)

9"

$5^{1}/_{2}$"

FRONT

$2^{1}/_{4}$"

9"

6"

$5^{1}/_{2}$"

ROOF

$7^{1}/_{2}$"

$5^{1}/_{2}$"

LUMBER
1 x 6 ($^{3}/_{4}$" x $5^{1}/_{2}$") X 6'

$5^{1}/_{2}$"	BACK	ROOF	FRONT	SIDE	SIDE	FLOOR	WASTE
	$13^{1}/_{2}$"	$7^{1}/_{2}$"	9"	9"	9"	4"	

NORTHERN FLICKER HOUSE

NOTES: Use 2½" entrance hole and tamp in sawdust all the way to the top to simulate a dead tree with soft heartwood. • Mount 4' to 6' high along fence rows bordering crop fields and pastures, either on existing fence posts or free-standing posts with predator guards. • Greater success may result by using 1½"-thick cedar boards for the house.

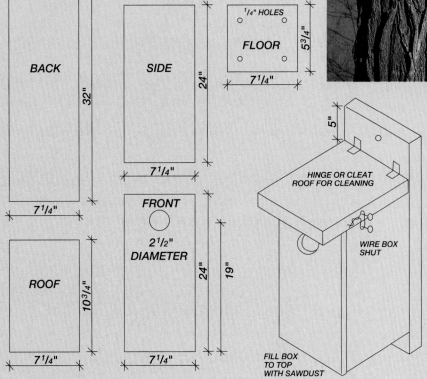

BACK
32"
7¼"

SIDE
24"
7¼"

¼" HOLES
FLOOR
5¾"
7¼"

ROOF
10¾"
7¼"

FRONT
2½"
DIAMETER
24"
7¼"

5"

HINGE OR CLEAT
ROOF FOR CLEANING

WIRE BOX
SHUT

19"

FILL BOX
TO TOP
WITH SAWDUST

LUMBER
ONE 1 x 8 (¾"x 7¼") x 10'

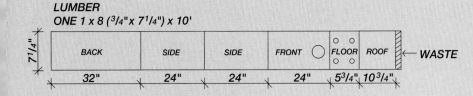

BACK	SIDE	SIDE	FRONT ◯	FLOOR	ROOF	← WASTE
32"	24"	24"	24"	5¾"	10¾"	

7¼"

The GARDEN HOUSE

A Bolt-Together Kit That Gives
You A Sunny Place Of Your Own

Andy Rooney has one. John Steinbeck had one, and so did that icon of nature appreciation, Henry David Thoreau: A special sanctuary, isolated from normal home activities and perfect for working, pursuing hobbies, contemplating, or just getting away from it all.

As recently as the Thirties you could find such outbuildings tucked away in a corner of the backyard, often behind sprawling trees or bushes. Most were simple sheds originally constructed as a place to store tools or to pot plants. Many of them served the purpose for which they were built, but many eventually were adopted by someone as a special retreat away from the rest of the world.

ONE-DAY WONDER

If you've been thinking you deserve such a place, or need extra space for serious utility purposes, you have three basic alternatives. You can build a structure from scratch. You can buy one ready-made from a home center or lumberyard to be delivered to your home. Or, if you are short on time but still want a hand in the construction, you can purchase a kit and invest a day of your time to make it your own.

You may be able to find backyard building kits locally; others are available by mail-order. One mail-order kit that stands out from most back lot buildings is the Green

The SunShed, opposite, is a versatile structure that combines the utility of a shed with the features of a greenhouse. It comes in eight prebuilt panels that bolt together using predrilled holes and supplied hardware.

Mountain SunShed. After it arrives, you and two helpers can assemble the panels on a foundation or a timber base in only two to four hours. Then, a coat of paint or stain, some shingles on the roof, and the building is ready to be used and enjoyed.

The SunShed comes from Gardener's Supply Company, which has its headquarters in the same town where Ben & Jerry's Ice Cream got started: Burlington, Vermont. It's available in an 8'x8' version for $1,195 or an 8'x10' rendition for $1,445 to $2,150, depending on the special options you choose.

Though it's not cheap, the unique little building has left a wake of enthusiastic owners who say it is one of the best buys they've made in years. For example, Andrew Metal of Cochiti Lake, New Mexico, reports that putting one together went like clockwork: "Each wall and roof panel locked in easily and perfectly. It's a handsome little building, and our neighbors think so, too."

With New England Saltbox proportions and details, the SunShed has a 12/12-pitch roof, a 30½"-wide hinged Dutch door, and a nine-pane side window for cross ventilation. Both sizes provide an 8' peak height for head room, and a roof rated at 50 lbs./sq. ft. to handle the heavy snow loads of northern states. The greenhouse windows are installed using a five-piece interlocking flashing system to minimize leaks.

The SunShed's exterior siding, of premium plywood in a vertical shiplap pattern, can be stained or painted as you wish. However, once it's assem-

bled, the most difficult decision may be how you want to use it.

For example, you can face its greenhouse windows to the south for growing plants. You can use it for bulky power equipment, such as lawn mowers, chipper/shredders, or tillers, as well as hand tools like rakes, hoes, or pruning tools and more. In the off-season you can shelter summer equipment, including the barbecue, lawn furniture, bicycles, or fishing gear. It also can be a place for things that never have a home, such as fertilizers, bird seed, or muddy garden boots.

Many do-it-yourselfers are tempted to use it as a well-lighted mini-shop or a hobby place where they can take projects and work in peace and quiet. It can be set up as a place to repair and recondition tools, build small projects, refinish a "find" from a country auction, dry herbs, or make flower arrangements.

ASSEMBLY AND FINISHING

Both the model sizes are available without floors. These versions can be set directly on a deck, or they can be used with a crushed stone, paver brick, gravel, or dirt floor. The 8'x10' is available with a tongue-and-groove plywood floor or a floor of treated wood. These models are set up with 8" of separation between the ground and the bottom of the floor panels. Foundations can be built using timbers resting on stones or concrete block supports at the sides and center of the structure. In areas where frost or high winds are common, fastening the shed to a permanent in-ground foundation helps prevent any movement.

All the kits come with a 16-page

The kit building also is a handy place to keep gardening tools, supplies, and equipment all in one place to cut down run-around time. It also can be used as a mini-shop to perform light repair or finishing work.

owner's guide which details the assembly, including tips on preparing the foundation. The assembly of the building starts with joining the floor panels together, if the shed has a floor, or bolting the wall panels directly to the foundation if the shed will not have a floor. Side walls and gable ends are tipped up into place one at a time and fastened using lag screws with washers. Next, the door and window are installed in the end walls before the roof panels are attached. It's best, before proceeding with the roof, to check that the floor and walls are level, and that the walls and ends are plumb at each corner, so the roof panels will fit perfectly.

The roof is attached in two sections, called the north and the south roof. The top ridge members of the two sections are fastened from the inside, again using lag screws with wash-

ers. Because the south roof section is heavier than the other panels, having a third helper makes the installation easier. The last steps are installing the trim and doing the roofing. You need enough shingles to cover 60 sq. ft. for the 8' x 8' shed, and 75 sq. ft. to cover the 8' x 10' shed. Three bundles of conventional shingles should be enough for either one, and the shingling shouldn't take any more than a morning.

From then on, the customizing and decorating is up to you. You can insulate the building or put up paneling if you'd like. You can add shelves, tool racks, or a potting bench. Some owners have put up window boxes out front as a place to plant their favorite perennials.

A final touch is to add an exhaust fan system, if you need it, to supplement the natural cross ventilation possible

using the side window and the door. The company has a fan kit that can be installed in either gable end for automatic venting. The kit includes a fan with exterior shutters, a wall-mounted thermostat, and an air intake shutter with motor. The system is good insurance to prevent overheating on sunny days. You can also construct your own method of shading from the exterior, or buy a shade kit that is offered by the company. ❧

Note: To get more information on the Green Mountain SunShed, contact Gardener's Supply Company by writing the company at 128 Intervale Rd., Burlington, VT 05401 or calling 800/477-9980 toll-free.

TECH NOTES: ASSEMBLING A SUNSHED

Owners delight in adding finishing touches to the SunShed, including paint, shingles, and exterior landscaping to blend the structure into its surroundings. Many run both electricity and water lines to it.

WAYS TO SET UP A FOUNDATION

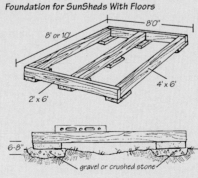

Foundation for SunSheds With Floors

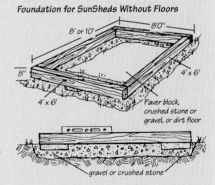

Foundation for SunSheds Without Floors

Models with or without floors need a sturdy timber foundation, as shown in the illustrations at right. They also can be erected on an existing deck or concrete patio, using the same type of foundation. To eliminate any movement, you can set the timber frame over an in-ground foundation.

Floor panels for models with floors are fastened directly to the foundation frame. The frame may be of redwood, cedar, or pressure-treated wood resting on stones or concrete block supports at the corners and center of the structure. Frame dimensions should match the structure exactly.

For models without floors, the walls are assembled directly onto the timber frame. For all foundations, excavating to a depth of 6" and filling with a level bed of coarse gravel or crushed stone is best. The foundation needs to be within $\frac{1}{8}$" of level over the full length of each side.

Spread Photo: Lindal Cedar Homes,
Seattle. Inset: Marvin Windows.

CLASSICS

PROJECT RULES OF THUMB

*Easy-To-Remember Nuggets Of Advice To
Help You Guess And Get Away With It*

That one ostrich egg will serve 24 people for brunch is a rule of thumb that might not be of much use to you unless you live in Australia. But there are hundreds of other gems of advice that do-it-yourselfers can put to good use as helpful "guesstimators" in a wide variety of projects.

Rules of thumb offer an easy-to-remember way to retain information, helping you instantly recall facts ranging from generalities, such as those in folklore sayings, to more specific data, such as scientific formulas. They are actually practical homemade recipes to help you make rough estimates, decide how to proceed, or keep you out of trouble. They fall somewhere between Newton's Law and a shot in the dark.

Some of the best rules of thumb are those that let you guess and get away with it. The rules of thumb assembled here come from professional how-to writers and trade professionals, as well as do-it-yourselfers who regularly collect these nuggets of helpful advice. You may know some of them already; pick and choose from the rest to add to your own collection. You never know when they will come in handy.

SIX-MARK SYSTEM
When using a carpenter's square to lay out a frame wall or partition, sharpen your pencil after every five or six marks. Using a dull pencil can add as much as an inch to the overall dimensions after about 20 feet, throwing the whole structure out of whack and mak-

ing it difficult to fit wallboard, sheathing, and other modular materials.

2x6 DECK RULE
When building a deck or other outdoor platform, don't use lumber wider than 6". Reason: Ponding water on wide boards can lead to cupping problems. Use two 2x6s, for example, instead of one 2x12.

THREE-FOOT OUTLETS
Over workbenches, install at least

one outlet every three feet. When wiring or rewiring the shop, consider installing outlets in the ceiling over major tool groups. Ceiling outlets are more accessible and eliminate tripping over power cords.

MARK-UP FACTOR
If you're making something in your home shop to sell, the cost of the materials shouldn't be more than 20% of the selling price. Put another way, the selling price should be at least five times the cost of your materials.

DOWEL SIZE GUIDE
The diameter of dowels in dowel joints should be half the thickness of the boards being joined. For example,

¾" stock should have ⅜"-diameter dowels; ⅞" stock should have ⁷⁄₁₆" dowels. The length inserted should be three times the dowel thickness. Thus a ⅜" dowel should be 2¼" long to penetrate 1⅛" into each member.

TWO-TUBE LIGHTING
To free work space in the home shop of glare and shadows, use two 48" tubes in a utility fluorescent light fixture, centered over the front edge of your workbench, 48" above the work area. For extra light to see details, use supplementary spotlighting. A lamp with a 50-watt reflector bulb can be clamped near task areas like vises and drill presses.

GLUING DOWELS
A good fit when gluing dowels is when you can push the dowel into the hole with your fingers, but not so large that the loose dowel wobbles. Don't put glue only in the hole bottom and hope that the glue will squeeze up. Apply the glue to both the dowel and the sides of the hole.

BENCH HEIGHT GUIDE
The height of workbenches is generally figured at about 4" higher than your waist. But also consider the height of your table saw. If you build the bench the same height, you can use it for extra support when sawing oversize materials.

TWO-THIRDS, ONE-THIRD
Select screws so two-thirds will go into the base material you are fastening to. In hardwood or wood likely to split, drill a pilot hole and a clearance hole for the shank. The shank

clearance hole is the same diameter as the screw shank, drilled one-third the length of the screw.

BAND SAW CIRCLES

The width of the blade and set of the teeth determine the minimum diameter circle you can cut on a band saw without damaging the blade or saw guides. Usually a ⅛" blade will cut a radius as small as ⅛"; a ³⁄₁₆" blade as small as ⁵⁄₁₆"; a ¼" blade as small as ⅝", a ⅜" blade as small as 1⁷⁄₁₆", and a ½" blade as small as 2⅝".

THINNER TO THICKER

When building a deck for your home, always nail a thinner member to a thicker member. Use hot-dipped, zinc-coated nails, and for maximum holding power, consider using ring- or spiral-shank nails to help reduce lumber warping.

WOOD SALVAGER'S RULE

If trying to decide the value of used lumber, recycling wood from standing buildings usually is only worthwhile if you can get it for little or nothing, because of the value of your labor.

BEST-SIDE SAWING

When sawing wood with a portable circular saw or saber saw, keep the good side down. For handsaws, scroll saws, band saws, circular table saws, and radial-arm saws, keep the good side up. Remember, have the tooth of the blade first exit through the back side of the board or panel.

PLYWOOD WEIGHT GUESSING

An easy way to estimate how much a sheet of plywood weighs is to figure about 25 lbs. per ¼" of thickness. A 4' x 8' sheet of ¼" plywood, for example, will weigh about 25 lbs.; ½", about 50; and ¾", about 75 lbs.

TWICE-OVER READING

After you read the directions for making or assembling a project, force yourself to read them again. You often will be surprised at what you may have overlooked, and chances are good you will pick up some fact that will make the project go more smoothly.

50-DEGREE FACTOR

Epoxy and acrylic adhesives need a temperature of 50 degrees F. to cure. If the temperature is lower, epoxies will soften, but will cure when the temperature rises. If acrylics are used below 50 degrees, however, they will never cure.

TWO-INCH ROUGH-INS

When making rough openings for interior doors, make the rough opening 2" inches higher and wider. For example, for a door 6'8" high, make the height of the rough opening 6'10". If the width of the door is 2'6", add 2" and make the rough opening 2'8" wide.

TOOL BUYER'S RULE

A common complaint of experienced shop owners is that their tools are underpowered by at least 50%. Many say they would have kept their first purchase if the horsepower had roughly been double. If buying a band saw, for example, get one with the deepest throat and the most power you can afford.

CFM REQUIREMENTS

The minimum airflow needed to handle debris from woodworking tools ranges from about 300 to 700 CFM (cubic feet per minute). Most home vacs provide about 100 CFM and industrial vacs about 120 CFM. Dust collectors operate on a different principle; even smaller ones can provide from about 700 to 1,300 CFM.

SHARPENING TIP-OFF

If you are having problems with weak glue joints, you may need to sharpen up your woodworking tools. Dull tools can loosen surface layers of wood, and glue may not be getting through the debris to solid wood.

FAUCET PRICE FACTOR

When doing home plumbing projects, consider that a higher-priced faucet may last as much as three times longer than a cheaper faucet. By going with better faucets, you not only save the cost of the second and third faucet, but also the trouble or cost of getting them installed.

TWO-WEEK SET

Don't take wood at cold or sub-zero temperatures into the shop and immediately start working on it. When starting a carving or turning project, give the wood a chance to equalize with your shop's heat and humidity, preferably two weeks or longer.

SCREWDRIVER FITTING

The right screwdriver for the job should fit snugly into the slot of the screw. If you let go of the screw and hold the screwdriver up in the air, the screw should stay on the end of the tool and not fall off.

TOOL HEIGHT GUIDES

For maximum efficiency, a bench or point of operation above the floor for an average person 5'9¼" tall should be 46" for band saws; 41" for lathes; 39" for radial-arm saws; 36" for hand-fed circular saws, shapers, and sanders, and 33" for jointers.

TOOL PRICE RULE

Because of market competition, you generally won't go wrong if you go by price. Usually manufacturers need a reason to charge more for a product. If you're wondering whether to buy a $500 tool or a $750 tool, go with the more expensive. The shortcomings of the cheaper tool will grow in your mind every time you use it.

PIPE PENCIL TEST

To determine if your water pipes need replacing, open the laundry tub faucet fully, then turn on your most remote fixture. If you are connected to a municipal water system, and you don't get a stream at least the size of a pencil at the remote fixture, your supply pipes may be corroded to the point where they should be replaced.

FASTENER SPACING

A fastener in sheetmetal shouldn't be any closer than 4 to 6 diameters from the next one. If you are using a ⅛" Pop Rivet, for example, the nearest rivet should be ½" to ¾". Using this rule reduces chances of damaging a part, and makes optimum use of fasteners.

TOOL LONGEVITY

For occasional home shop work, a low-price clamshell tool is fine. For the serious worker, a light-duty industrial tool is better. For a contractor, a heavy-duty industrial tool is a must. A good industrial tool will last 20 times longer than a lower-price consumer tool.

MARBLE TEST

To check floors for level when looking at "handyman special" houses, set down a marble at various intervals along the walls. If the floor has a smooth surface, the marble will roll to the low spots. How fast it rolls will indicate how level the floors are.

TABLE FORMULA

When planning to make a round dining table, you can figure the maximum number of people it will seat will be twice the table's diameter in feet. For example, a 5½'-wide table would seat 11 people. The circumference would be 207", allowing 18¼" per place setting.

WIRING GENERATIONS

If your home is at least 20 years old, you can expect to find as many as three "generations" of wiring and up to a dozen minor infractions of the National Electrical Code.

STAIR BUILDER'S RULE

When building stairs, the 25" factor is handy in calculating a safe and comfortable ratio of tread width to riser height. Figure that twice the riser height, plus the tread width, should equal about 25". For example, steep stairs with 9½" risers and 6" treads would be 9½ + 9½ + 6 for a total of 25"; low broad steps outdoors with 5" risers and 15" treaders would be 5 + 5 + 15 for 25".

BENDING DECISIONS

The radius of the bend in metal should be no less than 1½ times the thickness. If you are bending a ¹⁄₁₆"-thick piece, for example, the smallest the bend radius used should be ³⁄₃₂". If the metal cracks when it is bent, increase the bend radius to two times.

WHITE OR YELLOW?

Aliphatic resins (the yellow glues) will clog sandpaper less during finishing than polyvinyl acetates (the white glues). Yellow glues also are stronger and more water resistant. Both set in an hour, and cure in 24 hours. ⁂

ESTIMATING RULES OF THUMB

FRAME FIGURING

To figure the total length of material you need for any framing job with miter joints (doors, windows, and picture frames), multiply the combined height and width of the inside dimensions of the frame opening by 2, then add the molding width multiplied by 8, and add an extra inch for saw kerfs. That's how much material you'll need, but cut carefully because this allows only ½" for error.

HALF-BOX RULE

When buying quantities of standard fasteners (such as screws and bolts), if you need almost half a box or more, buy a full box. The second half is virtually free, compared to the higher per-piece costs. For example, 45 individual screws will cost about the same as a box of 100.

REMODELING PROJECTS

Working from scratch may be as much as 100% easier than remodeling. Keep this in mind and always allow for some extra time for the unexpected when, for example, you will be uncovering walls in a remodeling project.

THREE-TRIP PLUMBING

For the typical do-it-yourselfer, most plumbing projects won't be complete until you've gone to the store three times for parts and materials.

PAINT TIME GUESSES

When painting a room with walls in good shape, plan on spending as much time on preparation as on the actual painting. If walls are in poor shape, nonpainting time may take longer.

PAINT COVERAGE

Most paints will cover about 400 square feet per gallon at a normal 4-mil thickness. Because latex is so easily applied, guard against stretching it so much that a second coat will be needed. Check the approximate coverage on the label, and subtract about 10% for waste when using a brush or roller.

FOOTING SIZE RULE

To figure footings for under concrete block or poured concrete walls, a rule of thumb is: Width, twice the wall width; depth, the same as the wall width. This means that a 12" block wall would need a footing 24" wide and 12" deep, while an 8" wall would take a footing 16" wide and 8" deep. Generally, footings carrying significant weight should rest on a 6" gravel base set below the frost line; check your local building code.

CEMENT MIXING RULE

A good rule of thumb when mixing is that approximately 6 gallons of water will be needed for every 94-lb. bag of Portland cement. (Each 94-lb. bag is 1 cubic foot.) An average shovel of sand will weigh about 15 lbs., and a cubic yard of sand will weigh about 2,700 lbs.

DOUBLE-TIME ESTIMATES

Unless you have considerable experience, when estimating time needed to complete a project, make a guess, then double it. If the project involves techniques you haven't used before, a lot of small parts to be bought, or factors beyond your control (like weather), triple or quadruple your first guess.

FRENCH DOORS

*Now Home Exterior Doors Can Be More
Than Just A Piece Of Sliding Glass*

If you're up late some evening and the 1939 movie *Midnight* is showing on TV, tune it in. It's an amusing story of a Paris cabbie (Don Ameche) chasing an American showgirl (Claudette Colbert) who is hired by a rich man to pose as a baroness. But that's not the only reason to watch it.

While Claudette Colbert performs her upwardly mobile antics in and out of Parsian hotels and country villas, notice the French doors. Every few minutes someone walks through the original, authentic double doors that have inspired America's newest obsession in door styling for new homes or for existing homes built

with aluminum "slider" patio doors that began showing up in the Fifties and Sixties.

Sensing the new fascination with French doors, manufacturers such as Marvin Windows & Doors have been quick to respond with a variety of offerings that simulate, if not duplicate, the door style firmly rooted in the land of Napoleon, wine, éclairs, and croissants. You can get them to divide interiors or to provide stylish access to a deck, patio, or manicured garden. The price tag per double unit in standard sizes will vary from about $500 to $1,000 or so, depending on such subleties as glazing and locks.

But what is an authentic French door? Experts at Marvin Windows, with headquarters near the Canadian border at Warroad, Minnesota, explain that true French doors have two doors that hinge at the side jambs, lock at the center, and swing in toward the interior of the home. (Two-door units that have hinges in the center and swing in are called Terrace doors by the company.) To cover the center joint between the two French doors, one of them has integral molding that, in door talk, is called an "astragal."

The big news in French doors, however, and one of the reasons they are becoming as popular as a good

French bakery, is that technical advancements have made them energy-efficient enough to be used in exterior walls, even in northern-tier states with glacierlike winters. Improvements in glass technology — such as the use of Low-E panes filled between with argon gas — have made their double glazing actually more energy efficient than triple glazing used to be. That, added to new-style sills and sealing methods used today, make them a feasible exterior door option in any home, and in any climate, hot or cold.

A major advantage of French doors is that, with both sides open, they offer a larger, unobstructed opening than other type of doors. For the most authentic French door look, you would choose those with divided sections of glass (called lites) and that swing inward. This style, in fact, is the most popular. Outward-swinging French doors, point out Marvin door experts, are somewhat less historically accurate but can offer advantages over in-swinging doors that eat up interior space and can limit decorating options. Drifting further away from the original French doors, but still suggesting the look, are the double center-pivoting Terrace doors or French-style patio doors.

Tip: If you like the authentic version, but need only one door to open,

Options abound for the French door look. The photo at top, opposite page, shows how they have been updated to allow use on exteriors and to swing outward, unlike traditional French doors, bottom left, which swing inward. Wider stiles and rails also can impart a French aura on newer versions of the patio door, bottom right, which have been redesigned from the ground up since the '50s.

French doors can be candidates for any living space, including condominiums, as shown at the top of this page. They also can be enhanced with transoms, arched tops, or other surrounding glass, as shown at right. Double French doors can be individualized with authentic divided lites (individual pieces of glass), as shown below, or with snap-in grills.

TECH NOTES: INSTALLING FRENCH DOORS

THE IMPROVED FRENCH DOOR

Heavy foam-filled weatherstripping around the frame and at astragal minimizes air infiltration

Wood doors can be ordered in 1⅜" or 1¾" thicknesses for either interior or exterior applications

Wide bottom rails and center stiles authenticate true French door style

A special four-finned sill sweep and drip cap help minimize air and water infiltration at the bottom

Doors, factory sealed top and bottom, swing on either four or five hinges on heavy wooden frames

A multipoint locking system uses three handle-controlled bolts on one door, two on the other

the "sister" door can be a non-functioning, fixed panel. If you are bored with the look of straight lines, you also can get arched French doors with an elegant radiused top.

Marvin Windows takes pride in the fact that it's entire French door line comes from a single source and is not assembled with components from a number of manufacturers. The company offers them unbored and without a lock, so you can choose the hardware you want. They also can

be ordered with a lock and deadbolt with a 2⅜" backset for added security, however. Doors come with a sill improved to provide 1,400 times the insulating value of aluminum, along with a special four-fin sweep with drip cap to keep out the elements.

Overall the company offers nearly 40 sizes of in-swinging doors, and a comparable range of sizes in the out-swinging style. They are designed for 2x4 or 2x6 walls, though you can get extensions to fit nearly any wall

thickness. Any French door style is available with all-wood framing or with extruded aluminum cladding on the exterior for maintenance-free service. To keep mosquitos out, you can get swinging combination screen/storm doors, or just swinging screen doors.

Rough openings generally should provide for 1" more free space width-wise, and ½" extra space height-wise, than the frame. Rough opening widths required for standard in-

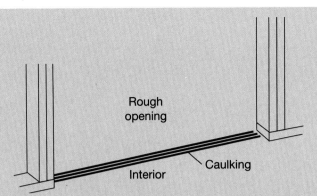

Rough opening

Interior

Caulking

Rough openings in wood walls, either existing or newly built, should be 1" wider than the frame, and ½" higher. Masonry wall openings should be ½" wider and ¼" higher.

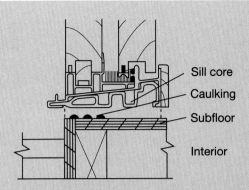

Sill core

Caulking

Subfloor

Interior

For best results the bottom of the rough opening should be both level and smooth. Caulk/adhesive is applied along the subfloor before the frame is installed.

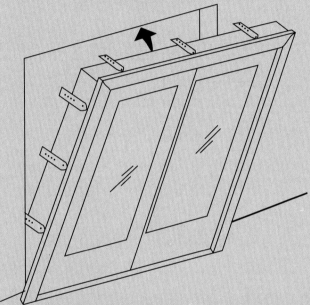

A helper is needed to assist positioning the doors into the rough opening. For exterior walls, the unit is inserted and the siding is marked to be trimmed off with a circular saw before final installation. The frame is temporarily held with 2" nails through installation brackets while square and plumb are checked before final fastening is completed.

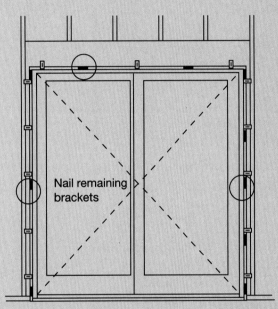

Nail remaining brackets

Shims are used to square the frame within the stud opening. (Any raising of the sill section is done with solid lumber, not shims.) After centering and checking diagonal measurements, shims (see circles) are secured, then scored with a utility knife and broken off. Factory jamb covers or interior trim hides the gap around the frame.

swinging French doors, for example, start at 2'8⅜" and increase in increments of 2'10⅜", 3'2⅜", 5'3⅜", and 6'3⅜". Rough opening heights start at 6'10¹⁵⁄₁₆" and jump to 7'2¹⁵⁄₁₆" and 8'2¹⁵⁄₁₆".

Openings for out-swinging doors and for masonry walls differ slightly. Glazing options include single-tempered or insulating-tempered glass or Low-E glass with argon gas.

Installing your own French doors is feasible (see TECH NOTES), and might save you about $150 or more per double-door unit. Installation handbooks are available to guide you through the steps, including removing the old door or building the rough opening, installing the new door, and completing the installation right through interior trimming. The most critical steps are making sure that the rough opening is of adequate size, raising the sill to a proper height if necessary (such as for high carpeting), and using shims to adjust the frame to be plumb and square for proper door operation.

*Note: For more information on how you might incorporate French doors in your home, contact Marvin Windows & Doors at P. O. Box 100, Warroad, MN 56763, or call 800/346-5128. The company has an excellent idea publication, **Before and After: Successful Remodeling With Marvin Windows & Doors**, available for $4.95, postage and handling included.*

The RAISED-BED GARDEN

How To Lift The Productivity Of Your Home-Grown Crops To New Levels

Harvest more produce from your garden with less work — it sounds almost too good to be true. Yet that's what happens when gardeners use the centuries-old technique of using raised beds of soil to improve growing conditions for home-grown crops.

The practice, which originated in the Orient, works with just about any crop or soil, according to experts at Garden Way, Inc., manufacturer of the famed Troy-Bilt garden tiller. You mound up the earth on each side of walkways to create more favorable conditions for plants. The plants respond with higher yields, while you save time and effort in the garden.

TWO-LEVEL ADVANTAGES

Raised beds offer more gain with less pain. Here are the specific advantages of switching from a flat garden to one with two levels:

More Produce. Raised beds increase the depth of fertile soil for your crops, even if you've been stuck with thin, rocky, or clay soils. The deeper topsoil promotes bigger root systems and better anchored, sturdier plants. Raised beds also eliminate foot traffic and standing water which compact the soil, restricting root growth and yields. The soil stays loose and aerated, with less surface crusting. That makes it easier for roots to get water, oxygen, and nutrients.

Earlier Planting. More soil surface is exposed to sun and wind than with level gardens, so raised beds warm up quicker and dry out faster. Assuming there is enough humus in your soil, you can be out planting while your neighbors watch, even if it rains every three or four days. Raised beds have been found to be up to 10 degrees warmer than flat gardens; this speeds seed germination and gives you a jump on the growing season. Tip: A raised bed or two made in the fall will

The centuries-old technique of raised beds offers multiple advantages. Soil for the beds comes from the aisles between.

provide a place for earliest possible plantings in spring.

Healthier Crops. Because air circulates better around raised beds, wet stems and leaves dry faster to reduce the risk of diseases. At the same time, the improved drainage of raised beds lessens the threat of plant rot during wet spells, which is important for crops like tomatoes and cucumbers. Raised beds help another way, too. Rain can drown or wash out germinating seeds and small plants. However, by forming raised beds in a contour across any slope, the beds will catch runoff in the furrows and keep such damage to a miniumum.

Other Benefits. With raised beds you don't have to stoop as far when working on home-grown crops. Those who have raised beds also say that with less compaction the hoe almost glides through the softer soil. Irrigation is simplified as well; you can simply lay a garden hose at one end and let water run between the beds. You are not restricted to a specific size or shape of bed, either. You can form beds in triangles, squares, and circles — even make beds at different levels, with some plants tumbling over the edges and down the sides.

STEPS TO RAISED BEDS

Typically, raised beds are 6" to 10" higher than the aisles between them. It's best to make them no wider than twice the reach of your arm, about 4'. That way you can work the bed from either side without having to walk on the bed.

Here's how to make your own raised-bed garden:

1. Till the site. Work up the soil to a depth of 6" or so where you want your raised-bed garden (a tiller works best). Work in organic matter, fertilizers, and lime at this time as needed.

2. Excavate the walkway. Use a shovel, a rake, or a spade to dig out a pathway about 18" wide and 6" deep, or use a tiller with a furrower attachment to make a deep furrow.

3. Form the bed. With hand tools, use a hoe and a rake to shape the soil excavated from the walkway into the bed. Angle the sides as steeply as possible, but not so steep that they will cave in or erode. If you use a tiller, the furrower will create the bed sides.

4. Consider side walls. Some gardeners use logs, railroad ties, or planks as side walls to build tidy-looking beds to varying heights, depending on whether they prefer to kneel, sit, or stand when working. A 3'-high bed, for example, can provide a person confined to a wheelchair easy access to gardening.

5. Prepare and plant. Flatten and smooth the top of the bed with the back side of a rake, then plant. Depending on the width of your beds, you can broadcast seeds of some crops instead of planting them single file in a row. Doing this allows plants to grow leaf to leaf, forming a living mulch that suppresses weeds, conserves moisture, and protects soil from rain erosion. This works well with beans, beets, carrots, peas, and most herbs.

Broadcasting also allows more plants per square foot, which can double, even triple yields. After seeding, tamp the seeds down, cover them with soil raked up from the sides of the bed, and tamp again. When seedlings reach ¼" to ½" high, drag a garden rake across them to thin out about a third of them; this also helps get rid of weed seeds that have germinated among the vegetables.

Plants that are set out as seedlings, like broccoli, cabbages, cauliflower, head lettuce, and peppers, can be planted in a staggered arrangement. Transplants that like tight quarters can be arranged in a 2-1-2 or a 3-2-3 pattern and kept thinned by harvesting the largest plants; the others usually will grow in quickly to fill

THE 10-MINUTE GARDEN

Row 5	**Pole Beans**		**Corn**
			Corn
			Corn
			Corn
Row 4	**Tomatoes**		**Cucumbers**
	Peppers		**S.Squash/Zucchini**
Row 3	**Broccoli**	**Cabbage**	**Cauliflower**
	Peas Followed By Beans		
Row 2	**Onions**		
	Beets		**Carrots**
Row 1	**Lettuce**	**Spinach**	**Chard**
	Dill	**Basil**	**Oregano**	**Parsley**

Garden Plan (20' x 25')

An activity-crammed schedule doesn't have to mean no garden. Here's a 20' x 25' plan designed for high efficiency, developed by Garden Way for people who don't have time to garden. The trick is to do a little gardening each day, say 10 minutes, rather than save all the work for the weekend. For example, on Monday, spend 10 minutes cultivating Row 1. Tuesday do Row 2, and so on. Later on you'll spend 10 minutes a day harvesting the fruits of your labor.

the void. Single-row crops can be seeded in double rows in beds at least 16" wide.

Keys To Success

To get the most from raised-bed gardens, you need to pay attention to factors such as organic matter, watering, weeding, and mulching. Raised beds can dry out faster and, once dried completely, they can be difficult to re-moisten.

Organics. Well-rotted manure or non-woody organic materials can be used to make soil more fertile and hold the right amount of moisture, or as a mulch to help shade and cool the soil and also smother weeds before they start. (Wood chips are okay among deep-rooted perennials.) Organic materials also help feed

earthworms, microbes, and other beneficial soil organisms. Add them at least once a year, applying a layer about 1" thick on established beds and working it into the top 6" or so.

Watering. When seeds are germinating, keep the top 1" to 2" of soil moist. Once plants are established, increase the moist soil depth to 5" to 6". You can water the soil directly, using a sprinkler or soaker hose, or irrigate the beds by flooding the aisles. When you water, water deeply to encourage deep roots.

Weeding. Usually a weekly shallow cultivation will control weeds between the rows and keep the soil loose and aerated. Within the rows, crops will shade out most of the weeds and reduce the time required for hand weeding. You'll find that the uncompacted soil in the beds will make the weeds easier to pull out.

Mulching. After planting and cultivating between the rows several times over a few weeks, you may want to put down a layer of mulch. Fill the walkways between the beds to prevent weeds from germinating and to help keep the beds moist. When temperatures rise, the mulch also will help keep the beds from becoming too hot. At the end of the season, you can till the mulch into your soil to increase its organic content.

Weather. Raised beds can offer you new ways to beat the weather, including drought, heat, or wet springs. Here are some tips:

• Plant early-season crops which need warm soils on top of the beds. After harvesting, till them in and then plant the next crop in the aisle between the beds. The beds will protect the new plantings from scorching temperatures and parching winds. They'll also provide water-saving shade early and late in the day.

• When water is likely to be scarce, or in dry locations, plant in the furrows or the walkways between the beds to make the most of the moisture you have. Another alternative is to plant on top of the beds and fill the aisles with mulch to slow evaporation.

• If you're plagued with wet soils in the spring, make your raised beds in the fall. The next spring the beds will drain and warm up as much as two weeks faster than a conventional garden. ❧

Note: For more information on raised-bed gardening and a free Great Gardens catalog, contact Troy-Bilt, 102nd St. and 9th Ave., Troy, NY 12180 or call 800/828-5500 toll-free.

MAKING RAISED BEDS

Use a tiller or a spade to work up your garden at least twice. Dig as deep as possible to leave the soil loose and thoroughly crumbled. Add any lime, organic matter, or fertilizer before your last tillage, mixing the materials well into the soil. If using a tiller, make the last pass perpendicular to the direction of your beds to help form straight beds and walkways.

Preparing the soil. Turn hard-packed soil into a loose, fluffy seedbed by making several passes at increasing depths.

Forming the bed. This can be done by hand or with a tiller with a furrower attachment, which can make raised beds as fast as you can walk.

Raking the top. After the beds are formed, rake the tops smooth with a garden rake. A raised bed can be from 8" to about 4' wide.

Planting the crop. Plant the crop as usual, using two or three single-file rows to a raised bed, or wide-row plant the entire bed.

NAIL HANDLERS

Nail Tools Can Save The Day, Whether You're Building Up Or Tearing Down

Unless you specialize in salvage work, chances are you'll hear much more about hammering nails than you will about pulling them. Carpenter Duane Clarke theorizes that the reason is that there is a stigma attached to the subject of pulling nails. It probably stems from the time when, as beginners, we associated pulling nails as a sign of incompetence, he says.

Another reason is the lack of hard-and-fast rules for pulling nails. How you do it depends not only on the tools you use, but also on the techniques you pick up by watching others and trying different ways yourself.

There are two basic kinds of nail pulling. First there is pulling nails that are bent while hammering or mistakenly driven into the wrong place. Anytime you watch a crew frame a house, you'll see a fair share of this. Knots, slippery hammer faces, defective or weak-shanked

Tool size, shape, and purpose are diverse in the nail handling arsenal. Catspaws (#1, #2, #3) can be a carpenter's best friend. Wrecking bars (#4 and #5) often are mistakenly called crowbars, and some (#6 and #7) have double heads for improved action. Prybars (#8 and #9) are cousins of the ripping bar (#10). The hand drilling hammer (#11) is the recommended tool for hitting nail pullers. The framing hammer (#12) can pull most nails 16d or smaller. The wedge (#13), commonly used for splitting firewood, can be helpful when two pieces of lumber need prying apart. Small prybars (#14, #15, #16) sometimes are called handy bars. The sliding-handle nail puller (#17) provides its own mechanical action.

nails, and awkward nailing positions can all lead to bent nails. So can poor hammering technique.

Then there is pulling nails in order to dismantle or recycle lumber. Here, nail pulling is often a secondary objective; the first order of business is to get that lumber apart, and then take care of the nails later.

The difficulty of removing a nail depends on the nail itself, how it was driven, and what it was nailed into. Hot-dipped galvanized nails, spiral or ring-shanked nails, and cement-coated nails are harder to pull because the shank surface creates a lot of friction. The resin-type adhesive on a cement-coated nail actually "sets" when the nail is driven, creating a bond between wood and metal. Duplex nails, on the other hand, are made to be pulled. These specialized nails are used for temporary fastening of such things as scaffolding, wall bracing, or concrete forms.

NAIL-PULLING LEVERAGE

Over the years hand tool manufacturers have come up with a variety of nail pullers. The photo opposite shows a sampling. These tools have either claws or slots to capture the nailhead, a prybar to loosen nails by forcing lumber apart, or a blade to sever nails. Many nail-pulling tools combine these features. Unlike other areas of carpentry, nail pulling hasn't been motorized. There are no pneumatic or electric nail pullers.

All nail-pulling tools use what physics teachers call first-class or second-class leverage. With first-class levers, the fulcrum (or pivot point) is between you and the load (the nail you are pulling). This is the leverage you get with hammers and other tools with claws at 90 degrees to the handle. The second-class lever has the load (the nail) between you and the fulcrum (the pivot point). This is the kind of leverage you get when you pull up on

tools with nail slots in the middle.

HAMMER CLAW PULLING

The basic hammer is the most widely used nail puller, though some carpenters hate to use it for that task for fear of breaking the handle. Clarke, for example, uses 22-oz. and 16-oz. framing hammers, and prefers straight claws to curved claws, for a couple of reasons. Straight claws can easily be forced between two pieces of lumber to pry them apart. And the straight claws don't require bending over as far to get the claws under the head of a nail. Other carpenters prefer curved claws because they provide better leverage for nail pulling.

Hammer handles can be wood, fiberglass, or steel. Wood and fiberglass have good shock-absorbing qualities, while a one-piece, steel-forged hammer is generally thought to be more durable. Any good-quality hammer should last through many nail-pulling sessions if the proper technique is used — a steady, smooth, pulling motion.

When you buy a hammer, it pays to evaluate it as a nail-pulling tool, as well as a driving tool. Make sure the claw is heat-treated and well tempered. The V of the claw should be clean and sharp so that you can get a good bite on a nail as big as 16d. Good claw hammers have ground and polished heads of drop-forged steel, not brittle cast iron.

The weakest part of any hammer is where the handle enters the head. To reduce breakage when pulling nails, many carpenters use a scrap of wood as an added fulcrum under the head. It can be a piece of 1x, or other available scrap. Gaining this extra mechanical advantage is especially helpful for deeply embedded nails or nails driven into hardwood.

To make extra nail-pulling leverage a permanent feature, some carpenters weld a short stub of steel rod across the

ADVICE ON BUYING NAIL PULLERS

The best nail pullers are made from heat-treated high-carbon (1078 or 1080) steel. The 10 stands for a straight carbon series steel; the last two digits indicate the percent of carbon. Many flat prybars are made of 1095 spring-tempered forged steel. The claws (or working ends) of the tool should be forged, ground, and painted.

As with other tools, a higher price usually means higher quality. Check how long the manufacturer has been in business. Many name-brand nail-pulling tools are made by companies that go back to horse-and-buggy days. Even these companies get tools returned to them occasionally, but usually less than 1% of them. Of these, most have been misused; many have been overly muscled with extensions, and others have been overheated during grinding, with a resulting loss of temper.

Nail-pulling tools forged in one piece generally will be stronger than those with welded parts. This does not mean you should avoid welded tools. If you are buying a tool that has been welded, however, take time to examine the bead closely. Pass up any tool with a bead that looks like it might have a defect. It is bad business to break such as tool, especially if it is being used under heavy pressure, and you are perched on a roof or wall, or standing on a ladder.

Tool manufacturers advise against striking a nail hammer or nail puller with another nail hammer. They recommend a hand drilling hammer, above, or a light sledge. Duane Clarke, top left, shows how to increase claw hammer pulling leverage with scrap wood. A double-headed wrecking bar, bottom left, allows a rocking motion for more speed and working comfort. **Opposite page***: Scraps of wood, top left, also can improve leverage when using pullers with center slots. The catspaw, top right, comes in various sizes and works well for removing nails hard to get at with hammer claws. A double-headed tool, bottom left, is used to remove flooring, siding, or sheathing. Set on rafter or joist, the twin prongs exert equal pressure on both sides. A second hammer, bottom right, often is used as a substitute for scrap wood to improve leverage.*

top of the hammer head, being careful not to ruin its temper. Improving leverage this way results in straighter pulled nails. Even though used nails haven't much status today, there are times when you run out of spikes and need just a few more to finish. That is when a bucket of used nails comes in handy.

Wherever the point of the nail protrudes, you can drive it back to make the head accessible. If the end of the nail just barely penetrates the lumber, you can use a nail set to back the head out enough to get your hammer claw under it. The cupped end of a 1/16" or 3/32" nail set will fit nicely over the nail's point to keep it from slipping off. Clinched or bent-over nails can be straightened for removal by using the claw of the hammer. Alternatively, you can pry the two boards partially apart, then hammer them back

together. This will expose at least some of the nailheads.

Once in a while, the head of the nail will break off when you are pulling it. If this happens, one solution is to push it as far into the V-notch of the hammer claw as possible, then twist the hammer a quarter turn to each side. The sharp inside edges of the V will groove the nail to provide grip as you pull it. Another way is to use pliers or nippers, along with a scrap wood fulcrum, if necessary, to inch the nail up and out.

Some beginners are tempted to use a second hammer to get a grip on tightly embedded nails, striking the face of the hammer that has the nail engaged in its claw. This can be extremely dangerous. Two hardened metal surfaces striking with force are likely to send brittle metal chips flying at high speed. As proof of this

hazard, Clarke still carries a small metal fragment from a crosshatched framing hammer in one eyelid.

Today, most hammers are sold with warnings that promote the wearing of safety goggles. This is sound advice. If you do need to snug up a hammer claw on a nail, it is best to use a mallet, a drilling hammer, or a short length of 2x lumber.

SPECIALIZED NAIL PULLERS

There are plenty of nail-pulling situations where a hammer isn't the tool of choice. If you need to pull nails that have their heads set below the surface of the wood, it is possible to expose the head by chiseling carefully around it so you can get the hammer claw under it. It is much easier (especially on your chisels), however, to use a catspaw.

The claws on catspaws — which usually are curved 90 degrees from

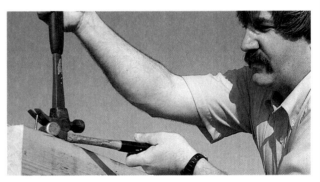

the handle, but also may be straight — are made to be driven into the wood and under a nailhead. Catspaws made of bar-steel stock are best struck with a drilling hammer or sledge. Nevertheless, you still should wear eye protection.

Nails bigger than 16d usually demand more leverage than a hammer or catspaw can provide, so wrecking bars should be used. The terms "wrecking bar" and "crowbar" often are used interchangeably. Technically, crowbars are 5' to 6' long, while wrecking bars generally are smaller, with one end that is slightly angled and another that is curved 90 degrees, gooseneck fashion.

On the racks of a well-stocked hardware store, you'll see some newer variations of the wrecking bar. Prybars and ripping bars are similar to wrecking bars, but flatter in section. A spe-

cialized type of wrecking bar has a double head, and looks something like a claw-tipped horseshoe attached to a steel handle at about 45 degrees. This tool can still be used to pry up flooring, siding, sheathing, and roof boards. Set on a joist or rafter, with its two-pronged head under the boards, the tool lets you use a fast rolling action to loosen wood. Homemade versions of this tool exist, but you have to be a fair welder to make one that is safe and will last.

The sliding-handle nail puller is one of the more expensive nail-pulling tools you can buy. It usually costs between $30 and $40, and is worth every penny if you need it. During general construction you won't get that much use out of it. It is a worthwhile investment, however, if you are removing plywood sheathing or if you are doing a lot of remodeling.

The tool has a sliding handle that acts like a pile driver, pushing one of its jaws under the nailhead. You simply push or pull the tool, and the second jaw grabs under the nailhead. As you continue the motion, the tool pulls the nail out.

While rarely considered nail-pullers, wood-splitting iron wedges can come in handy for unfastening nails. Wedges are especially helpful when you need to separate large nailed-together beams or headers. Instead of trying to pull nails out individually, put the lumber on edge and, with prybars or wrecking bars, use the buddy system to separate the pieces. When you get the wood separated enough at one end, insert a wedge. Then, keep moving down toward the other end of the lumber. Keep adding wedges as the split opens up while you work from one end to the other.

Diminutive prybars, above and top right, can earn their keep when you must remove trim work or delicate molding. The Stanley tool shown at right resembles a screwdriver but has a miniature claw on the working end. It makes fast work of removing misplaced or unwanted staples.

TRIM AND MOLDING

Salvaging lumber can sometimes call for a more delicate touch, particularly if you are pulling nails from trim or molding that you want to reuse.

Clarke carries two small, flat pry-bars, the Wonderbar (Stanley Tools, Slater Rd., New Britain, CT 06050) and the Superbar (Vaughan & Bushnell Mfg. Co., 11414 Maple Ave., Hebron, IL 60034) for this kind of work. The Superbar is the less expensive of the two ($3 or $4). Clarke grinds an end of one bar to get a very fine edge that won't leave an indentation when he slips it behind a piece of molding. After the molding has been raised slightly, he inserts the second bar, then uses both bars alternately to pry off the trim.

Another way to remove trim is to use a nail set to punch the nail completely through the wood. Large trim that won't pry off easily is a good candidate for this treatment, but it can only work if the trim is fastened with finish nails. The disadvantage is that you end up with larger holes in the wood. Smaller holes will result if you pry off the trim and then pull the nails through the back of the trim with a hammer or pliers. For this job Clarke uses nippers or a pair of channel-lock pliers. Nippers, because of their sharp bite, can really grab a nail, but to exert strong pulling pressure you need a long-handled pair.

If trim is attached with flathead nails, you can first pry out the molding, then push it back in the hope that some nailheads will be exposed so that you can pull them out. The only problem here is that flathead nails — especially when they've been set and covered with wood putty — often will tear out some of the surrounding wood as they are hammered out head first.

To remove doors and windows installed with casing nails, what works well for Clarke is to use a Sawzall or a hacksaw blade to cut the nails off between the jamb and the rough opening. Then, after pulling the unit out, he can back out the nails or leave them in place and nip off what is left on the back side.

What about hardened cut nails in concrete? If you are removing walls and prying up a bottom plate, cut nails usually will pull right through the 2x stock, so you end up with nails sticking up out of the slab. If they don't pull out easily, one solution is simply to break them off. Cut nails are brittle, and a whack with a sledge does the job. (Be sure to wear protective goggles.) If the plate was glued down, as well as nailed, your only answer may be a sledge and ripping bar, though this approach generally will leave you with kindling wood. ❧

The ——
BACKYARD RESORT

*How To Use A Deck To Create
An Economical Backyard Paradise*

Combine an economical above-ground swimming pool with a deck surround and you have a family summer recreation center that is hard to beat. If you have a home with a first floor level at least 4' above ground, plus a sloping backyard, decking can provide an above-ground pool with many of the advantages of an in-ground pool for a fraction of the cost.

ACCESS AND STORAGE

As an example of how this can be done, Monte Burch of Humansville, Missouri, used one large deck to integrate a 24'-diameter above-ground pool into his backyard. The pool is easily accessible from the house and from his two-story office/garage, which has its second floor about 18"above the deck level. Two steps and a small platform at the sliding patio door of the office provide for easy access to this private backyard resort.

Monte's deck also extends all the way around to another side of the home, where a "privacy deck" off the master bedroom also provides access to the pool. Besides linking living areas to the pool, the space below the deck provides handy, out-of-the-way storage for items such as ladders, garden hoses, and other yard gear. The pool filter system, with all the unsightly hoses and mess, also is situated under the deck, out of the way and unseen,

yet readily accessible.

Pressure-treated wooden latticework seals off the deck sides, providing an attractive appearance while allowing air to circulate under the deck. In the yard adjacent to the deck is a small brick patio. Monte's family loves to barbecue, "but no matter

A well-designed deck can attractively integrate an above-ground pool at low cost, and provide other benefits as well.

how hard we'd try, grease and spills would cause unsightly stains on the wood deck," he says. The answer was to create a completely separate barbecue area just below the deck. The bricks, laid in sand, absorb the grease and are easily hosed down. An alcove under the deck and next to the patio provides storage for barbecue equipment.

One factor that must be considered at the outset if you plan to install a pool, says Monte, is whether you need a fence around it. Many municipalities require a pool to be fenced, and if your yard is not, the pool surround may have to have one on top of it. "In our case," he says, "the pool surround only goes around half of the pool. But a raised deck with a fence could be built around the entire pool and deck project if it were required."

Yet another advantage of installing an above-ground pool with a deck surround is that you can do it yourself. Installing an in-ground pool is almost impossible for the average homeowner. But even a beginner can erect an above-ground pool, although it does take work and attention to detail to make sure the pool is safe and lasts. Building a deck to surround the pool can be done by a homeowner with a few tools, a bit of knowledge, and the time to do the work. The cost savings is substantial compared to hiring professionals to do the job.

TEST OF TIME

Most deck projects shown in magazines and books are sparkling new, so you cannot judge how well they stand the test of time. The deck and pool project shown in these photos is more than six years old and has withstood Missouri's blazing hot

Installing a swimming pool can be a do-it-yourself project if you use an above-ground pool. Adding a deck surround makes it more attractive and easier to use. Monte's deck of pressure-treated wood successfully linked up the home, his office/garage, and the above-ground swimming pool. The area under the deck hides pool equipment and other yard gear behind latticework attached to the deck sides. Steps to ground level, shown at left, provide an ideal spot for table and chairs. The pool is in view of both the home and the office/garage, shown bottom left. The walkway to the privacy deck off the master bedroom, below, also provides access to the pool.

summers and freezing winters, not to mention numerous teenage pool parties.

Monte says this deck project was the second one he built. "Our first deck, without a pool, was constructed some years ago of standard 2x6 lumber left over from another building project. Within five years the deck boards had rotted and the deck had become unsafe. When we decided to rebuild the deck and add the pool, there was no argument that the wood used would be pressure-treated."

After some research, Monte chose Wolmanized wood, and he reports that the deck still is as sturdy, level, and attractive as it was when it was first built. Due to the constant splashing of chlorine-treated water, it has become weathered to a beautiful shade of light grey. Although Wolmanized Extra wood has a protective water repellent forced into it, it was not available when the deck was built so Monte applied a penetrating oil coating for added protection.

How to proceed? Monte says the construction of the deck and instal-

lation of the pool is fairly straight-forward, but enough planning must be done to make sure that the pool is situated correctly, and that the deck fits properly to the house and the pool. To review the steps he followed for the installation, see TECH NOTES. "Granted, your conditions may not be the same as ours with a sloping lot ideal for an above-ground pool," Monte says. "But how we approached the installation should give you some ideas on how you can start planning your own project." ❧

TECH NOTES: CREATING A BACKYARD RESORT

In our project, the deck support members were installed, then the pool, and finally the deck surface. This allowed us to rough-cut the deck surface boards where they overhung the pool, then chalk-line them and cut a straight line for the coping. Then the coping or fascia was installed, the oil finish added, and finally the pool filled — the moment we were all eagerly awaiting. Following is a step-by-step review of how we proceeded. — Monte Burch.

1 The first step is to determine exactly where the pool should be situated. A pool should not be located under electrical power lines, or over septic tanks, drainage fields, soft sand, or low spots that may collect water from higher ground. The pool also should not be placed on built-up or filled ground that may shift or settle. We set a stake in the approximate center of the pool location, then drove a nail in the top of the stake and tied on a string the length of the radius (one half the diameter of the pool). Then, using small wooden stakes, we outlined the circumference of the pool.

2 Using the string, we shifted the pool outline until it was just right. It is important that the pool be absolutely level to within 1" and rest on a smooth surface. With the position of the pool determined, and before beginning deck construction, we excavated as needed to make the area level and smooth. This surface preparation was extended at least 1' further than the outside edge of the pool. We removed all grass, weeds, and clumps of turf from within the pool area, and also cleared the area where the deck was to be built.

3 With the pool area located and prepared, the next step was to lay out the deck and fasten the ledger (board) to support the deck against the house. This must be fastened securely using lag screws, bolts, concrete anchors, or spikes, depending on your home's construction. Measuring from the ledger, we sited the positions of the support posts to find where postholes would be dug to below the frost line. This can be done by hand, or you can rent a power posthole digger, which makes the job a breeze.

4 Support posts may be set on concrete piers and fastened in place with special metal plates, or with a large bolt set in the pier to fit in holes in

TOP VIEW OF DECK AND POOL

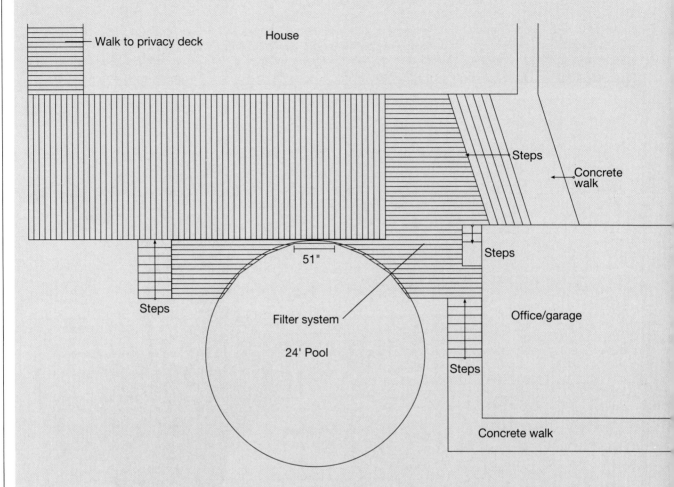

Walk to privacy deck

House

Steps

Concrete walk

Steps

51"

Steps

Filter system

Office/garage

24' Pool

Steps

Concrete walk

the posts. Posts also can be placed in the ground on prepoured concrete punch pads, with concrete poured around them, or simply placed in the ground in solid areas. A check with local building codes will dictate the type of post support needed for a safe, long-lasting deck.

5 In most instances, placing the posts on concrete pads and pouring additional concrete around them is the easiest and most effective method. If you use this technique, rough-cut the posts to a little longer than the correct height. The height can be determined by placing one end of a straight, smooth board on the ledger on the side of the house and holding it level at the post site. Measure from the top of the board edge to the bottom of the posthole or top of the concrete pier. We placed the outside posts in position first. Then we poured the

punch pads, allowing them to cure for three days. We then put the posts in place, measuring exactly in all directions to make sure they were positioned correctly.

6 It's important to make sure the sides of the posts are square and plumb because an angled post can cause a great deal of trouble when nailing joists and other supports in place. With the posts plumb in both directions, we braced them with 2x4s and stakes. Then we poured concrete around them until slightly higher than ground level, then smoothed the top of the concrete and allowed it to cure.

7 Once the concrete was set, the braces were removed and the joist header was attached to the front of the posts, then to the joists between the header and the ledger, and to each post. Make sure there is at least ¼"

slope per foot from the house to the outside edge of the header. We cut the posts off flush with the tops of the joists and headers using a hand saw. On a deck such as this, with decking running in several directions, the joists must be run in opposite directions for each decking pattern.

8 An alternative to this type of construction is to place beams on top of the posts, then toenail the joists or fasten them to the beams with special deck joist hangers. This method may be required by the building codes in some areas. Be sure to check with local authorities on the type of construction allowed. Your local building supply dealer may also be able to offer advice.

9 With the deck supports in place, the next step was to install the pool. This was the third above-ground pool

SIDE VIEW OF DECK CONSTRUCTION

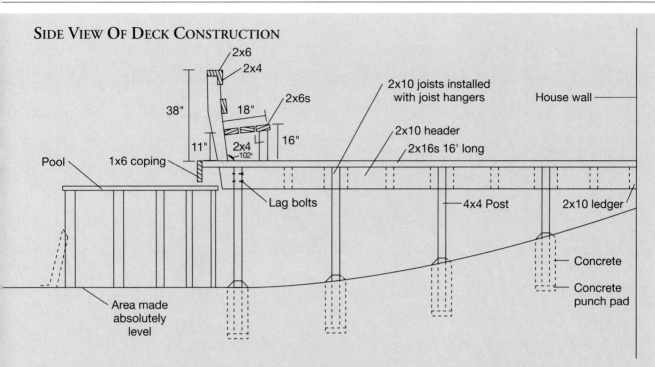

I've installed and I can definitely say it's a do-it-yourself project. But you'll need help; it is not a one-person job. It will take a day or two to erect the pool, not counting the time preparing the site. Follow the manufacturer's directions explicitly for your particular pool. Our pool called for placing patio blocks around the circumference of the pool, and digging the blocks down flush with the leveled ground. The bottom wall channels were then fastened together and placed down on the channel plates on the concrete blocks.

10 Next came the erection of the side wall. This is one of the hard chores. Don't do this on a windy day, don't allow the metal wall to buckle, and make sure you have enough help on hand to hold the wall in place until the top wall channels are installed. At this point, the bottom of the pool was covered with heavy-duty polyethylene plastic sheet (drop cloth) and extended 8" up on the wall. Sifted dirt or mason's sand was then placed on top of the plastic sheeting to create a wedge around the inside edge of the pool. (This keeps the pool liner from creeping back under the bottom wall channel.) With this done, a 1" layer of mason's sand was placed over the plas-

tic that covered the entire bottom surface of the pool.

11 The next step required the help of at least two people, one inside the pool and one outside. It helps to have even more. With the pool bottom properly prepared, the vinyl liner was placed in the center of the pool, folded out, and placed so the edge of the perimeter seam came to the covered wall channels. We removed a section of top wall channel and installed a channel plate at one end. Then we lifted a section of the pool liner wall over the metal wall, and placed a piece of plastic coping over it to hold it. This was done around the entire perimeter of the pool wall until the liner was in position.

12 We smoothed out excess liner material and wrinkles, then started filling the pool with 1" to 2" of water. This smooths the liner firmly in position. We filled the pool slowly and watched the water level carefully. If water collects in one spot, the pool foundation is not level. The water depth must not vary more than 1¼". Once the water starts to fill the pool, don't attempt to pull or straighten the liner because even the weight of ½" of water can damage it. Once we started

the liner installation, we didn't stop until it was complete, including the installation of top plates and uprights.

13 After filling the pool, we began attaching the top plates and uprights according to the manufacturer's directions. Next, we filled the pool to a depth of about 8" and gathered the excess liner over the sides and straightened it as needed. The rest of the pool side support frame was installed and the pool filled. At this point we installed the filter system below the deck.

14 With the pool in place, we nailed the decking boards onto the deck. We used galvanized nails, but have found that they tend to work up with all the activity that takes place on our deck. If I were to do it again, I'd use galvanized screws instead. The deck overhangs the pool by about 9", including a wood coping fastened to the protruding ends of the deck boards to provide more comfortable seating and access to the pool. The pool ladder was fastened directly to the pool deck. The final details included adding the seating, rails, and steps, and closing off the bottom of the pool surround with lattice work of pressure-treated wood.

All Star DO-IT-YOURSELF HINTS

Handy, Helpful, And Downright Valuable How-To Advice

Handy hints, you might say, are the currency of how-to knowledge, passed on from father to son, neighbor to neighbor, friend to friend. They are the folklore of do-it-yourselfers and encompass a wide range of subjects, from solving a common problem to overcoming a unique difficulty in once-in-a-lifetime construction projects.

This choice collection of how-to advice is the result of an extensive review of hundreds of handy hints generated by both professionals and do-it-yourselfers. You can put some to work immediately; many others will be fresh ideas that may get you out of a tight spot in projects ahead. Each has the potential to fortify your own self-sufficiency, and most of all, help you finish what needs to be done.

ORGANIZING

Checking Levels. You can check a level for accuracy: Lay one working edge on a flat surface and check the bubble. Reverse it end for end, and check the bubble again. It should be in the same position. Now try the opposite working edge. Take a reading, and switch it end for end and take another reading. The bubble should be in the same position. You can check for plumb by holding the level against a flat, per-

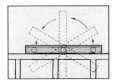

pendicular surface. Check the bubble. Then, turn the level to use the opposite working edge. The bubble should be in the same position.

No-Fall Pegboard Hooks. One way to keep pegboard hooks from falling out when you remove tools and other items is to use your staple gun. Shoot a ¼" or larger staple over the hook, as far down on it as possible.

Buying Hammers. Experienced carpenters, though they use a 16-oz. claw hammer for most jobs, also will carry a 20- or 22-oz. framing hammer for the heaviest nailing jobs with big spikes. For lighter work, a 13-oz. curved claw hammer may be useful. A 7-oz. hammer might come in handy for small jobs, such as making picture frames.

Must-Buy Hand Tools. When equipping a shop, consider two of the handiest tools from old-time shops: a drawknife and spokeshave. A drawknife can be used instead of a router for champhering work. It is faster and leaves a much finer cut. You don't have to go back over the work, and there won't be chatter marks. A spokeshave is like a plane with handles, so you can control the depth of the cut for a fine finish.

Making Tool Boards. To keep tools

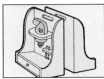

together, or at least in bunches, make some tool boards. They can be as simple as a section of pegboard nailed to a base of 2x4s, or more elaborate to include small drawers or inserts for small power or hand tools. You can make them to organize tools and materials by project (home fixing), or by function, (drilling, fastening, gluing, or soldering). You can make them to hang on the wall in your shop, or keep an area open under workbenches for slide-in storage. Used at the bench, slide them out only part way; for out-of-shop projects, carry what you need to the job site.

Used Air Compressors. If you buy a used air compressor, make sure the pop-off valves and the controls that govern the upper and lower pressure limits (activating and deactivating the compressor pump) are checked and tested. If you are not sure these parts are good, replace them. It's better to spend a few dollars than risk a tank explosion.

Making Shims. Precision wood joints often call for a thin shim between dado blades and chippers. To make them without a large punch, put the shim material (like file folder cardboard) over a metal opening that is the size needed. Place the ball of a small ballpeen hammer over the opening, then strike it with another hammer (use eye protection) to cut a clean hole. Trim, and you have an ideal shim.

Shop Storage Wall. To conveniently store sheetrock, paneling, and plywood, as well as other long boards, build a second wall out about 2 feet from your shop wall, floor to ceiling, in one corner of your shop. Behind this new wall, you can build shelves as nec-

essary to house long dimensional lumber boards as well. You also can set up a bench to the outside of the new wall and install pegboard above it. Tip: Build enough shelves for long boards so you don't have to unload the whole bunch to get a board near the bottom.

Small Part Storage. You can use milk and water jugs for small parts storage by cutting out a section just opposite the handle. The contents of these handy containers can be marked easily by using a hot glue gun to fasten on a sample of the part being stored inside — nails or screws. Survey the jugs and bottles you are throwing out; even used detergent containers can work.

Glue Fix For Hooks. Another solution to keeping wire hooks on pegboard from coming off when tools are removed is glue. Simply insert the hook into the pegboard, then glue the hole with an electric hot glue gun. In a minute or so, the hook is fixed, although you can wrestle it off when you want to rearrange your tools.

Installing Lights. If you are

installing new shop lights, or positioning a bench in your shop, a simple test can help you move the light or the bench for best illumination. Hold a pencil or dowel vertically, then check the shadows. Reposition your setup to reduce shadows as needed. If you have strong shadows on one or more sides, consider installing more lighting.

Storing Round Stock. If you are having problems organizing and storing dowels, pipes, and other short-length stock like molding, try this. Find or buy a length of plastic plumbing pipe or plastic downspout material. Cut it up into sections about a foot or so long. Set them vertically next to each other, then tie them together, build a small wooden frame around them, or set them in spaces that will

keep them together, such as between studs in a garage wall.

Organizing Materials. To organize smaller materials, buy a number of cardboard boxes all the same size instead of scrounging various-size boxes from the grocery store. This way, you can stack them neatly, they will have covers, and they will be sturdy for years to come. Mark each box on all four sides and on the top with a big letter and number, like A-1, A-2, and so forth. Use a three-ring binder for a list of box numbers and the contents of each box.

Sandwich Bag Trick. To save small parts like screws, small bolts, and the like, don't overlook plastic sandwich bags or the small bags used at the grocery store for fruits and vegetables. Throw the parts in the bag and tack the bag to the wall. Then, if you don't get back to the job right away, all the little parts will be there waiting for you. The idea works well while doing electrical wiring, too. Put receptacle screws and covers in a bag and tack the bags next to the outlets as you work on them.

Shop Nylons. Worn-out nylons can be used to hold tools on pegboard if you run out of pegboard hooks. Knot up one end, feed it through the back, and loop it through appropriate holes for the tools you want to hang. The nylons will stretch nicely around various tool shapes, and will actually hold them more securely than regular pegboard hooks.

Storing Nail Sets. The containers used for push-up, stick-type deodorants can be recycled into excellent holders for items like nail sets, small drill bits, saber saw blades, and other small parts. Besides keeping items in one place, the little containers have caps and the bottoms can be pushed up to expose smaller items. Soak the container to remove the label, then use a felt-tip pen to mark what's inside.

PLANNING

Plastic Drawer Tip. Small cabinets with multiple plastic drawers are handy, but the key to making them functional is to mount them at eye level. That way you can see where items are and don't need to pull out all the drawers to find what you want.

Temporary Sealer. Don't start a project such as a large bowl turning or carving and leave large areas of end grain exposed to heat and low humidity. If the project can't be completed and the final finish applied, always apply some kind of temporary sealer, such as paste wax, shellac, or lacquer, which can be removed easily before finishing.

Outline Patterns. You can quickly make your own outline patterns for small projects with just a piece of white paper and an awl. Position the paper over the piece you want to duplicate, then rub around the edges with your finger. Remove the paper, and lay it over your new wood. Following the creases created by the rubbed edges, punch small holes with the awl into the wood. To mark straight lines on your pattern, make a hole at each end of the line. On curves, the holes should be closer together. Remove the paper, and draw a line between the holes. You can make the holes to the outside of the pattern line, then cut directly through the holes.

Making Patterns. To duplicate complicated edges, you can  buy a contour gauge with sliding wires, which you push against the contour to be copied, then tighten the wires in position. The inexpensive tool is available at hardware stores and can be a life-saver when you need to duplicate complicated curves.

Place For Plans. To store building plans, reference materials, and project clippings, keep at least one two-drawer file cabinet in the shop. You may be able to tuck cabinets under existing workbenches or, if you are building new workbenches, design them to accommodate file drawers.

Room For A Shop. Maybe you have a shop set up in the basement, but are tired of cramped quarters and constant cleanup. If you have a single-car garage, an inexpensive way to at least double the space is to split it in half and fill in the middle. You can use the whole space for your shop, or you can set up shop on one side and still have room for a vehicle. After splitting the garage in half, slide one half over onto a newly poured extension of the slab, then fill out the roof, back, and front. You can use a new double-wide garage door, or keep the same door if you only need access for one vehicle.

Lumber Rack Advice. When planning a shop, consider building a lumber rack on casters. Divide it into sections for lumber of varying lengths and widths. You also can store lumber near the ceiling of your shop using pipe floor flanges screwed to ceiling joints and ¾" pipe sections screwed to tees and elbows.

Disposal System. If you don't yet have a sawdust collection system in your home shop, an intermediary step is to use plastic trash bags under tools like a table saw. Clip the bag below it with snap-type clothespins. The sawdust that doesn't fall in can be scooped up and thrown into the bag. This is a good alternative if you can't stand the noise of shop vacs.

Dressing Lumber. A key to project success is taking time to set up equipment as accurately as possible. Professionals use tools capable of precision adjustments. With saws, for example, they'll use 10" or even 12" table saws, while you might have to make do with an 8" bench-top saw. They will use high-quality blades kept in top condition. The professional also will run lumber through a planer and jointer to make sure it is precisely square. If you don't have this equipment, find someone who does and who will dress up your project lumber. Wood from the lumberyard probably won't be precisely square and true, and if you try to build a project to critical dimensions with it, you're likely to be disappointed.

Small Tool Sets. Don't shortchange yourself on small tools like screwdrivers, pliers, and open-end wrenches. If you find yourself running after such tools, buy multiple sets and keep them in the places where you use them, such as the shop, garage, and house.

Using Pegboard. When remodeling your shop, consider lining the walls with pegboard, the tool owner's friend. If you don't have or like pegboard hooks, try using short sections of ¼" dowels pounded into ¼" pegboard.

Sharpening Advice. To get a cut-ting edge sharp, the most critical factor is the relief, or the gradual tapering of the blade above the edge. When sharpening, try to keep the blade at less than a 25-degree angle. Generally, the smaller the angle, the better the edge. To get an idea of the angle, fold a piece of paper with square edges in half at the corner. That will be 45 degrees. Fold that angle in half again and you have a 22½-degree angle.

ADAPTING

Vise Conversion. Need a woodworking vise? You might be surprised to learn that in some professional woodworking shops the vises are machinist vises. To use a machinist vise for woodworking, simply make up wood inserts to fit inside the jaws. The inserts can be roughly 8" x 8", cut to set over the vise shank, and fitted on the back side to fit the vise jaws. With the inserts in place, you don't have to worry about jaw marks on your wood, and with the inserts removed, the vise can be used for other purposes as well.

Positioning A Vise. Position the 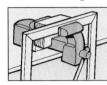 machinist's vise on your workbench to work with you instead of against you. Used in conjunction with a 2x4 spacer, a vise can be positioned so that when the spacer is set against the back jaw, the work will be in front of the bench and reach all the way to the floor. Also position the vise so that, when the 2x4 spacer is set against the front jaw, the work will set on top of the bench. To position your own vise, set any spacer you will be using against the back jaw, then line up the front of the spacer with the front edge of the bench.

Precision Part Polishing. To deburr or polish small precision parts, buy a roll of flexible, small-diameter abrasive cord (round) or tape (flat). Aluminum oxide or silicon carbide abrasives are used for deburring; crocus is used for ultra-fine polishing. The cords are flexible enough to reach inside and around precision parts, such as seals, bearings, or bushings, and also work well for finishing metal, plastic, and glass surfaces.

Instant Scaffolding. If you find yourself from 1' to 4' short on projects, use salvaged plastic milk or pop cases for temporary scaffolding. They can be used individually, or stacked into temporary work platforms. They are solid to stand on, and are interlocking to increase stability. When not used for scaffolding, they can be set on their sides and used for shop shelves.

File Hand Protectors. If your files don't have handles, you can use electrical wire connector nuts large enough to fit over the sharp file tang for protection. Just screw them on. You also can use items such as short sections of doweling, drilled to accept the tang, but don't use golf balls. The balls are manufactured with centers under extreme high pressure and may explode if you drill into them.

Long-Reach Drill. New or broken bike spokes can be reworked into long drill bits, especially handy for drilling pilot holes in hardwood for finish nails. Pound the point flat, then regrind it like a drill bit. You can make some from 4" to 6" long, which will keep the drill chuck away from the sides when you work in a corner. You can make them up in several sizes and lengths.

Wheels On Tools. Use casters to keep major tools, even workbenches, portable. Wheeled tools and benches allow you more flexibility and let you reposition for specific jobs or to take advantage of natural daylight. If stationary tools don't have casters, you can make up a base from double ¾" plywood large enough to accommodate the tool legs. Put casters on one end, and use 2x4 stock at caster height at the other end.

Portable Shop. If you live in  cramped quarters and don't have room for a workbench for home projects, consider making a special set-in-place section that can fit over a kitchen, wet bar, or laundry counter. You can even outfit it with a clamp-on vise and a tool rack. When the job is done, tuck it away in a closet or in a protected area outside.

Mortar Soap Trick. If you are having trouble keeping mortar elastic enough to work with, mix a little dishwashing liquid with the water when mixing it up. This keeps the mortar elastic long enough to finish the job.

Miter Saw Inset. If you want to 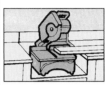 keep your miter (or chop) saw on a bench, consider building a drop-down section so the miter saw table is level with the rest of your bench. If you can't do this, consider building a false top on one side to support lumber being cut.

Shop-Made Clamp Pads. To keep from marring wood, you can easily make your own clamp pads for pipe and bar clamps. Scrap rubber, rubber shoe soles, even broken car mud flaps will work. Cut the pads ⅛" oversize, using a saber saw to cut a kerf and undersize circle in one end of the pad. The kerf allows the pad to stretch in place over the pipe without your having to remove the lock end of the pipe.

Guide Wheel Helper. Adding a wooden guide wheel onto the fence of a table saw used with a dado head will help you out a couple of ways. Screw on a little round wheel directly over and above the dado blade, the exact thickness of your boards. The wheel will hold the wood firmly on the table. Even if the piece is slightly bowed, the wheel will assure that the depth of any rabbet you are making is uniform throughout the cut. Also, if you plane wood before making a rabbet cut, the wheel will remind you if you have forgotten to do the planing. Unplaned wood won't fit under the wheel.

Homemade Sandpaper. You can save money on adhesive-backed sandpaper discs by buying sandpaper in larger quantities and making your own discs. Give the sandpaper and metal disc a coat of rubber cement, wait about 30 seconds until both surfaces are tacky, then slap them together and you can begin sanding almost immediately. When it is time to change sandpaper, just peel it off the metal disc with a putty knife.

Portable Tools. If you are working in different areas outside your shop, running for tools can waste time. Instead, stack all the tools you'll need into a wheelbarrow. Then, wheel off to the job. For smaller jobs, consider using large five-gallon plastic pails, like those that hold sheetrock mud. Put related tools in individual pails.

CUTTING

Accurate Miter Joints. Trying to cut an accurate miter joint on a table saw? Just use the table saw to cut close to the joint line. Then, for an accurate miter, use either a manual miter trimmer (like the Lion Miter Trimmer) or a disc sander. The 12" disc sanding attachment on a Shopsmith works well. Because the wood is fixed, and the sander is moved into the wood, you get remarkably precise and smooth cuts.

Saving The Threads. Before hacksawing an overly long bolt to shorten it, thread a nut onto the bolt, down past the proposed cut. This permits you to re-form the damaged threads by turning the nut off the bolt when you finish the cut.

Quick Pipe Cutting. If you are trying to cut or thread a section of pipe when you are not set up for it, try this. Pick up the pipe with a pair of pliers and tighten the vise against the plier jaws. In the vise-tightened pliers, the pipe should not slip.

Cutting Tubing. You can make cutting copper tubing with a hacksaw easier if you first insert a length of wood doweling the same size as the tubing inside it, as far as the cut line. The insert will provide added rigidity to the tubing.

Sawing Sheetmetal. When selecting a hacksaw blade for sheetmetal, at least three teeth should touch the metal at all times to give a smooth cut. If the material is too thin for even your finest blade, try sandwiching it between pieces of thin plywood. When plywood

isn't a practical approach to a job, cut out the shape with a pair of tin snips.

Saw Unjamming. If you are sawing a board through wide, thin lumber, such as plywood, saws have a tendency to stick and jam in the kerf. You can fix this by using two clamps and short pieces of scrap wood. Clamp the kerf the proper distance apart at the end of the sheet where you began cutting.

Sawing For Drainage. When building outdoor projects, even with pressure-treated wood, bevel the tops of upright structurals and joist ends with an angle of 30 to 45 degrees to reduce moisture absorption. While pressure-treated wood resists end rot, it remains subject to splitting, checking, and chipping caused by moisture-induced swelling and shrinkage.

Precision Cutting. To achieve 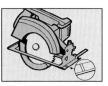 accuracy with a portable circular saw, take time to scribe lines onto the top of the base, in front of both sides of the blade. Then you will always know where the saw kerf will be. To scribe the first lines, use a square flat against the blade and mark with a sharp awl.

Sawing Multiples. To hold two or more pieces of wood together while you saw them, try using strips of double-coated pressure-sensitive adhesive tape. The tape keeps the pieces from slipping. Place strips of tape on the surface of one piece, and press the second firmly onto it.

Triangle Saw Tool. To make sure

you get a true 45-degree miter cut on your radial-arm saw, use a draftsman's 45-degree triangle. With the blade over the table, hold the triangle against the blade to position the auxiliary fence before clamping it to the table. A 30/60-degree triangle also can be used for those angles.

Upside Down Hacksaw. If you need to hacksaw through an existing pipe or rod, but space above it is limited, try this: Remove the blade, straddle the pipe with the frame of the saw, then re-install the blade upside down. Cut through the pipe with the upside-down blade. In many cases, this will allow the space you need to complete a cut.

Little Story Pole. To duplicate multiple measurements in precision cabinetwork, use a piece of 1x2 stock as a story pole. It should be longer than the longest cut required. Carefully mark the height, width, depth, and length of different project parts on the 1x2. By using it for all measurements, all parts will be cut correctly.

Oversize Compass. To draw or scribe very large circles of the same size, you can use an adjustable curtain rod that has right-angle ends as an oversize compass. Tape or tie a pencil or scriber to one end of the rod. Do the same at the other end with a nail. After adjusting, use a small C-clamp at the center of the rod to keep the compass the length you want as you go from circle to circle.

Marking Wood. Writing instructions in pencil on soft pine (such as top, bottom, and right side) leaves indentations in the wood that require extra sanding to remove. It's better to use white chalk for these markings. They are easy to read and are quickly removed with a damp cloth.

Quick Saw Guide. If you need to

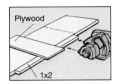

cut a number of pieces of lumber with straight or angle cuts, making a homemade saw guide will save you time. A simple guide can be made for cuts with a portable circular saw from a piece of plywood and a 1x2. Double-check to see that it is at the angle you want before putting it into use.

Workbench Measuring. For hand-free measuring, rip a yardstick in half and fasten it to the front edge of your workbench. You can use a router to make the measure flush with the bench top. You also can line up the measuring device with the side of the bench and fasten a small block at one end so that you can butt the stock you want to measure up against it.

Cutting Foam Rubber. To cut a straight line through a thick piece of foam rubber, compress the foam pad to a fraction of its normal size. Lay the pad on a protected flat surface. Put two boards on the pad along either side of the cut line. Leave space between the boards for the knife blade, then draw the boards down against the work surface with C-clamps. The knife should produce straight, even

cuts through the material.

Sheathing Cuts. Professional carpenters know this, but you may not if you are working on a once-in-a-lifetime construction project. If you are putting up sheathing of the fiber variety, you can save time by making your cut marks with a chalkline instead of a carpenter's pencil. Hook the end of the line at one end, hold it down, and snap to make the line. The chalkline works for sheetrock, too.

Modified Miter Box. A small modification can extend the useful life of a handsaw miter box. Insert a piece of 1x stock to the inside bottom of the box when it's new to add years of service. The saw blade will come in contact with the false bottom without cutting into the miter box itself. Slide the wood back and forth, and turn it over to spread out the wear. When it is badly cut up, replace it.

Modified Sawhorse. Drill holes in the top of your sawhorses and insert wooden pegs to help keep lumber from slipping under the pressure of sawing. Drill the holes at closely spaced intervals, extending at least 16" across the sawhorse. With a peg inserted in a hole close against either edge of a board being sawed, simple downward pressure applied by hand will keep the work in place.

Small Part Pick-Up. If you are making projects with small parts produced from your saw, let your shop vacuum pick up the pieces for you. It's faster

and much safer than getting your hand close to the saw blade. Clean the vac out well, and wire or clamp the suction hose so the small pieces are sucked in. Then, simply collect the small wood parts out of the shop vacuum when you're done.

Cutting Veneer. If you've tried to cut or trim veneered pieces, like a flush panel door, you know that splintering can be a problem. A solution is to use a sharp utility knife and straightedge to mark the trim line. Make sure to mark both sides, and cut in deeply. You can complete the cut along the lines, using either a saw or a plane without making a mess of things.

Blade Change Help. To make changing blades on a band saw easier, use your small spring clamps. A new band saw blade tends to slip off the top while you try to get it on the lower wheel. Use a couple of small spring clamps to hold the blade on the top wheel while you slip it over the other wheel and apply tension. Take the clamps off before making final adjustments.

Chiseler's Technique. To get square

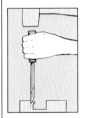

shoulders when you are chiseling wood with a hollow-ground or double bevel chisel, always begin inside your marked lines and cut into the waste wood. Rough out the entire cut, then carefully pare the waste down to the mark for any final finish trimming.

BUILDING

Precision Measuring. For more precise measurements, use the 1" mark on your steel tape, take the total measurement, then subtract the 1" for the reading. When cutting smaller pieces for a project, check for precision by measuring a number of the pieces at once. If you have four pieces that should be exactly 8" long, lay them end to end

and measure. This multiplies small errors hard to detect in only one piece. For example, if the four pieces measured 32⅛" instead of 32, then you know that each of the four pieces is ⅓₂" too long.

For Plumb Posts. Want to hold round or square posts plumb in a hole until you can pack dirt around them?

Make a couple of wedges of 2x6, 30" long. Mark one side at 6" and make an angled cut from that mark to the opposite corner of the 2x6. Use one of these on each side of the post. The larger the hole, the further the wedge will go down in the hole.

Folding Rules. If you use folding rules, you can be more accurate if you turn them on edge, rather than flat on your work.

Deck Spacers. Instead of using nails

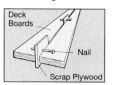

as spacers when installing deck boards, you can use small scraps of plywood of a selected width. Drive a nail through the scrap to make the spacer, and insert, as necessary, to space the boards. They can be used over and over, and don't pinch your fingers the way nails do.

Lying Tapes. If you are doing the measuring and someone else is doing the cutting but the cuts are always off, compare your tapes. Draw both tapes out on a board to see that the measurements are the same. One may be reading short because the end is bent slightly.

Growing Patterns. When making repetitious cuts, use only one pattern for marking cuts. If you always use the last board cut as a pattern, small errors will accumulate. If each cut is off $\frac{1}{16}$", after cutting four pieces you can be off $\frac{1}{4}$".

Easy Division. To divide a board in half, you can use a compass. Put the pivot at the end and draw an arc. Do the same at the other end. Where the two arcs cross will be the middle. You also can draw an "x" diagonally from opposite corners to find the center.

Outside Diameters. You can use your metal measuring tape to measure outside pipe diameters. Wrap the tape around the pipe so it overlaps, keeping a couple of inches or so extra on the end. Read the measurement edge to edge, then subtract the extra tape.

Glue First, Machine Later. When gluing, start with straight boards slightly oversize and machine the wood after gluing. Glue pieces up to rough size, then joint one edge and cut the other with a carbide saw blade. Gluing oversize lumber means that you don't have to worry about using clamp pads or waste time trying to protect a

piece already cut to size. Don't do any machining on the wood for 24 hours. Glue will swell the fibers slightly at the joints. If you machine too soon, before the swelling goes down, you will remove swollen fibers. Then, after the wood returns to normal, you will have depressions at the glue joints.

Big Project Square. A handy tool for the shop is a sheetrock square, a T-square 4' long. It's especially handy in laying out patterns or cuts on full sheets of plywood or particleboard. The square is accurate and stable, and gives you a full 48" straight line. Newer versions come with a head that can be adjusted to various angles and clamped in place.

Equal Pieces. To divide a board into equal pieces, lay a square on the board, with the start of the scale on one corner. Angle it so you get a number easily divisible by the number of pieces you want. If you want three, for example, use numbers like 9, 24, and 27. If you use 9, mark and cut at 3" and 6" to get three equal pieces. For four pieces, use numbers like 8, 12, and 16.

Squaring Walls. To determine if

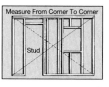

a wall you are building is square before it is raised, simply measure diagonally from corner to corner, from the top of one side to the bottom of the other. Do this on both sides. When both measurements are the same, the wall should be square.

Shop Marking System. Using white chalk instead of pencils offers no-mar marking. Because you don't have to worry about markings on project parts, you can be more liberal with them and use special marks to remind yourself which pieces were cut to length, or which have already been run through the planer or jointer. For example, a large "L" can be used to indicate that a board has been cut square and run

through the jointer. Mark it so that the long part of the "L" is next to the jointed edge and the bottom of the "L" is next to the square-cut end.

Hammer Cleaning. If using cement-coated nails, or working around glue or adhesives, the hammer face can get dirty or slippery and cause bent nails and black marks on the wood. Regularly run a piece of fine sandpaper or emery cloth over the face.

Finding Slope. You can use a level

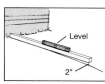

to find slope by placing it on top of a straight 8' 2x4. If, for example, you want a brick walk to slope $\frac{1}{4}$" per foot, you would have a 2" drop at one end when the bubble indicates level. Some torpedo levels have marks indicating $\frac{1}{8}$" or $\frac{1}{4}$" pitch to make it easy to position plumbing pipes to drain properly.

Tight-Fit Fastening. Often screws and bolts need to be installed where two hands can't be used. Use a piece of masking tape to keep the parts on the tool to make starting them a one-handed job. For a screw, punch a hole in the tape, then fold the tape over and around the screwdriver shank to hold it in place. For a bolt, lay a piece of tape in a socket with the sticky side facing the socket walls. This makes a tight fit for the bolt to be pressed in. When the bolt is installed and properly torqued, it's easy enough to take off the socket with the tape still in place.

End Nail Sizes. If you are end-nailing shelving, where you are driving nails through the side supports into the shelves, use this guide: Select nails about three times as long as the side boards are thick. If driving through $\frac{3}{4}$" stock, use 6d (2") or 8d (2½") nails. In some case it may be possible to find 7d (2¼") nails.

Avoiding Bent Nails. Beginners often bend a lot of nails because they try to push the hammer instead of swinging it. Professionals advise holding the hammer at the end of the handle, which allows you to swing it like the pendulum of a clock. Another secret old-timers know is that you need to keep your eye on the nail, not on the hammer.

Split Preventers. To reduce splitting, drill a pilot hole about three-quarters of the diameter of the nail. One method for dense or brittle wood is to grind the sharpness from nails. You can avoid splitting wood when using ordinary nails by blunting the point of the nail. A blunt nail will tear, rather than spread, the wood fibers.

Driving Small Nails. To avoid whacking your thumb when driving small nails, punch a nail through the corner of a 3x5 file card. Then, hold the opposite corner when driving the nail.

Large Bit Drilling. If a centerpunch mark you've made to drill through metal is too small to keep a large-diameter bit from wandering, try this: Use a small-diameter bit to drill a small pilot hole. After the pilot hole is made,

it will guide the large-diameter bit when it's used to expand the hole.

Avoiding Split Ends. Sometimes it's possible to avoid splitting wood when nailing near the end of a piece of lumber by cutting the wood longer and letting it overhang as you nail. Then simply trim off the surplus wood that has taken the nails without splitting.

Pilot Hole Drill Bit. Nailing jobs often call for pilot holes the same size as the nails. You can produce any number of holes rapidly and with ease with a power drill and one of the nails. Just clip off the head, and chuck it into your drill. The nail "bit" will drill holes the exact size needed, as deep as required.

Drilling Thin Metal. To make the job easier, sandwich thin metal between two pieces of wood and clamp in a vise for rigidity. Drill until the bit almost cuts through the metal, then turn over the work. Use a file to cut through the protruding bulge on the reverse side of the sheet to remove the last thin layer of metal and expose the hole.

Screw Wax. You don't have to buy

beeswax from mail-order catalogs for your screws. Instead, go to your local hardware store and buy a wax seal for a commode. It is beeswax processed in a solution to stay soft for easy workability. It's also much cheaper than paying about $9 a pound through the catalogs.

Toenailing Tricks. When toenailing, it's best to drive nails in the stud at about a 30-degree angle. If you have trouble with the stud or joist moving when driving the first nail, you can first drive a holding nail on one side to keep the board in place, then remove it after you have driven two nails into the opposite side. You also can use 2x2 or 2x4 spacer blocks, cut to hold studs in place while you drive the first nails.

Spinning Nails. You can avoid splitting wood like molding with a nail spinner. With the device in your drill, insert the nail, then drill it into position. The nail will go to within ¼" or so of final depth. Drive the nail home with a hammer and nail set. This technique works especially well with dense wood like oak.

FINISHING

Super-Wide Clamping. Need to hold extra-wide work for gluing or for driving screws? Hook either end of a pipe clamp over your work, then turn the other end 90 degrees so it lays flat. Hook a second pipe clamp to it, and if it reaches the other end of your work, turn that end 90 degrees and tighten. If two clamps won't reach far enough, add a third clamp between the first two. Add as many as you need. Just make sure the handle of the last clamp overhangs the end so you can turn it.

Carpenter's Triangle. When dry-fitting boards to be glued, here's how to make sure you will get them back together in the desired position: Draw a large triangle across all of the boards of a section. The boards will be easy to get back in the right order. Use a pen-

cil with a light touch or white chalk so the markings can be removed easily.

Inside Measurements. To take inside 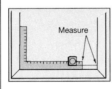 measurements, use a metal tape from inside edge to inside edge. Take the reading and add on the length of the tape housing. Another way is to use a combination or carpenter's square. Position upside down in one corner, draw the tape to the square's blade. Then add the measurement on the blade.

Project Protection. Covering a foot or so of one end of a sawhorse with scrap carpeting provides a non-scratching base for working finished wood or furniture.

Quick-Change Sanding. The big

secret in finishing wood is the sanding. If you spend more time at this process, the rewards will show up later. To speed up sanding of flat surfaces with a vibrating sander, insert two pieces of sandpaper into the sander at the same time. When the top layer is worn, simply tear it off and the next layer already will be in place.

Glue Removal Tools. A couple of very sharp paint scrapers and a sharp wood chisel ½" wide are good tools to help remove excess glue after it has dried slightly. Press the sharp scraper square to the surface, and in a couple of swipes you can eliminate any glue squeeze-out. Use the chisel to scrape excess glue from inside corners or next to moldings. Make sure scrapers are sharp. Touch them up with a fine file or sharpen on a 1" belt grinder. You can use the shank of a screwdriver to burnish the edge and roll it over to get more of a "hook" on it.

Fast Gluing Tool. To spread glue without creating a mess, make a disposal spreader using a large paper clamp and a 3" x 4" section of window screen. Just fold over the screen without creasing it, then clamp the ends in the paper clamp. Dip the tool into the glue and draw it lightly across the work. It holds small or large amounts for controlled spreading.

The Tape Clamp. Sometimes you need to clamp two pieces together for gluing, but they are such an odd size or configuration that normal clamps won't work. A solution is to use banding or filament tape. Draw a number of pieces tightly over the glued joint to hold both pieces firmly together.

Radial Saw Clamp. Your radial-arm saw can be used as a clamp. Take off the blade and guard so the motor can be lowered to rest on top of the sheets or wood strips that need clamping. To clamp, crank the motor assembly down plus another 1/16". The motor weight will rest on what you want clamped.

The motor also can be used to form a rigid stop for horizontal clamping.

Curved Sanding Block. You can make a curved sanding block from a section of 4" rubber hose. Slit it lengthwise and fit it with a piece of sandpaper 4" wide and 1/2" longer than the outside diameter of the hose. Fold down 1/4" of each edge, wrap the sandpaper around the hose, and insert the creased edges into the slit. The slit hose snaps together to clamp the sandpaper in place, and the tool conforms to small curvatures.

Baseboard Molding. One way to 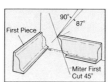 handle corners is to put the first piece in with a square end. Then, to overlap the second piece, miter it at 45 degrees to expose the molding face, and cope along the edge of the profile to provide a 3-degree undercut angle, away from the joint on the backside. This allows some leeway if the room isn't perfectly square, and allows the showing edge a tight fit.

Tight-Fit Molding. For tight-fitting miter corners on molding, use a carpenter's pencil while cutting it on

a miter saw. Put the pencil under the molding, about an inch from the blade, on the side of the board you want to use. This angles the front side of the molding slightly wider than the side that will be next to the wall. The front will touch first, and any gap is hidden at the back of the joint.

Saving On Glue Costs. Instead of buying contact cement and white glue in the smaller containers, buy it in larger quantities and use a pump-type oil can to dispense it. It's more convenient and economical. Put a small electrical wire connector over the end of the spout to keep the glue from drying out between jobs.

Sizing End Joints. To prevent starved glue joints on end grain, first size the end grain with a mix of glue diluted with water. Dilute just so that, when applied, glue drops don't form at lower edges of wood.

Undenting Wood. When driving finishing nails into wood that is to be finished and you miss your mark and dent the wood, try this: Have a wet rag on hand and slightly soak the dent. After puttying the nail hole and sanding, the dent will be minimized.

TROUBLESHOOTING

Crooked Floorboards. To muscle  bent floorboards into place, one method is to nail a 2x4 at an angle on the subfloor with duplex nails. Position a block made by sawing off its tongue onto the crooked board. Then drive a wedge between the block and your 2x4. The wedge should move the block so the tongue-and-groove floorboard edges into place.

Gluing Helper. Need to get glue or cement through a small opening? Try using a new disposable medical syringe, fitted with a needle of adequate bore and length. To use some cements, you may have to dilute first with a suitable thinner. If you plan to use the syringe and needle again, promptly clean it with an appropriate solvent.

Regluing Trick. Warm vinegar will soften old glues for regluing. Except on some antiques, remove old glue, paint, wax, dust, oil, and grease before gluing. Dip parts in warm water and let dry completely. Warming parts also helps open up wood pores before regluing.

Tack Holder. Need a long arm to put in a small tack near the ceiling or other hard-to-reach place? Just make a small

square of doubled-over masking tape, with sticky sides on both sides. Put it on the face of your hammer and press on your tack. Hit the first blow hard enough so that the tack will pull off of the masking tape.

Pressure Situations. Many puncture wounds happen when something is difficult to remove and you start applying too much pressure. Especially with tools such as screwdrivers or needle-nose pliers, consider what will happen if that tool slips off. If there is any chance that it will contact your body, use another method.

Cleaning Out Holes. When drilling

blind holes in iron or steel, fine metal bits usually fall into the hole. To remove them, use a strong magnet and a soft iron or steel rod that's smaller in diameter than the hole. Push the rod to the hole bottom, and press the magnet to its upper end. Keep the magnet to the rod, pull it out of the hole, and brush away the bits of metal. Repeat until all metal bits are removed.

Easy Taping. With tape that is not in a dispenser, do this: After you have cut off what you need, turn the tape back underneath itself about a quarter inch. This way you always have a starting tab the next time you want to use the tape. You can easily grab the tape end without searching for the end of the tape on the roll.

Cool Adhesives. Refrigerate epoxies to increase working time. Mixed two-part epoxies undergo heat-releasing chemical reaction. By storing them in the refrigerator, you gain more time before the mixture cures.

Carriage Bolts. A problem with  carriage bolts in wood is that they start turning when you attempt to tighten a nut. If this happens, and you have access, use a hacksaw to cut a groove into the head. Then, you can use a screwdriver to keep it from turning while you tighten it.

Emergency Sawhorse. When you get caught somewhere outside the shop without a sawhorse and you need to cut lumber, reach for the step ladder. Keeping the ladder in an open position, lay it down on its side on the ground. It will give you temporary support for quick cuts or ripping.

Long Blowgun. Blowgun nozzles can be lengthened by adding a piece of soft copper tubing. This lets you reach motors and interior machine parts for cleaning without getting a face full of dust. The end of the tubing also can

be bent to reach around the back side of motors or edges. Tip: Also use your shop vacuum in any cabinet opening when blowing dirt out of motors to keep dust out of the shop.

Protective Pliers. Soft-jawed pliers can be made for use on polished objects by brazing a layer of brass onto the jaws of an old pair of pliers. You also can epoxy scraps of leather to the jaws of a pair of pliers or adjustable wrench to protect such items as chromed bolts or nuts.

Lost Part Insurance. When working where you can cause a major problem if a washer or nut drops into an assembly, save yourself lots of grief. Tie a long piece of dental floss to the part, and tie the free end to something solid. When the parts are finally installed, the dental floss can be cut off or, in the case of a nut, it will come right off because the threading action will cut it.

Versatile Heat Guns. A heat gun is ideal for stripping paint. It also can soften window putty, remove bumper stickers, defrost freezers, char-stain wood, dry out wood for painting, disinfect animal cages, heat surfaces before gluing, burn weeds from cracks in sidewalks and patios, light charcoal, loosen rusted or overly tight nuts, and solder pipe joints. The gun also can be used to bend certain plastic pipes.

Vibrating Tools. If a small air compressor or similar tool in your shop vibrates, you can soften it with special foot pads of corrugated cardboard squares. Make pads 1½" to 2" thick by gluing several squares together for each leg. To increase the strength of the pads, glue the squares so the corrugation of one piece lies at right angles to that of the next square of cardboard.

Broken Bulbs. It can happen in the shop or elsewhere: The glass part of a light bulb breaks off, leaving the metal part still screwed in. Instead of trying to dig it out with a needle-nose pliers, try using a thick dowel that fits just

inside the metal base. You also might try a section of dry sponge. Carefully push it in tightly and turn.

Depth Gauges. For precision wood-  working, buy depth stops that fasten to the bit. For general construction, use masking tape on the bit to indicate the proper depth. You also can use a block of scrap wood of the proper thickness to keep the drill hole at the right depth.

Running Wires. If you need to thread fine wire through cabinet frames or wall studs, try this trick. Use a plastic straw to follow the path of the drill hole that you made. Because the straw is stiff, it will follow the hole easily. The little wires will slide through without binding or catching on the wood or the frame.

Glue Containers. Use glass or plastic containers for glue. Using coffee cans may lead to black glue lines, more likely with white glue than yellow glue. That's because glues with pH lower than 7 absorb iron from the can and the dissolved iron can react with wood to leave black glue lines.

Grease Remover. Instead of using gas or hand soap to get dirty grease off your hands, reach for the vegetable or olive oil. Apply about a half teaspoon, rub, and wipe it off with a paper towel. It works as well as some of the more costly commercial preparations, and is easy on your skin, too. It also can be used to remove paint.

Broken Screws. There's a solution for wood screws which have broken off below the surface of the wood. If you don't want to risk damaging the wood by digging it out, try driving the screw deeper into the wood with a nail set. Then just fill the hole with a filler, and drive a new screw next to the broken one.

TYPE OF CUT. File cut should be selected for the material of the workpiece, the desired removal of material, and the surface finish.

SINGLE CUT
Cuts steel.

DOUBLE CUT
Cuts steel, cast iron, brass, and bronze.

RASP CUT
Cuts hard plastics, wood, aluminum, and spongy materials.

MILLED TOOTH
Cuts steel, brass, bronze, hard plastics, wood, aluminum and spongy materials.

MULTI METAL
Cuts steel, cast iron, brass, bronze, hard plastics, and wood.

FILE KNOW-HOW

*The Lowly File Can Fortify Your Arsenal
Of Project Ammunition*

Ask your average homeowner about metal files, and chances are good you will get a blank look. Yet some do-it-yourselfers in the know will tell you that the basic file would rank at the top of a list of the most under-utilized tools found in the home workshop arsenal.

It's not that they haven't been around. Like other basic tools, files and rasps evolved from stone implements. In fact, the first recorded use of files can be found in the Bible, during the reign of King Saul about 1090 BC. By 1490 AD, early toolmakers attempted to cut files by machine, using concepts found in a Leonardo da Vinci invention. It wasn't until 1750, however, that the Frenchman Chopitel came up with a machine that could do the job successfully.

If you check the catalogs of major file marketers today, you'll quickly see one reason why files remain a mystery to many of us. From its humble beginnings, the basic file has spawned relatives in literally hundreds of shapes, styles, and variations. (One major tool company catalog lists no fewer than 528 types of metal files for various applications.)

FILE TYPES

If there is a need for it, file makers have it — whether you're a cabinetmaker, machinist, silversmith, forester, locksmith, watchmaker, farrier, or homeowner who needs a basic set of files for occasional projects. (You can even find a special file called the "screwhead file," which is designed to enlarge and clean out the heads in screws.) The key to sorting out which file to use for a project is to first get familiar with file terminology.

File Length. Each part of the file has a name, and files are categorized by length, type, and shape. The length is measured from the point to the heel, not including the tang. The length of a file gives you an idea of its coarseness, its stroke distance, and its speed in removing material.

File Type. It is the cross-sectional shape or style of the file that determines its type: round, square, triangular, knife, or flat. These sections are further classified by their contours, such as taper files (which taper from heel to point) and blunt files (which are the same width the entire length).

File Cut. The cut refers to the character of the teeth with respect to the coarseness. Single-cut files have a single set of parallel, diagonal rows of teeth. Double-cut files have two sets of diagonal rows of teeth; the second is cut in the opposite diagonal direction, and on top of the first teeth. (The first set is called the "overcut," while the finer second set is called the "upcut".) Rasp-cut files have individually punched teeth entirely separate from one another. Curved-cut files have teeth arranged in curved contours across the file face.

File Coarseness. This refers to the number of teeth per inch of file length. Most American pattern files are available in three grades of cut: bastard cut, second cut, and smooth cut. The degree of coarseness is greater in longer files, but the differences between bastard, second cut, and smooth versions are still proportionate.

SELECTING FILES

File specialists at CooperTools advise that single-cut files generally are used with light pressure to produce a smooth surface finish, or to put a keen edge on knives, shears, or saws. The double-cut file is used with heavier pressure than the single-cut, and removes material faster from the workpiece. The rasp-cut file gives a rough cut, and is used mostly on materials like wood, aluminum, and lead. The curved-cut file is used primarily in auto body shops for smoothing body panels.

If you are just beginning to collect a set of files, consider the starter sets packaged for basic homeowner needs. One Nicholson-brand handyman's home file pack comes with four files that cover most uses around the home. It contains an 8" Mill Bastard, 8" Four-In-Hand, 6" Slim Taper, and 6" Round Bastard,

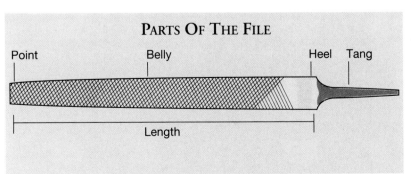

PARTS OF THE FILE

Point　　　Belly　　　　　　Heel　Tang

Length

with suggested uses right on the plastic pouch.

File makers try to make it easy for the casual do-it-yourselfer to get the right tools. For example, you can find files labeled "Home and Garden," which are sold specifically for sharpening knives, scissors, and the coarse steel cutting edges of implements like garden hoes. Or, you can find files labeled "Combination Handy," which are a good bet for multiple jobs. Such files give you a single-cut on one side for sharpening edged tools and smoothing metal surfaces, and a double-cut on the other side for rapidly removing metal. One side edge has teeth, while the other edge is "safe" or blank.

When selecting a file, try to fit the file's shape, size, and coarseness to the job. Select a file shape that fits the area to be filed. For example, a triangular file is best on acute internal angles, to clear out square corners and

sharpen saw teeth. A flat file is good for general-purpose work, while a square file works well for enlarging rectangular holes. Use a round file for enlarging round holes. A half-round file can be used for dual purposes: the flat face for filing flat surfaces and the curved face for grooves.

It is best to try to match the file to the specific metal. Metal properties vary greatly. Soft metals need a keen file used with light pressure. Hard metals require a file with duller teeth to keep them from biting too deeply and breaking off under pressure. Hard plastics need files with high, sharp teeth. Soft plastics, which file in shreds, are best worked with shear-tooth files.

Because the size of a file and its coarseness are directly related, the larger the file, the more stock it will remove. The smaller the file, the finer the finish it will leave. Likewise, the coarser the cut of the file, the rougher

the finish. Genererally speaking, bastard-cut and second-cut grades are used to remove stock quickly, while smooth-cut files are used for finishing.

RASPS AND RIFFLERS

For jobs such as shaping wood, files cut smoother. Rasps, with their individual teeth, work faster and are less likely to clog, however. Basic rasp types include the wood rasp and the cabinet rasp, as well as special rasp combinations. The wood rasp offers a coarser cut than the cabinet rasp, and is made primarily for rapidly removing stock. For finer woodwork, the cabinet rasp often is used for jobs like fitting mortise-and-tenon joints. Rifflers, offered through catalogs such as Garrett Wade, are specialized woodworker tools. Available up to nearly a foot long, their handles have rasps or files at both ends.

Another descendant of the file and rasp family especially suited to shap-

FINE POINTS OF FILING

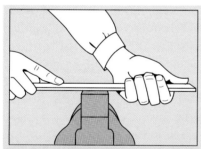

The Grip. For two-handed filing, grasp the handle with your right hand and the point of the file with your left. Rest the file handle in the palm of your right hand, with the thumb pointing along the top of the handle and the fingers gripping the underside. Grasp the point of the file between the thumb and the first two fingers of your left hand, with the thumb on top of the file. With heavy filing strokes, the thumb of the left hand is normally in line with the file and the tip of the thumb is pointed forward. For lighter strokes, you can turn the thumb to almost a right angle to the direction of the stroke.

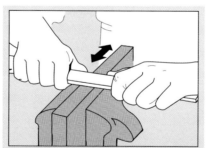

Drawfiling. When done right, drawfiling can produce a finer finish than straight filing. Grasp the file firmly at each end and alternately push and pull the file sideways across the work. Normally a standard Mill Bastard file is used for drawfiling, but where a considerable amount of stock has to be removed, a Flat or Hand file (double cut) will work faster. However, this roughing can leave small ridges that will have to be smoothed by finishing with a single-cut Mill file. Note: A file with a short-angle cut shouldn't be used for drawfiling; it will score and scratch instead of shave and shear.

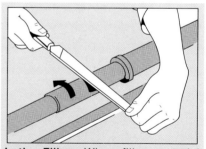

Lathe Filing. When filing material revolving in a lathe, don't hold the file rigid or stationary, but stroke it constantly on the work. A slight gliding or lateral motion will help the file clear itself and eliminate ridges and grooves. When filing metal materials in the lathe, the recommended surface feet per minute for cast iron is approximately 150; annealed tool steel, 175; machinery steel, 350; and soft yellow brass, 500. Tip: Don't run a hand over your lathe work because oil and moisture can coat the surface and make it difficult for the file to take hold.

ing materials such as wood, plywood, composition board, and soft metals is the Surform Tool from Stanley Tool. Its unique "cheese grater" design is available with different cuts, plus you can fine-tune its work by adjusting stroke direction. For maximum removal, you hold it at 45 degrees to the direction of stroke. To remove less material and get a smoother surface, you reduce the angle so the tool is parallel to the stroke. By using a slightly reversed angle, you can get nearly a polishing effect.

FILING TECHNIQUES

With conventional files, there are three basic ways they are put to work. There is straight filing, when you push the file lengthwise — straight ahead or slightly diagonally — across the workpiece. There is drawfiling, where you grasp the file at each end and push and draw it across the workpiece. And there is lathe filing, which consists of stroking the file against material revolving in a lathe.

For normal filing, work held in a vise should be about elbow height. You might want the work slightly lower if you have a great deal of heavy filing to do. Or, for work that is fine or delicate, you can raise it up to eye level. (Note: If there is a chance that the work could be damaged in the vise, you can use protectors made of wood, zinc, copper, or aluminum between the work and the vise jaws.)

For normal flat filing, try to carry the file forward on an almost straight line in the same plane, changing its course enough to prevent grooving. Too much pressure can result in a rocking motion, causing a rounded surface. It is possible to ruin a good file by applying too much — or too little — pressure on the forward stroke. In general, use just enough pressure to keep the file cutting.

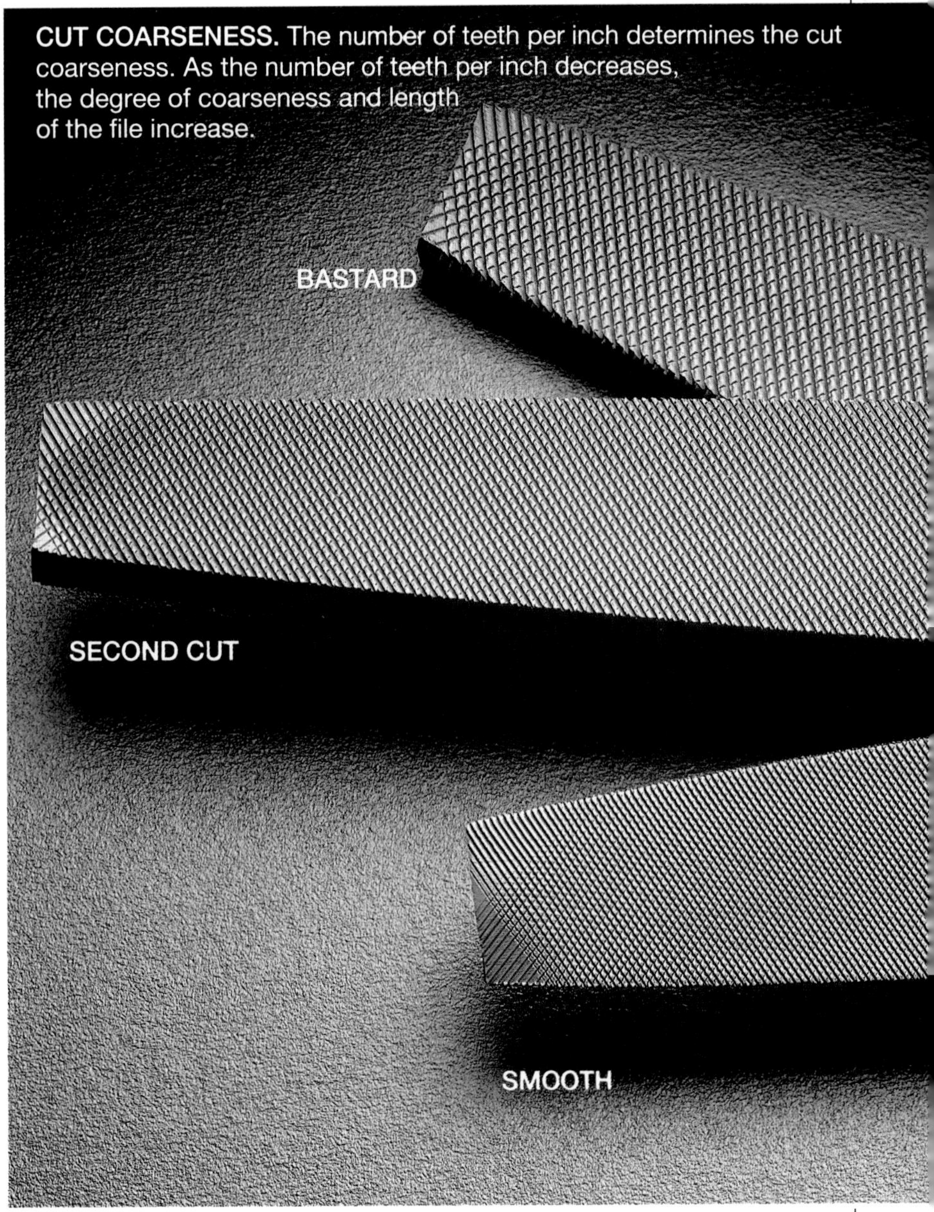

CUT COARSENESS. The number of teeth per inch determines the cut coarseness. As the number of teeth per inch decreases, the degree of coarseness and length of the file increase.

BASTARD

SECOND CUT

SMOOTH

If allowed to slide over the harder metals, the teeth of the file can dull fast. If they are overloaded by too much pressure, they are likely to chip and clog.

On the reverse stroke, it is best to lift the file clear of the work, except on very soft metals. Even then, pressure should be very light — never more than the weight of the file itself.

CARING FOR FILES

For safety reasons, a file should never be used without a tight-fitting handle. Files are available with handles already attached. If your files have bare tangs, you can get handles specifically for various-size files. Protect the teeth of files not in use by hanging them in a rack or keeping them in a drawer with wooden divisions.

Files always should be kept clear of water or grease, which can make them less effective. It also is a good idea to wrap a file in a cloth to protect it whenever it is carried in a toolbox. Keep file teeth clean at all times by using a file card or a wire file brush to clear the grooves between the teeth. ❧

Spread Photo: Lindal Cedar Homes,
Seattle. Inset: Matt Straw.

CHECKPOINTS

Home — EMERGENCY REPAIRS

*A Baker's Dozen Of Common Problems
And How To Deal With Them*

Leaking pipes, appliances that quit working, plugged-up or overflowing toilets — the list of home repair emergencies is nearly endless. But what is a home repair emergency? Simply put, it is an event that fouls up the normal use of your home. At worst, it endangers those who live there, renders the home or its many systems inoperable, or puts their long-term use in question.

Once you start counting, there are roughly a couple dozen home emergencies that call for immediate action. Other problems may or may not be emergencies, depending on the problem and your coping skills, and usually can be taken care of over a longer period of time. What you may consider an emergency, your next-door neighbor might laugh off as a simple technological glitch. Your reaction depends on whether you know how to correct, or at least minimize, a malfunction.

Learning how to handle repair emergencies yourself can pay back much more that the money you save. Understanding what causes home repair emergencies also will help you in the future by helping you understand how to prevent them and how to deal more effectively with professionals when you need to hire them.

The following tips are selected from *The Home Repair Emergency Handbook*, recently published by Taylor Publishing Co. Compiled by how-to author Gene Schnaser, the book explains that one thing home emergencies have in common is that they are almost always unexpected. Another thing they have in common: Most can be nipped in the bud by simply knowing how to turn things off in your home. If those in your household know how to turn off the main electrical switch, the main water valve, and the main gas valve, what ordinarily might become a potential disaster can easily be reduced to a small problem.

Besides providing tips on more than a hundred home repair emergencies, the new troubleshooting book also provides a handy section for listing the location of critical home system shutoffs, as well as the phone numbers for emergency electrical, plumbing, and heating system services.

THE PLUGGED-UP TOILET

When a toilet does not flush at all, or flushes only partially, often it is caused by nonbiodegradeable items, such as combs, bath toys, and the like which fall in and clog the trapway. A toilet that does not flush properly may indicate defective toilet plumb-ing or problems within the waste-drain-vent system beyond the toilet.

What To Do: First try using a rubber-cupped plunger, often called a "plumber's friend." Coat the outside lip with petroleum jelly, and make sure the cup is covered by water. Plunge vigorously for a few minutes, then pull sharply away. Try several times. If plunging doesn't work, try using a wire hanger, or what is called a closet or toilet auger (a special "plumber's snake" with a sharp, spiral hook on

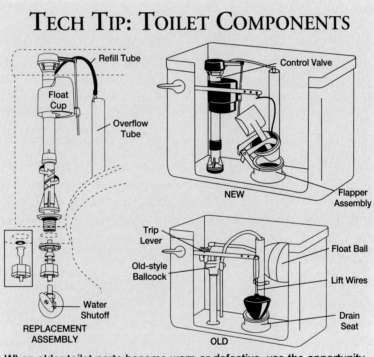

TECH TIP: TOILET COMPONENTS

Refill Tube
Float Cup
Overflow Tube
Control Valve
NEW
Flapper Assembly
Trip Lever
Old-style Ballcock
Float Ball
Lift Wires
Drain Seat
Water Shutoff
REPLACEMENT ASSEMBLY
OLD

When older toilet parts become worn or defective, use the opportunity to update with more modern, trouble-free components.

one end of a flexible length of cable and a handle on the other).

Use an auger carefully to avoid scratching the porcelain, and push it into the trap while turning the handle until the auger bites into the clog. Once you think the blockage is removed, try flushing with wet toilet paper. If the water goes down, but not the paper, an obstruction is still in place. Try the auger again. In extreme cases, you may need to remove the toilet to clear the blockage or gain access to the waste pipe below.

Special Advice: Do not use commercially available drain cleaners, or bleach solutions, in a toilet. Also do not use the balloon-type devices that are attached to a garden hose; the pressure they exert may break the toilet.

Helpful Hint: If you suspect a foreign item is causing the blockage, you can try holding a small compact-size mirror down into the opening, and shining a flashlight onto it to illuminate the passageway. Once you see the object, try working it out with a wire or toilet auger.

THE RUNNING TOILET

When water continually runs after the toilet is flushed, lift off the tank cover, flush, and observe the interior parts for any obvious problems. Specific repairs will depend on the age and style of the toilet. Both older and newer styles have a mechanism to actuate an inlet valve to let water into the tank, and a mechanism attached to the trip lever to allow water to flow out of the tank. The tips below apply to older-style components.

What To Do: On the inlet side, older ballcock mechanisms have a valve that is opened and closed by the rod connected to the float ball. As the ball rises in the tank, it shuts off incoming water. On the outlet side, older toilets generally have a device that fits into a seat at the bottom of the tank to hold water until the toilet is flushed. This device is variously known as a stopper ball, tank ball, or flapper.

If the tank does not refill, first check to see that the stopper ball or flapper is in good condition and seating properly. Adjust its chain or its guide arm, lift wires, and trip lever so the ball falls straight onto the seat. Scrape away any corrosion from the valve seat. If this fails, the easiest way to correct the problem is to replace the stopper ball and valve seat with a new-style rubber flapper assembly, or replace a worn-out flapper.

If the stopper ball or flapper works okay, check the float ball and rod assembly. Make sure the float ball does not touch the tank wall. The float ball may not rise high enough to shut off the inlet valve; if so, gently bend the float ball rod up, using both hands to avoid damaging the ballcock assembly. Also check for a leaking float ball, which will keep it from rising high enough to shut off the water. If the ball leaks, it is easily replaced by unscrewing from the end of the rod.

If the float ball is set too high, however, it may allow water to flow over and down the overflow tube. In this case, bend the float arm down to lower the water level to about 1" below the top of the tube. If the float ball is set right, but water continues to flow, the inlet valve in the ballcock assembly is probably defective. You can attempt to replace the valve washer, replace the entire inlet valve, or replace the entire ballcock assembly.

Special Advice: In some cases, the cause of a running toilet may be a refill tube end down too far in the overflow tube, with its end below the water level. The refill tube then can become a siphon, draining water out of the tank. To correct, reposition the tube so there is space between the end and the water level. Also, when troubleshooting a running toilet, examine the base of the overflow tube. Corrosion can create holes that allow water to continually drain from the tank.

Helpful Hint: Low-cost toilet tank repair kits are readily available for both older and newer-style components. Depending on the problem, installing newer-style components may be the best bet for more trouble-free performance.

THE LEAKING WATER PIPE

A leaking pipe can occur at any time, especially in older homes. Whenever a pipe leak is detected, first turn off the water supply to that area at the nearest valve. Or, if necessary, turn off the water at the main supply valve. (All members of the household should know where the main supply valve is located in case of this type of emergency.)

What To Do: After the water is turned off, decide whether to call a plumber or to try to fix the problem yourself. For smaller leaks in pipes, hardware stores and home centers carry a variety of clamp-in-place devices that can be used on pipes at least 1½" in diameter. (Chewing gum or tape will not stand up to the water pressure in pipes.)

You may, however, be able to stop leaking at pipe joints with epoxy, at least temporarily. Turn off the water, clean the metal well, and apply the epoxy in a thick layer around the leaking joint. If the joint still leaks, the only option may be to replace the fitting. Joint leaks in galvanized threaded pipe sometimes can be stopped by tightening the threads. Because this opens up the next set of threads, however, you have to work back to what is called a "union." Bad sections of copper, galvanized, or plastic pipe can be sawed out and replaced using special couplings.

Special Advice: When working with old galvanized steel pipe systems, it's best to use two pipe wrenches. Avoid banging or applying excessive pressure to the pipes or you may cause more joint leaks in the system. Whenever a pipe leak develops, also inspect the rest of the water supply pipes. Entire sections may need to be replaced, especially if water pressure is low. A professional plumber can offer an opinion.

Helpful Hint: If local codes allow, sections of metal pipe may be repaired with plastic pipe and fittings that are easier to work with than metal. Special transition fittings are used between the old metal and new plastic pipe. Check with home centers or other suppliers of plastic pipe and fittings for what you need.

THE FROZEN WATER PIPE

When water supply pipes become frozen, they should be thawed out promptly to avoid any possible bursting. A bulge may show the location of the frozen area in soft copper or lead pipe, but bulges may not show up in pipe of other metals. If frozen pipes have split open, they will spray out water, when unthawed, if the water is not turned off. Sections of bulged or split pipe must be replaced.

What To Do: When thawing water pipes, it's best to start on the supply side toward the water main and keep a faucet open to indicate when a flow starts. A good way to defrost pipes is to restore central heating to the area. Otherwise, you can wrap old cloths around pipes and pour boiling water over them, or you can use a heat gun, heat lamp, hair dryer, or electrical heating tape. (Keep in mind that concentrated heat from a propane torch may cause steam that could burst the pipe. Also, keep heat lamps at least 6" away from walls.) Electrical heating tape, covered with insulating tape, can be wrapped around pipes that freeze and left in place so it can be plugged in during extremely cold weather.

Special Advice: With waste or sewer

pipe, it's best to start at the lower end and work upward, if possible, to allow the water to flow away as the ice melts. You may be able to thaw frozen traps, waste pipes, drains, and sewer pipes by pouring boiling water into them through the drain opening or trap. If that doesn't work, consider calling a plumber.

Helpful Hint: In many cases, pipes near an outside wall tend to freeze because of a lack of insulation. Wherever pipes become frozen, consider adding insulation to the outside of that area. (You may need to open up a portion of the wall to gain access so you can add the insulation.) If pipes next to an outside wall freeze occasionally, consider keeping the wall open at that point and installing a louver so home heat will keep the temperature above freezing.

THE CLOGGED FIXTURE DRAIN

Most blockages occur close to the fixture's trap, especially if they occur quickly and don't affect other fixtures. If you can run a volume of water into the fixture before it backs up, or if other fixtures are affected, the blockage may be farther in the drain system. If the blockage is in the main house drain, it may first show up at bottom-level floor drains.

What To Do: Drains can be unclogged using several methods, including using a force cup with handle ("plumber's friend"), removing the trap to clean it, or using a flexible coil spring auger, hydraulic device, or chemical drain cleaner. (Note: If the trap below the fixture is accessible, put a bucket under it, remove the clean-out plug and try clearing it with a bent coat hanger. If the trap doesn't have a clean-out plug, you'll need to remove the entire trap. Be careful collecting waste water if any chemicals have been used.)

If a plunger is used, partly fill the sink or bowl with water and plug the overflow drain. (On tubs you need to

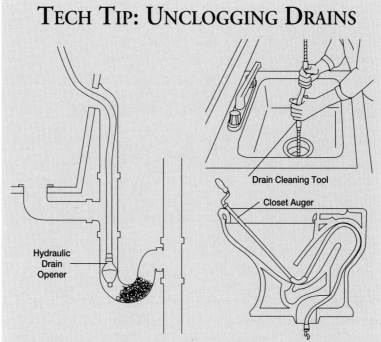

TECH TIP: UNCLOGGING DRAINS

Drain Cleaning Tool

Closet Auger

Hydraulic Drain Opener

A plunger is the first-line defense, followed by a drain clearing auger, top right, a toilet closet auger, below right, or hydraulic openers (except in toilets), left.

remove the pop-up or trip-lever drain stopper mechanism to plug the overflow opening. On double sinks you need to plug the second drain. Don't use a plunger if chemicals have been used.) Coat the lip of the plunger cup with Vaseline and force the plunger up and down several times. After the pipe is cleared, pour boiling water through the drain to clear the waste line.

If plunging doesn't work, you can try an inexpensive drain clearing tool that has a corkscrew-like auger on one end of a coil spring cable. An offset tube handle with a thumb setscrew slips over the cable. The cable's auger end is pushed into the drain until the clogged area is reached, then the handle is moved toward the drain, the thumbscrew is tightened, and the offset handle is cranked. As progress is made, the screw is loosened and more cable is fed into the drain. (Note: A special version of this type of tool, called a "closet auger," is sold for toilets.)

The tool's spiral auger can be threaded through drains with crossbars. For pop-up drains, you can try to remove the drain plug by turning and lifting. If that doesn't work, loosen the screw and nut on the lift rod under the sink and withdraw the lift rod. If the tool can't be worked through the drain opening, it can be fed through the trap's clean-out plug, if there is one.

Special Advice: Hydraulic drain openers (also called expansion nozzles or "blast bags") also are available for clearing fixture and main drains. They connect to a garden hose and expand inside the drain to form a seal, then pulsate water under pressure to loosen and clear blockages. These units are not intended for toilets, or where chemical drain cleaners are present. One brand is Drain King, sold in three versions for different pipe sizes.

To use in a bathtub, the overflow plate is removed and the unit is inserted at least 10" into the overflow pipe.

For showers, the drain plate is removed and it is inserted at least 8" into the drain. For kitchen sinks, you must remove the trap from under the sink and insert it at least 24". For washing machine drains, it is inserted at least 18". To clean out main drains, the unit is pushed into the drain at least 4' — further if inserted into the clean-out or roof vent closest to the clogged area. To deflate the unit to remove it, water to the hose is turned off, and the hose coupling is loosened at the faucet.

Helpful Hint: A plunger and a small cable auger should be sufficient for most home uses. Try to avoid using liquid drain cleaners when possible because they can be hard on pipes and drain traps.

THE STUBBORN FURNACE

Often what are thought to be furnace emergencies are caused by the thermostat not being set or operated properly, no power to the furnace, or no fuel or pilot light. *Important:* If you detect natural gas odor in your home or in the furnace area, take immediate precautions. Do not try to light any appliance, smoke, turn on light switches, or use the phone. Shut off any valves to appliances suspected of leaking gas, then call a technician. If in doubt about what to do, or if the gas odor is strong, leave home immediately, call your gas supplier from a neighbor's phone, and follow the supplier's instructions. If you can't reach the gas supplier, call the fire department or 911.

What To Do: If the furnace doesn't come on, and you don't smell gas, first see that power is reaching the furnace. Check the circuit breakers or fuses at the main service box. If reset breakers or replaced fuses blow again, call a service technician. Check to see that any switches on or near the furnace are turned on. Make sure the thermostat

is set in heat position, and that it is set above room temperature. If the furnace doesn't come on after an interval, check the furnace itself. If you have a gas furnace, the gas valve should be turned to ON. For an oil furnace, check the fuel level in the tank. If the furnace has a pilot light, check to see that it is lit. If not, relight carefully, following instructions in the owner's manual or on the unit.

(*Warning:* If you smell gas, leave the area immediately and call a technician. The lighting instructions for a gas furnace should explain the procedure to use to see if the gas valve is good. If the test procedure indicates the gas valve is bad, turn off the furnace gas valve and main gas valve, and call a technician. Also call for help if the pilot light does not stay lit after several tries.)

Special Advice: Most furnace controls will have a reset switch. If the furnace starts after the reset switch is pushed, but shuts off again, call a technician. Gas furnaces equipped with an electronic ignition device instead of a pilot light have a gas valve designed for slow opening. It first opens part way to let just enough gas through for safe ignition of the burners. After a few seconds, it opens fully to allow proper flame height. The burners should light within two seconds after the gas valve opens. If air in the valve and lines prevents the flame from being established within seconds, the system will go into "lock-out." To reset, wait one minute and turn the thermostat to a setting below room temperature. Then turn it back up to a setting above room temperature; this should restart the ignition cycle.

Helpful Hint: If the furnace works, but heat is not circulating, the problem may be with the blower or the blower belt. If the flame on the burner is yellow or blue, or lifting off the

burner, call a technician to adjust it. Check your owner's manual for annual maintenance suggestions, including keeping the furnace and its components free of lint or dirt accumulation.

THE SIZZLING WATER HEATER

If you hear sizzling noises when the heater's burner comes on, the tank may be leaking onto the burner, or water caused by condensation may be dripping into the burner area. Whenever the heater is filled with cold water, some condensation will form while the burner is on. This usually happens: 1) when a new heater is filled with cold water for the first time, 2) when gas burns and water vapor is produced in heaters, particularly high-efficiency models where flue temperatures are lower, and 3) when large amounts of water are used in a short time and the refill water is very cold.

What To Do: Heaters with tank leaks should be replaced. Don't assume a heater is leaking, however, until there has been enough time for the water in the tank to warm up. A heater may appear to be leaking when, in fact, the water is condensation. Excessive condensation can cause water to run down the flue tube onto the main burner of a gas-fired heater and put out the pilot. This condition may be noticed during the winter and early spring months when incoming water temperatures are lowest. After the water in the tank has warmed up (one to two hours), however, the problem should disappear.

Special Advice: If condensation is heavy, also check the venting system of a gas-fired heater. Good venting is essential for the heater to operate properly, as well as to carry away products of combustion and water vapor. Inspect the venting system once a year. Look for obstructions that may block combustion and ventilation airflow, as well as damage or deterioration that can cause improper venting or leakage of combustion products. If discovered, have the flue and venting cleaned or replaced before continuing to use the heater.

Helpful Hint: An undersize water heater will cause more condensation. The heater must be the proper size to meet your home demands, including dishwashers, washing machines, and showers.

THE NOISY WATER HEATER

Some noises from a water heater may be normal, such as the expansion and contraction of metal parts during periods of heat-up and cool-down. Sizzling and popping also may be caused within the burner area by normal condensation during heating and cooling periods. Sediment buildup on the tank bottom also may create various noises (and if left in the tank, may cause premature tank failure).

What To Do: If the water heater is making crackling, sizzling, or popping noises, check the heater to see if it is a leak or normal condensation. In some cases the temperature-pressure (T&P) relief valve may be dripping because the water supply system has pressure-reducing valves, check valves, or backflow preventers. When these devices are not equipped with an internal bypass and no other measures are taken, the water system may not allow for the expansion of heated water and the T&P valve may drip to

relieve the excess pressure. Call a technician to install a bypass and/or an expansion tank to relieve the pressure from thermal expansion.

In some cases, the cause of a leaking T&P valve may be that the water heater temperature is set too high; in other cases, the valve may be bad. A too-high temperature setting can also cause pounding and rumbling or a surging sound in the heater.

Special Advice: Tank sediment

buildup can cause noises as water gets under the sediment and turns into steam when heated. Drain the tank to clean; if the problem persists, contact a technician for a professional cleaning. Similar sounds can be caused in electric water heaters because of scale-encrusted heating elements; if so, the elements can be replaced. Sediment buildup can be reduced by regularly draining a few quarts of water every month from the drain valve at the lower front of the tank.

Helpful Hint: The T&P valve should be manually operated at least once a year. Check your owner's manual for recommended procedure. Make sure no one is in front of or around the outlet of the discharge line, and that the extremely hot water discharged will not cause damage. (If, after manually operating the valve, it continues to release water, close the cold water inlet, follow draining instructions in your manual, and contact a technician to replace the valve.)

THE DEAD AIR CONDITIONER

A central air conditioning system pumps heat out of your home. There are two main types, which technicians call the "package" systems and "split" systems. The package system has the compressor, outdoor coil, indoor coil, fan, and blower motors in the same housing outside the home; it connects to ducts in the home through an outside wall. The split system has a compressor, fan, and condensor coil outdoors. The evaporator coil and blower motor (or existing furnace blower) is indoors, and refrigerant lines run between the two sections.

What To Do: If your air conditioner does not start up or isn't working, first check that it is getting electrical power. Check the circuit breakers or fuses and load center handles in both indoor and outdoor locations. Study the user's guide. Check that the thermostat is set to COOL or AUTO,

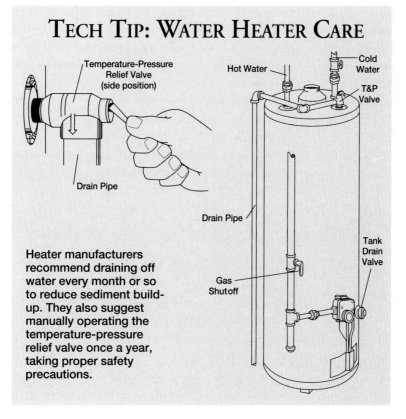

TECH TIP: WATER HEATER CARE

Temperature-Pressure Relief Valve (side position)

Drain Pipe

Hot Water

Cold Water

T&P Valve

Drain Pipe

Gas Shutoff

Tank Drain Valve

Heater manufacturers recommend draining off water every month or so to reduce sediment build-up. They also suggest manually operating the temperature-pressure relief valve once a year, taking proper safety precautions.

and that the fan switch is set on AUTO or ON for continuous operation. The set point should be below room temperature. Check the coil outside to see that the fan is running. Make sure grilles, registers, and filters indoors are not restricting airflow. (Dirty filters are a common cause of poor cooling and compressor failure.)

Call a technician if you hear new, unusual noises, or if the air conditioner is short-cycling (turning on and off rapidly) and not cooling properly. When performing any maintenance, be sure to shut off all electrical power. Manufacturers suggest you leave the power on to the outdoor unit at all times. To prevent damage to the compressor, do not use the air conditioner until electrical power has been turned on for at least six hours.

Special Advice: Never use the outdoor coil as a stand for garden hoses or tools. To assure free airflow, keep the coil clean and free of grass clippings, weeds, and other debris. Keep fences and shrubs at least two feet away.

Helpful Hint: Replace throw-away filters when dirty. Clean plastic fiber or foam filters by soaking them in a mild detergent and rinsing with cold water. Aluminum mesh filters can be washed with detergent and water, but they should be recoated according to the manufacturer's instructions. These filters won't filter out dust or dirt as effectively without the adhesive coating on them.

THE JAMMED SINK DISPOSAL

Occasionally, in-sink disposals become jammed by foreign objects accidentally dropped into them, or by trying to grind high-fiber waste such as corn husks, lima bean pods, or artichoke leaves. Most vegetable and table scraps are no problem, but whole rinds, grapefruit skins, or cobs should be cut into smaller pieces before being fed into the disposal.

What To Do: Clearing a sink disposal usually is relatively easy; however, take care to avoid personal injury or damage to the unit. To free a jam, turn off the water and turn the disposal power switch to OFF. Remove as much food waste as possible using a pair of long-handled tongs or pliers. The manufacturer may have supplied a small wrench to clear jams. Insert one end of the wrench into the hole in the bottom of the disposal, and work it back and forth until it moves freely for at least a complete turn. Remove the wrench, wait five minutes to let the motor cool, then press the reset button at the bottom of the unit. Turn on the disposal and water and let it run until thoroughly flushed.

If your unit does not have a wrench, or if you can't find it (wrenches are best kept taped to a nearby pipe under the sink), try a broom handle or something similar.

Special Advice: Do not put your fingers or hands in the disposal. To avoid possible injury by materials that may be expelled by the unit, do not use it for clam or oyster shells, glass, china, plastic, large whole bones, or any metal. Don't put chemical drain cleaners or lye into the disposal.

Helpful Hint: If the motor does not restart, make sure you have pushed the reset button. If it still doesn't work, check for blown fuses or tripped circuit breakers. If units without a reset button won't start, the overload protector may be defective and the motor may have to be replaced.

THE ELECTRICAL SHORT CIRCUIT

Background: If a fuse is blown, the fuse window appears discolored and the metal strip running across the inside of the window is broken. This indicates a short circuit caused by two bare wires touching or by a hot lead grounding out to a metal object somewhere in the circuit. Circuits protected by cartridge fuses will give no visible indication of a short circuit. Circuits protected by circuit breakers can be identified by the handle of the tripped circuit breaker being in the tripped or OFF position.

What To Do: Identifying the cause of a short circuit is the same for fuses or circuit breakers. Disconnect all lights and appliances on the circuit with the blown fuse or tripped circuit breaker. Then, replace the blown fuse or turn on the tripped circuit breaker. If the fuse blows or the circuit breaker trips with all of the appliances unplugged from the circuit, the short is in the circuit wiring itself and the wiring must be repaired or replaced. If the circuit is good, reconnect each light and appliance on that circuit, one at a time.

Special Advice: Use extreme caution when reconnecting lights and appliances. Do not connect suspiciously frayed cords to outlets. When you turn on the faulty light or appliance, the fuse will blow or the breaker will trip again. Carefully check appliances for bare cords, broken light sockets, or damaged plugs before plugging them back into the circuit.

Helpful Hint: If one particular fuse blows several times, shut off all wall switches and appliances on that circuit, and remove all line cords from the sockets. Remove the fuse and screw a 100-watt light bulb into the fuse receptacle. If the bulb lights with all of the appliances unplugged from the circuit, a short exists within the circuit. If it doesn't light, connect each of the appliances, lamps, and line cords one at a time. If the bulb lights at the fuse panel and the appliance fails to work, you've located the short. Remove the bulb from the panel before disconnecting the faulty appliance.

THE WANDERING THERMOSTAT

A thermostat may work, but cycle the furnace on and off rapidly, cause major swings in temperature, or have readings other than the setting. If the thermostat has been recently installed, consult the instructions that came with the unit. For other older thermostats, try to locate a copy of the owner's instructions.

What To Do: If the thermostat turns the furnace on and off too often, the problem may be that the "burner-on" period is too short. Check for an adjustable heat anticipator lever inside the thermostat. Adjust the lever one scale mark higher and wait several hours for the thermostat to stabilize. If the thermostat allows major swings in temperature, the problem likely is a "burner-on" period that is too long. In this case, adjust the heat anticipator lever one scale mark lower. Again, wait several hours for the system to stabilize.

Special Advice: If the thermostat setting and the thermometer reading disagree, the thermostat may not be level, it may be affected by drafts or radiant heat, or it may be out of calibration. To see if it is level, place a bubble level or a plumb line against the unit. If the thermostat is affected by drafts and heat, it may need to be relocated. If it is out of calibration, check the instructions for the unit on how to adjust it, or call a technician.

Helpful Hint: Normally a thermostat should be placed at least five feet from the floor, away from sources of heat, including sunlight, and on an interior wall. Position it away from corners and dead spots behind doors and in closets. It should not be located on walls that have ducts or pipes, and should be protected from airflow within the wall.

THE DEFECTIVE GARAGE DOOR

Reasons for an electronic garage door opener not activating can include interrupted power supply, antenna out of position, defective transmitter, expired remote battery, or defective push-button switch inside the garage. First, make sure the unit's receptacle inside the garage is receiving power and that the opener is plugged in.

What To Do: To see if the transmitter or its battery are bad, check the opener with the push button inside the garage. If it works, check to see that the unit's antenna is not bent out of position. Try replacing the transmitter's battery. If the transmitter still doesn't work, its button may be defective. Try cleaning with electrical contact cleaner. If that doesn't correct the problem, you may need to replace it. Conversely, if the transmitter works but the push button inside the garage doesn't, turn off the power and try electrical contact cleaner on the push button. If that doesn't fix it, turn off all power and replace the switch. Simply remove and detach the two wires from under the screws on the back, and reinstall the new switch.

Special Advice: When a power failure traps your car inside the garage, you can use the emergency release located on the opener track. Usually, this will be a cord hanging down between the motor and the door. Pull it down and away from the door to release. *Important:* If you disengage the release during a power failure, be sure to unplug the opener, too. After the power is back on, pull on the release again to re-engage the opener. Make sure all drivers in your household know how to use the release mechanism.

Helpful Hint: For routine adjustments, consult the owner's manual. If you don't have an one, contact the manufacturer and request a copy. The model number should be on the back of the power unit.

Note: The new 200-page **Home Repair Emergency Handbook** *is especially valuable to first-time homeowners or single-parent households; it's available at bookstores for $14.95, or can be ordered directly from Taylor Publishing Co., 1550 W. Mockingbird Ln., Dallas, TX 75235 (800/677-2800).*

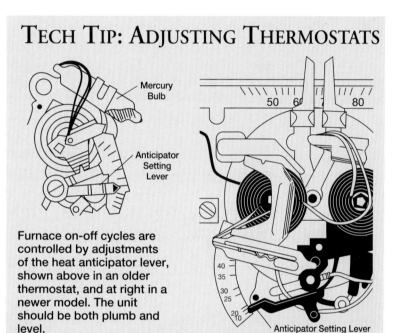

TECH TIP: ADJUSTING THERMOSTATS

Mercury Bulb

Anticipator Setting Lever

50 60 80

40
35
30
25
20
10

Anticipator Setting Lever

Furnace on-off cycles are controlled by adjustments of the heat anticipator lever, shown above in an older thermostat, and at right in a newer model. The unit should be both plumb and level.

Smart
BOAT RIGGING

*How To Select And Install Gear For More
Rewarding Fishing*

Many an angler spends $5,000 or more for a fishing boat, then reluctantly shells out only $50 or so on rigging it. According to Al Lindner, fishing expert of *In-Fisherman* fame, that's a big mistake and a pure waste of investment.

"Rigging a boat is as important to fishing success as presenting the right bait in the right place at the right time," he says. "But rigging is more than just equipping a boat; it involves the fine art of properly placing the tools of fishing so you can maximize fun and cut out the hassles. In other words, good rigging can facilitate your enjoyment of fishing."

More precisely, proper rigging means that while you are riding the waves in pursuit of lunkers, you can hold onto your rod while reaching for switches, rod holders, and grippers. It means you can see the loran or sonar, whether you are fore or aft. It means being able to operate trolling motors smoothly when a giant musky dives under the boat. And it means room for bait, maps, rods, reels, and tackle.

Ultimately, he says, it means more fish in the boat.

Boat rigging involves more than wiring, placing transducers, or planning deck configuration. Those are basic mechanics. The soul of rigging is integrating those mechanics with your needs as an angler. A prop-

erly rigged boat requires the planning of everything down to the last Velcro strap — so you won't have a wrench in your hand instead of a rod or have to scramble for a net, bend over to look into a cabinet to see the flasher, move around the boat to turn things off, or lose track of a school of fish because the trolling motor is not wired right.

But before you rig a boat, you have to buy one. Before you buy a boat and motor, it's a good idea to first rig it out on paper. The diagrams on the following pages will give you starter ideas on how to rig boats four ways to fish big lakes or rivers, or to pursue bass or general fishing.

Photos: In-Fisherman

Al Lindner, left, discusses the fine points of rigging his own boat with Jim Wentworth, who has outfitted boats for 22 years.

THE BOAT

An angler who fishes only rivers needs a river boat, probably a flat or tunnel bottom with room for accessories. A tournament bass fisherman needs to get down the lake quickly and fish from a comfortable casting platform. The weekend angler who dreams of trolling on big water for leaping king salmon needs a long, wide, stable V-hull to handle heavy wind and waves.

Al Lindner emphasizes that various boat designs serve different functions. "A lot of presentation techniques — back trolling, vertical jigging, and trolling — are geared into the hull design and how the boat is laid out.

Bass boats are highly evolved rigs, for example, but if I could only have one boat, it would be a multispecies design."

What's the best multispecies boat? "I know I'm pushing it," he says, "but I have an 18'10" Lund boat with a 90-hp tiller motor. I use it for walleyes, muskies, crappies, bass, even tarpon, in shallow or deep water. The advantages of tiller over console controls include more space and more precision when trolling or back trolling. With higher horsepower engines, however, console models are easier to handle and run long distances. The windshield protects you. And, with the same hull, console models are typically rated for at least one-third more horsepower than tiller models."

Aluminum, fiberglass, or Kevlar? An aluminum hull is lightest; fiberglass is heaviest. With the right keel, heavy boats stay on track and follow a contour more efficiently. But with identical outboards, weight reduces acceleration and maximum speed. Aluminum hull boats also are easier to tow.

Other features to look for include enough flat space in front of the angler to mount units to be visible while fishing or cruising. Check for room to snake wires and position transducers. Check for ample space, including functional battery compartments, rod lockers, livewells, and storage. Also eyeball reachability; will trolling motors, switches, sonar, bait, and rod holders all be accessible from the fishing station?

If the hull is the body of the modern fishing boat, wiring could be considered the circulatory system, and electronic accessories, the brains. Rigging today not only includes sonar, space-age versions of early "fish finders," but also loran, which uses low-frequency radio waves to determine positions over long distances, as well as the latest breakthrough, global positioning systems (GPS), which use satellites to calculate precise positions

Input from the *In-Fisherman* staff resulted in this diagram of a rigged multispecies hull. Controls are within reach of the tiller station. The bow station is outfitted simply, but efficiently. Everything is in its place and strapped down. Sonar is within reach, in sight, yet out of the way.

A modern multispecies boat should include battery monitor, compass, dual sonar systems, live well, front storage for deep-cycle batteries, front trolling motor, and rear kicker (or extra electric).

Options include loran with receiver built into a 180-degree, ratcheting base bracket, a "jumper system" for trolling motor operation, Ultra Mount sonar brackets, dual-bilge systems, built-in tackle trays, interior lighting, on-off foot controls (with trip guards) for trolling motors surrounding both fishing stations, and more.

THE MULTISPECIES BOAT

splash guards

mounting board for transducers wiring through hull

semi or modified V-hull

transducers

rubber covered entry slit in splash guards for electric motor

powerful variable speed electric motor (gas "kicker" in larger boats)

screw eyes for bungy cords to secure tackle boxes, coolers, etc.

rod holder

pedestal mounts for further seating options

antenna strap or end cap that pulls end into boat

8-foot antenna for marine band radio

ratchet bracket for raising and lowering marine-band antenna

on-off switch for trolling motor with safety guards

easy-access tackle trays (under seat and in-deck)

all-angle, multidirec handle extension for trollin motor

3-prong plug-ins for trolling motor and "jumper system"

storage compartm for crankir battery

foot controls

powerful electric

front storage for deep-cycle batteries

marine band radio compartment

velcro rod straps

landing net

Control panel:
1. bilge switches
2. livewell timer and pump controls
3. tachometer
4. navigation lights
5. fuel guage
6. tilt gauge
7. clock

pedestal seat

livewell(s)

built-in tackle tray (under seat)

cleats/grippers

velcro rod straps

push pole

tiller drive with kill switch/electric start

on/off

foot-trim switch

dry storage

trim switch

battery monitoring system

rod holder

LCG or paper graph flasher or side-viewing sonar wired to cranking battery in back

plug-ins for trolling motor and "jumper system"

front deck

loran antenna

locking in-deck rod lockers

180° ratchet bracket for loran antenna— has loran receiver built into base

strap or end cap

paper graph/side-viewing sonar (optional)

flasher

LCG with loran capability

rod holder

cleats/grippers

liquid-filled compass

THE RIVER BOAT

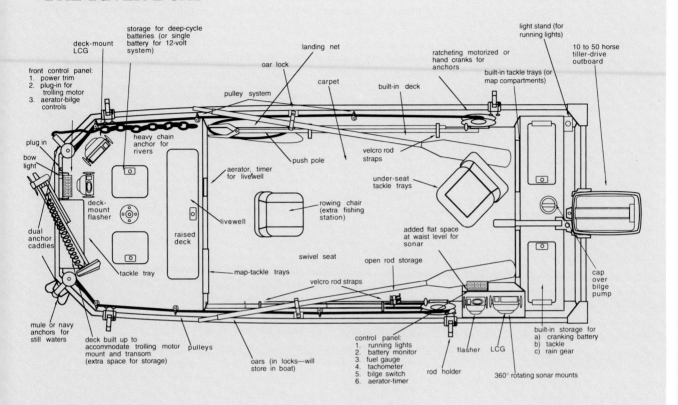

storage for deep-cycle batteries (or single battery for 12-volt system)

deck-mount LCG

landing net

oar lock

light stand (for running lights)

ratcheting motorized or hand cranks for anchors

10 to 50 horse tiller-drive outboard

front control panel:
1. power trim
2. plug-in for trolling motor
3. aerator-bilge controls

carpet

built-in deck

built-in tackle trays (or map compartments)

pulley system

plug in

bow light

heavy chain anchor for rivers

push pole

velcro rod straps

under-seat tackle trays

deck-mount flasher

aerator, timer for livewell

rowing chair (extra fishing station)

added flat space at waist level for sonar

dual anchor caddies

livewell

raised deck

swivel seat

open rod storage

cap over bilge pump

tackle tray

map-tackle trays

velcro rod straps

control panel:
1. running lights
2. battery monitor
3. fuel gauge
4. tachometer
5. bilge switch
6. aerator-timer

built-in storage for
a) cranking battery
b) tackle
c) rain gear

mule or navy anchors for still waters

deck built up to accommodate trolling motor mount and transom (extra space for storage)

pulleys

oars (in locks—will store in boat)

flasher

LCG

rod holder

360° rotating sonar mounts

THE BASS BOAT

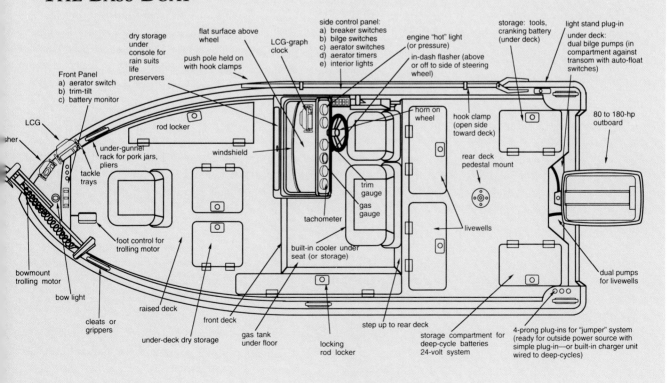

dry storage under console for rain suits life preservers

flat surface above wheel

push pole held on with hook clamps

LCG-graph clock

side control panel:
a) breaker switches
b) bilge switches
c) aerator switches
d) aerator timers
e) interior lights

engine "hot" light (or pressure)

in-dash flasher (above or off to side of steering wheel)

storage: tools, cranking battery (under deck)

light stand plug-in

under deck: dual bilge pumps (in compartment against transom with auto-float switches)

Front Panel
a) aerator switch
b) trim-tilt
c) battery monitor

LCG

rod locker

windshield

horn on wheel

hook clamp (open side toward deck)

80 to 180-hp outboard

under-gunnel rack for pork jars, pliers

rear deck pedestal mount

tackle trays

trim gauge

gas gauge

livewells

dual pumps for livewells

foot control for trolling motor

tachometer

built-in cooler under seat (or storage)

bowmount trolling motor

bow light

cleats or grippers

raised deck

under-deck dry storage

front deck

gas tank under floor

locking rod locker

step up to rear deck

storage compartment for deep-cycle batteries 24-volt system

4-prong plug-ins for "jumper" system (ready for outside power source with simple plug-in—or built-in charger unit wired to deep-cycles)

THE GREAT LAKES BOAT

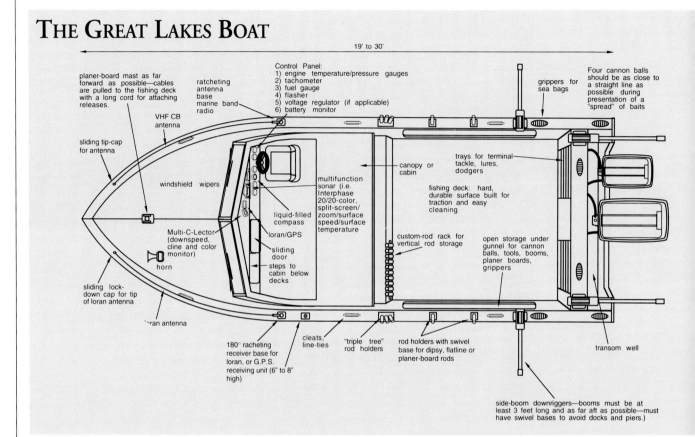

19' to 30'

planer-board mast as far forward as possible—cables are pulled to the fishing deck with a long cord for attaching releases.

ratcheting antenna base marine band radio

VHF CB antenna

sliding tip-cap for antenna

windshield wipers

Multi-C-Lector (downspeed, cline and color monitor)

horn

sliding lock-down cap for tip of loran antenna

loran antenna

Control Panel:
1) engine temperature/pressure gauges
2) tachometer
3) fuel gauge
4) flasher
5) voltage regulator (if applicable)
6) battery monitor

multifunction sonar (i.e. Interphase 20/20-color, split-screen/ zoom/surface speed/surface temperature

liquid-filled compass

loran/GPS

sliding door

steps to cabin below decks

canopy or cabin

fishing deck: hard, durable surface built for traction and easy cleaning

custom-rod rack for vertical rod storage

grippers for sea bags

Four cannon balls should be as close to a straight line as possible during presentation of a "spread" of baits

trays for terminal tackle, lures, dodgers

open storage under gunnel for cannon balls, tools, booms, planer boards, grippers

transom well

180° racheting receiver base for loran, or G.P.S. receiving unit (6" to 8" high)

cleats, line-ties

"triple tree" rod holders

rod holders with swivel base for dipsy, flatline or planer-board rods

side-boom downriggers—booms must be at least 3 feet long and as far aft as possible—must have swivel bases to avoid docks and piers.)

anywhere on earth.

Here are tips from Al Lindner and boat riggers who work with the *In-Fisherman* magazine staff in each of these areas.

THE WIRING

Batteries are the heart of any boat, according to Jim Wentworth, a boat rigger for 22 years and owner of Fish-Lectronics in Nisswa, Minnesota. He likes a built-in battery monitoring system that monitors voltage output, as well as the remaining charge. Ideally, a switch lets you check energy levels in three or more batteries with one monitor.

And he prefers a 12/24-volt system. "You need at least two 100-amp batteries for a 200-amp-hour total," says Wentworth, "to create a reliable 24-volt system; 150s are better yet. The most important items on board are batteries; without them you go nowhere. But they're practically

worthless without proper wiring. Boats need at least 8-gauge wire running end to end. I rig with 6-gauge, which will carry 80 amps 16 feet with no loss of voltage. If the wire isn't heavy enough to carry the juice, you can get only half power from your trolling motor."

Wentworth rigs accessories — bilge pumps, sonar, livewell aerators, loran, trim control, lights, and radios — all off the starting (cranking) battery. The battery is continually being recharged and can handle lower-draw accessories. A monitor tells if and when you should charge the cranking battery. Tip: Maximizer circuits in most trolling motors affect the way sonar operates, so it's a mistake to rig them on the same battery. Trolling motors draw the most energy, so connect them to deep-cycle batteries.

"And always," says Wentworth, "pro-

tect each electrical device — trolling motors, lorans, sonars, and downriggers — with circuit breakers. Pre-wired boats come with circuit breakers and fuses, but anglers who do it themselves sometimes forget fuses." He protects trolling motors and jumper-system plug-ins with 40-amp circuit breakers because at full load they can draw over 30 amps. He protects sonars, lorans, lights, and other accessories with individual breakers ranging from 1 to 5 amps, depending on the draw of each device.

THE ACCESSORIES

"Consider sonar placement at least three times before putting a hole in a boat," Wentworth advises. "Will the sonar unit be in the way? What else should be put there? Where will the transducers go? What will the final arrangement look like? Map it out ahead of time or you may be sorry."

He says two other things are critical: sonar 1) must be viewed easily while running and while fishing and 2) must be within reach for changing modes or viewing angle, and for turning on and off. "If you have to set your rod down to mess with accessories," he says, "your rigging is costing you fishing time. Some boats have built-in cabinets for sonar, but they're worthless if you can't see the units while you are standing."

What to buy? LCD (liquid crystal display) technology is taking over the sonar market, Wentworth observes. "LCDs are nice, but you can't always see the screen in bright sunlight. And you can't always see bottom in thick plankton blooms or heavy weeds, either. That's when a flasher comes in handy; you can see it easily with peripheral vision."

Most serious anglers have one or two sonar units, and the majority choose LCDs. LCDs have many features, including fish alarms, loran capability, zoom, backlighting for night use, and readouts on surface temperature, boat speed, voltage output and, of course, depth. But so many anglers have bought LCDs that some companies have eliminated flasher models. Other companies, Wentworth fears, will drop their flasher line if Japanese manufacturers stop making them.

Some fishermen are now buying extra flashers to store because they are afraid they will not be available in years ahead.

Flashers detect fish when you are running full out. On the other hand, with LCDs you don't have to be glued to the screen to see fish — there's a running history for a short period. Graphs are great, too, because they offer more detail than LCDs, and give a complete running history for reference. Each can have a purpose onboard; one isn't a complete substitute for another.

Wentworth has paper graph, LCD, and flasher sonars at his main station at the back of his own boat. The graphs and LCD help him visualize the bottom, allow him to check one scenario against the other, and serve as backups for each other.

But how do you keep things simple with added antennas, boxes, panels, and screens to rig? One option is to use units that do double duty. Units like the Bottomline 6600 EZ, the Eagle A-9500, and Lowrance LMS 200 provide LCD graphs with optional loran capability, speedometers, and

ELECTRICAL RIGGING SOURCES

Below is a sampling of electrical rigging components, assembled by the *In-Fisherman* staff.

Battery Saver. Batteries lose charge and lifespan over periods of disuse. The Mity Mite shuts off when a battery is fully charged and comes back on whenever the battery drops one volt. It mounts permanently in the boat without getting in the way. Schumacher Electric Corp., 7474 Rogers Ave., Chicago, IL 60626.

Bilge & Live Well Pumps. A backup bilge pump with its own power supply is handy. The Johnson Pro-Line pumps 1,000 gallons per hour; the Rule, 700. Johnson Pump of America, Inc., 4825 Scott St., Suite 306, Schiller Park, IL 60176. Rule Industries, Inc., 70 Blanchard Rd., Burlington, MA 01803.

Pulse Modulator. Older or smaller trolling motors often don't have pulse modulation, which means less efficiency and less time on the water without recharging the battery. The Chopper is an add-on that increases motor efficiency. St. Louis Power, Inc., 4963 Fairview, St. Louis, MO 63139.

Dashboard Monitors. These companies offer instruments to monitor engine temperature and performance of engine and prop. Faria Marine Instruments, 385 Norwich-New London Turnpike, Uncasville, CT 06382. Teleflex Marine, Inc., 640 N. Lewis Rd., Limerick, PA 19468.

Smart Charger. This unit charges two 150-amp deep-cycle batteries in under five hours with no danger of boil over. The Super Smart Charger generates the exact maximum charge, and shuts off when the battery is charged. Deltona Power Supply, 801 U.S. Hwy. 92E, Deland, FL 32724.

Engine Mount Trollers. These trolling motors mount to the cavitation plate of an outboard or inboard, offering console control for docking or slow trolling. SystemSport, Inc., 2500 West City Rd. 42, Burnsville, MN 55337. Goldeneye Products, Inc., 6213 Bury Dr., Eden Prairie, MN 55346.

Four-Prong Plug-Ins. Good plug prongs reduce electrical resistance, so trolling motors and charging systems utilize full power. Marinco Marine Electrical Products, One Digital Dr., Novato, CA 94949.

Hand-Held Battery Monitor. Without a built-in monitoring system on board, or on boats that don't monitor the cranking battery, hand-held models show you how much fishing time is left. Altus Technology, 11569 Encore Circle, Minnetonka, MN 55343.

24-Volt System With Jumper Charging

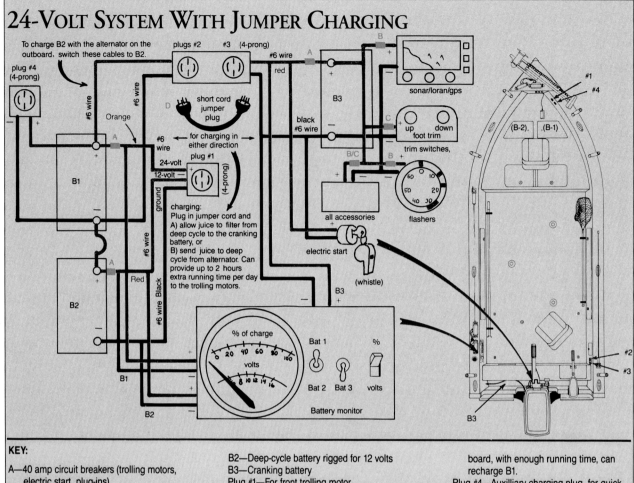

KEY:

A—40 amp circuit breakers (trolling motors, electric start, plug-ins)

B—1- to 3-amp circuit breakers (sonar, radios)

C—3- to 5-amp circuit breakers (bilge pumps, trim switches)

D—Dual 4-pronged plugs on a short cable for "jumper system"

B1—Deep-cycle battery rigged for 24 volts

B2—Deep-cycle battery rigged for 12 volts

B3—Cranking battery

Plug #1—For front trolling motor

Plug #2—For back trolling motor and jumper cable

Plug #3—Leads to B3. When connected to plug #2 with jumper cable, the deep cycles can charge a dead cranking battery in 5 to 10 minutes. Or, the alternator on the out-

board, with enough running time, can recharge B1.

Plug #4—Auxilliary charging plug, for quick plug-in charging in the yard or garage, or even (properly rigged) for charging off the alternator on a truck or car. Leads to B1. Plug #1 also is an auxilliary charging plug for B2.

---

built-in surface temperature gauges. These devices reduce dash clutter, but present one drawback. If one function breaks, you sacrifice the other functions while the unit is being repaired.

Wentworth mounts his loran antenna on a 180-degree rotating base that allows him to slap the unit down on the gunnel and clip it out of the way while fishing and running full out. The base of the antenna is the receiving unit, which also saves space.

"Loran is going to be around for a long time," he observes. "But global-positioning satellite systems (GPS) are going to give it a shove. When GPS gets down to around $1,000, which could happen soon, it's going to be one of the hottest things on the

market." GPS comes packaged in double-duty units that incorporate sonar, like the Lowrance LMS-300 GPS. But it's more commonly available in stand-alone units like the Si-Tex GPS 77 or the Raytheon 590. The antennae on GPS units are only inches high, requiring much less space than loran.

Wentworth uses a variety of mounts for sonar, loran, and GPS screens, but one model stands out: the Ultra Mount III (T&L Products, 7856 Reinbold Rd., Reese, MI 48757). Its 360-degree rotating swivel base acts like the business end of an expensive tripod. For viewing a unit at all angles while fishing, this one is hard to beat.

Al Lindner notes that every fisher-

man he knows who uses this mount likes it. "Little things add up," he says. "A few seconds here, a minute there, and before you know it, you are catching more fish. The ability to instantly refer to your sonar from any position will save time and cut down on the frustration factor."

*Note: The In-Fisherman Communications Network produces **In-Fisherman** magazine ($16 for seven issues), national In-Fisherman television and radio programs, as well as videos, books, and newsstand specials of interest to serious anglers. Write to In-Fisherman, P.O. Box 999, 651 Edgewood Dr., Brainerd, MN 56401.*

TOOL POWER

Smart Tool-Buying Advice Straight From Those Who Make Them

Tool experts say that having good tools that work well is half the battle in creating successful home projects. Take the advice of these experts to accumulate the right tools for the job. Here are suggestions to help you get set up right, both from hand tool experts at Stanley Tools and power tool experts at Skil Corporation. A quick review can help you plan your purchases and prevent mistakes, whether you are a beginning do-it-yourselfer who needs to outfit a toolbox with the most basic tools, or an advanced craftsman equipping a complete workshop.

One of the handiest measuring tools you can buy, the combination square, above, allows fast, accurate marking at either 45- or 90-degree angles.

QUICK-REFERENCE TOOL CHECK

——— HAND TOOLS ———

Beginner Level: Portable 19" toolbox • 30' tape rule • 16-oz. wood handle hammer • Screwdriver set or four-way rachet screwdriver • ⅜"-drive socket set • 6" slip-joint plier • Crosscut handsaw • Miter saw and miter box • Utility knife • 24" level • Plastic-cased chalk line • Awl • Carpenter's square

Intermediate Level: 20" or larger toolbox and/or tool chest • 16-oz. steel-handle hammer • ¼" and ½" socket sets with deep sockets • Larger screwdrivers • Needle-nose pliers • Heavy-duty utility knife • Miter box with 10- and 90-degree range • C-clamps and bar clamps • 48" level

Advanced Level: 32" portable toolbox, plus tool chest and/or cabinet • 100' tape rule • 16-oz. fiberglass-handle hammer • Quality screwdrivers with triangular grip • Diagonal-cutting pliers • Heavy-duty utility knife • Wallboard saw • Hacksaw • 72" level • Assorted squares • 100' chalk line

——— POWER TOOLS ———

Beginning Level: ⅜" variable-speed drill • Cordless screwdriver • ⅜"-drive cordless power wrench • 7¼" circular saw • Jig (or saber) saw • Finishing sander • Benchtop power grinder

Intermediate Level: 10" benchtop table saw • Scroll saw • Benchtop drill press • ⅜"-drive cordless or electric drill • ⅜" hammer drill • 5½" trim saw • Reciprocating saw • Belt sander

Advanced Level: ½" electric drill • Cordless drill/driver • Power miter saw • Plate joiner • Laminate trimmer • Router • Specialty sanders

HAND TOOL CHECKLIST

Before buying tools, review your budget, experience level, and available space. To save money, experts at Stanley Tools suggest buying the best you can afford, so later purchases will be additions instead of replacements.

BEGINNING LEVEL

Following are basic tools that most homeowners or do-it-yourselfers should have available. To house them, Stanley experts suggest using a 19" all-purpose toolbox.

❑ A tape rule that rolls up into a case for measuring distances from 1/16" to 30'.

❑ A curved-claw, inexpensive wood-handled hammer with a 16-oz. head for hanging pictures and shelving or removing nails.

❑ A set of screwdrivers of varying lengths and tip sizes, or a four-way ratchet screwdriver. A 3/8"-drive socket set to save both time and effort on tightening or removing nuts on bolts of various sizes.

❑ A set of combination wrenches for simple adjustment of nuts and bolts. A pair of 6" slip-joint pliers with two-position milled jaws for all-purpose work.

❑ A general-purpose crosscut handsaw with eight teeth (points) per inch. Some newer saws actually cut 50% faster than conventional saws because the teeth cut wider than the blade's thickness.

❑ A plastic miter box and miter saw to cut molding, chair rail, baseboards, and picture frames at 45- or 90-degree angles.

❑ A retractable utility knife for light jobs, such as cutting wallpaper, packing tape, cardboard, and ceiling panels. Some newer knives have a snap closure to change blades without a screwdriver.

❑ A 24" level for jobs such as leveling appliances, shelving, and curtain rods.

❑ A chalk line to mark perpendicular lines on walls for wallpapering, for example, or on floors for laying tile.

❑ An awl to mark through holes on the backs of items to show where to place screws.

INTERMEDIATE LEVEL

Here are suggestions if you consider yourself an intermediate do-it-yourselfer. To carry and store these tools, experts suggest using a 20" or larger portable toolbox and/or a tool chest.

❑ A 16-oz. steel-handled hammer with cushion grip to absorb shock.

❑ Additional, larger screwdrivers than the basic set. Look for those with comfortable handles.

❑ Additional socket sets in 1/4" and 1/2" sizes, plus a variety of deep sockets which are useful when a nut is recessed or when a bolt extends beyond a nut.

❑ A pair of needle-nose pliers to use for getting into tight spaces or for cutting wires.

❑ A metal-bodied retractable utility knife with a multiposition blade, for cutting flooring and plastic.

❑ A miter box with a range from 10 to 90 degrees for more intricate woodworking, such as making furniture.

❑ Basic clamps, including C-clamps or bar clamps, for holding wood together for gluing.

❑ A hacksaw for cutting metal. Consider one with a D-handle to prevent scraped knuckles.

❑ A basic file set to smooth out burrs or to sharpen chain saws or lawn mower blades.

❑ A 48" level to build structures, such as workbenches, decks, or storage sheds.

ADVANCED LEVEL

Basic hand tools for advanced do-it-yourselfers may be additions to what you have, or replacements for tools you initially bought. For these tools, a 32" portable toolbox, plus a tool chest and/or cabinet, is suggested.

❑ A long steel tape to measure distances from 50' to 100'. Most use a hand crank to return the blade, but models are available with automatic blade return.

❑ A 16-oz. fiberglass handle hammer with cushion grip for extensive hammering jobs.

❑ A set of professional-quality screwdrivers with large triangular grip and tips of special alloy steel.

❑ A pair of diagonal-cutting pliers to reach where needle-nose pliers cannot, such as inside an electrical box.

❑ A heavy-duty utility knife with interlocking nose design that prevents the knife halves from spreading, for cutting shingles or for scoring wood.

❑ A crosscut saw with flexible blade and more than eight teeth (points) per inch to allow a fine and slow cut.

❑ A wallboard saw for jobs such as cutting out holes for electrical outlets.

❑ A hacksaw with a tubular frame that stores blades inside.

❑ A 72" level for large-scale construction projects.

❑ A selection of rafter squares, combination squares, and try squares for special measuring jobs.

❑ A 100' chalk line encased in a metal body for rugged use.

POWER TOOL CHECKLIST

To select tools wisely, experts at Skil recommend making a mental estimate of how often you will actually use the tool, how much experience you have had with similar tools, and what projects you have planned for the future.

BEGINNING LEVEL

If you are a beginning do-it-yourselfer, and your needs are infrequent, you can get by with tools in the lower price range. However, compare costs; nice-to-have features may not cost that much more.

❑ A ⅜" variable-speed electric drill to drill holes for projects such as assembling swing sets or hanging draperies.

❑ A cordless power screwdriver for a variety of household chores, from hanging shelves and curtains to changing light switches. Look for fast recharge (5 hours or less), a pistol handle for more grip on larger screws, and a rocker switch so you don't need to manually slide the switch from forward to reverse.

❑ A ⅜"-drive cordless power wrench for such jobs as installing metal shelving and garage door openers, repairing bicycles, and other work. Look for long run-time, and quick recharge with an LED charge indicator light.

❑ A 7¼" portable circular saw for jobs such as room paneling or shelf building. A vari-torque clutch helps minimize kickback and prevent motor overload. Also check for on-saw blade wrench storage, a lower guard lift lever for making pocket cuts, a textured nonslip handle, and a lateral lock "off" button to avoid accidental starting.

❑ Additional power tools for a beginning workshop might include a jig (or saber) saw for cutting curved shapes, a finishing sander for fine finishing work, and a benchtop bench grinder for sharpening items, such as lawn mower blades, screwdriver tips, or chisels.

INTERMEDIATE LEVEL

For intermediate and advanced do-it-yourselfers, benchtop power tools priced under $200 can help you move into beginning woodworking without the expense or space required by stationary power tools.

❑ A 10" benchtop table saw for all-purpose cutting. Check for improved, self-aligning rip fences.

❑ A scroll saw for intricate cuts. Newer models have more stable workpiece hold-downs that adjust to 45 degrees.

❑ A benchtop drill press, which can meet most drilling needs and complement portable and stationary tools.

❑ A combination belt/disc sander.

❑ A ⅜" cordless drill for drilling into steel, as well as wood. Newer versions have forward and reverse speeds of 240 and 600 rpm, and a recharge time of 3 hours.

❑ A ⅜" electric drill, if preferred over a cordless. Check for die cast aluminum gear housing and a larger 5-amp burnout protected motor.

❑ A ⅜" variable-speed hammer drill, for drilling through concrete or masonry.

❑ A 5½" professional trim saw for lighter-duty work, such as cutting 2x4s and baseboard trim.

❑ A reciprocating saw with a variety of blades for cutting wood where nails may be found, doing scroll cuts in metal, cutting plaster, or pruning trees. Check for ball- and roller-bearing construction and variable speed from 0 to 2,400 strokes per minute.

❑ A compact, lightweight belt sander for easy handling. Good features include a vacuum system with dust bag, one-lever belt changing, and a front handle for control.

ADVANCED LEVEL

While advanced do-it-yourselfers have more experience with tools, they need to ask the same questions anyone else does, including whether the tool has enough power and features to do an adequate job, whether it will save time, and whether it offers good value for the dollar.

❑ A ½" industrial-quality electric drill for more challenging projects, such as installing door locks. With more torque than ⅜" models, the ½" accepts a wide range of accessories, including hole saws to drill large holes into metal or wood, and self-feeding bits that can make large holes with a minimum of feed pressure.

❑ An industrial-quality cordless drill/driver has high-torque gearing to handle large screws when hanging doors, installing built-in appliances, and building walls. Look for variable-torque clutch for precise positioning of screws, 1-hour recharge, and a ready light to indicate full charge.

❑ A power miter saw to make precision cuts in materials such as molding and trim. Look for a cast-iron base for stability and accuracy, ball and roller bearings, and electric brake for quick blade stops.

❑ A selection of specialty tools, which may include plate joiners, laminate trimmers, routers, and a wide assortment of specialty sanders.

HEAD-START BUILDING

Selecting The Right Plan And Lot
Can Save You Big Money Before You're Done

Thousands of families every year ask themselves if they should buy or build. Unless you've gone through it before, you may be in for several learning experiences if you decide to build. The key, say experts, is to keep those experiences from costing you big money.

A home is a complex blend of mechanical systems, as well as aesthetic considerations. It's the final cost that usually is the limiting factor. As a general rule, building a new home will run between $60 and $100 per square foot of living space. If you are pressed on budget, one way to reduce up-front costs is to use a stock home plan rather than hiring your own architect.

For sale at larger newsstands and bookstores, home plan publications offer thousands of designs by architects from all over the country. Construction blueprints can be ordered from these sources at a fraction of the cost of custom-designed plans. (For example, seven sets of blueprints for the popular home shown on page 173 are available for under $500.) This can save you several thousand dollars that can rescue a squeezed budget or allow you to invest more into the home itself.

CHOOSING THE PLAN

The experts admit there is only one major goal involved in picking a home plan: choosing one that best matches your present and projected needs to what you can afford. Here are some tips to help you analyze a plan that strikes your fancy.

Be sure it fits your lot. This seems obvious, but sometimes it is easy to forget to check into setback and side-yard requirements of local building codes. Some areas even have height limitations.

Make sure you can afford it. Check with local lenders, builders, lumberyards, or home insurance agencies to get a range of square-foot building costs in your area. Costs vary widely, depending upon local material and labor costs and on the complexity and quality of the home you decide you want to build.

10 FEATURES OF A GOOD HOME PLAN

1 **Exterior.** This one is a judgment call. Look for a facade that fits the neighborhood, matches your taste, and looks graceful. Decide if you want traditional or contemporary styling, or a blend of the two.

2 **Openness.** Many quality plans lend themselves to convenient outdoor living, with decks and porches. Others bring the outdoors inside with the use of sun rooms, abundant windows, and skylights.

3 **Front Entry.** A sheltered entry is always a nice touch, and an interior hall or foyer is the mark of a good design. A guest coat closet is desirable; a powder room even better.

4 **Traffic Flow.** Hallways, rather the individual rooms, should carry the heaviest traffic. You may, for example, want to avoid designs that require traffic to and from the back door to go through the kitchen.

5 **Interior Zones.** Homes contain three basic zones: 1) working zones (kitchen and laundry), 2) living zones (family, dining, and living rooms), and 3) quiet zones (bedrooms, dens, and studies). A well-conceived design separates these zones as much as possible.

6 **Adaptability.** Most home builders today prefer open, adaptable plans to the more rigid and confined homes of the past. Multiuse spaces, such as family rooms, can change as families grow.

7 **Master Bedrooms.** Homes being built today almost always include a deluxe master bedroom suite, with a private bath and abundant closet space. Dressing rooms, double vanities, and whirlpools are other luxury touches.

8 **Kitchens.** With today's lifestyles, the kitchen often becomes the center of a family's activities. Large, open kitchens with abundant countertop space, breakfast counters, nooks, islands, and pantries are desirable.

9 **Ambience.** The general feel of a home is influenced by its basic design, as well as by decor and furnishings. High or vaulted ceilings, skylights, clerestory windows, curved stairways, and other special touches can boost a home's value.

10 **Utility.** Today's families have an abundance of possessions to store. They appreciate big closets, extra garage space, attics, linen closets, bookshelves, and other built-in or potential storage areas.

Match it to your lifestyle. Make a list of priorities you and your family can agree upon. Few of us can afford everything we want, so compromise almost always becomes necessary. Consider your entertaining needs, family size and ages, and other factors important to you.

Consider your life stage. Young families may need a plan with flexibility and "bonus space" that allows changes and additions as the family grows. For a retirement home, watch for steep stairs, multiple levels, narrow hallways, small bathrooms, confined kitchens, and other situations that may create future mobility and access problems.

Look ahead to resale value. After you've looked at the broad picture, you can focus on the finer points of the home you plan to build. You want it to fit your family's needs, but the home also must have resale value. To attract a good price, the design should include features that are popular with a majority of home buyers.

Choosing The Lot

Design, real estate, materials, and contracting costs are the four areas that offer new home builders opportunities to save. Observers at HomeStyles in Minneapolis say that land costs will depend on location, whether it is developed, and whether the site poses potential problems, such as difficult terrain, an unusual configuration, or complicated zoning requirements.

In some areas, you may not have much selection. If you do have alternatives, here are some factors to consider.

Lot Location. Decide if the convenience of being close to workplaces, stores, schools, and churches is more important than the quiet and privacy of a remote site. Consider the neighborhood's appearance and local taxes. Also check commuting distances, traffic, public transportation, road conditions, airport noise problems, and zoning laws, as well as water, sewer, and drainage factors.

Lot Terrain. The slope of a lot can influence what you build. It is usually cheaper to build on flat or gently sloping lots, and yard work also is easier. Some slope is good for drainage, however. Hilly or sloping lots provide more creative potential for multi-level homes and walk-out basements, but landscaping costs can be higher and maintenance more difficult. Retaining walls can be costly, but also can add interest to a lot.

Up-sloping lots lend themselves to split entries and tuck-under garages. Down-sloping lots offer potential for decks and walk-out basements in the rear. Side slopes work well for split levels, and also may allow for lower-level garages and walk-out basements. Also check for rocks; big boulders can be expensive to move, but also may offer landscaping opportunities.

Size Of Lot. Although a large lot is considered desirable by most buyers, some actually prefer a smaller, low-maintenance lot that won't require hours of yard work. If available lots are narrow, you can find many home designs that take advantage of such sites. In some areas "zero-lot-line" building is allowed, which means you may be able to build right to the lot line. Check with local building officials.

Hidden Costs. Building on a five-acre lot miles from town may involve extra costs. Check to see if water, sewer, and gas lines, as well as electrical, phone, and cable TV lines, run by the property. Also check for any special environmental requirements for private water supply and sewage disposal systems.

If the lot is in a new development, check to see if the necessary facilities are in, and consider potential costs of present and future assessments for sidewalks, curbs, gutters, water, and sewer. In established neighborhoods, find out the costs of water and sewer hookups and other legal requirements.

Don't Forget Landscaping

The lot you buy can influence the home plan you select and the costs of completing your building project. The main goal is to avoid surprises.

The biggest question usually is what can you afford. "But you may not even be able to determine what is affordable if you don't know what questions to ask when buying a lot," says Rod Keppel, who operates Arbor Heights Nursery in Webster, New York. "Hidden costs can push you way over budget if you are not careful. In our area, the terrain can be quite hilly, with dramatic and drastic grade changes. Landscaping often is much more expensive than a builder bargains for," says Keppel.

He advises developing your master landscaping plan before you begin building. Such a plan can reduce the overall cost and help you set a reasonable landscaping budget. "When money runs low, landscaping sometimes gets reduced to a lower priority. The result may be a less-than-functional design that doesn't take full advantage of the site."

Completion Costs. Once you have your lot and blueprints, experts advise you to develop a master landscaping plan. It can give you a good idea of costs so you don't get caught short halfway through.

Draw out your plan on graph paper, and try to develop a budget. If you don't have money to hire a landscaping contractor, ask local plant nursery suppliers to help you. If you can't do all of the work at once, try to plan it in stages that can be done as your budget permits. ❧

ANATOMY OF A BEST-SELLER

HomeStyles, which sells plans from about 40 designers, reports that its plan E–3000 from Breland & Farmer Designers, Inc., has been its best-seller for four years in a row. According to the plan marketing firm, the features that make this stylish 3,035-sq.ft. home so popular include: 1) gracious, stylish exterior; 2) large porch and deck at rear; 3) inviting front porch entry; 4) smooth traffic pattern throughout; 5) good interior zoning; 6) visually open and flexible family room; 7) luxurious master suite; 8) large, accommodating kitchen; 9) either formal or casual atmosphere; and 10) abundant closets and other storage space. Blueprints, with or without a basement, are available from HomeStyles, 800/547-5570.

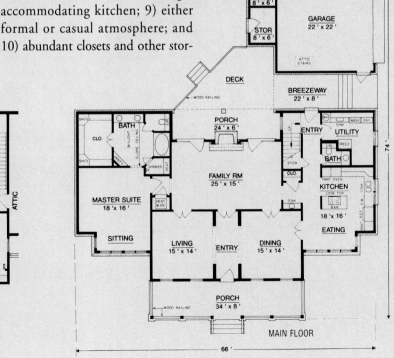

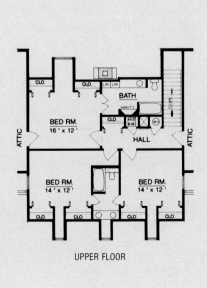

EASIER WAYS TO FINISH UP

Much of the backbreaking work associated with landscaping can be eliminated by renting a skid-steer loader, such as the Bobcat shown here, from a rental equipment dealer or by hiring a contractor with the equipment. Equipped with attachments, skid-steers make short work of grading, preparing seedbeds, planting trees, and handling landscaping.

Lawn seedbed preparation can be simplified using a skid-steer with a landscape rake that pulverizes and smooths the soil while removing rocks and debris.

Equipped with an earth auger, a skid-steer can dig holes for trees in short order. Augers up to 36" in diameter are available for plantings and smaller versions for post holes.

A bucket or pallet fork on a skid-steer loader is ideal for transporting trees and heavy shrubs to the planting site. They also quickly move other materials, such as posts and timber.

Larger trees can be moved easily to new positions on your property with "tree-spade" transplanter attachments, available for larger skid-steer loaders.

Backhoe attachments on small loaders can take the sweat out of excavating jobs, and also are good for tearing out old landscaping, including shrubs and small stumps.

A main advantage of skid-steer loaders is that they can maneuver well in tight quarters. Several model sizes available can squeeze in where other equipment can't.

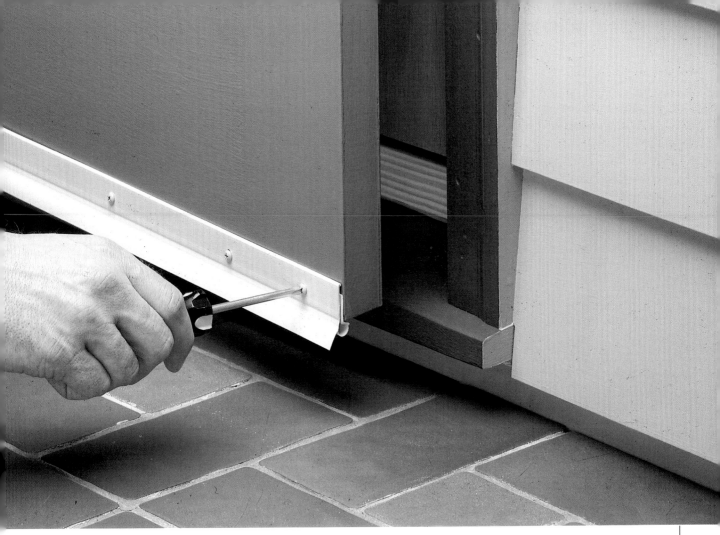

Photos: 3M

SECOND-GENERATION WEATHERPROOFING

*Tightening Up The Home Has Created
New Challenges With Condensation*

Two serious energy crises and rising costs have left older homes with upgraded R values and newer homes built to be more energy efficient. Steps to save energy have presented many homes with a secondary problem that begs for attention, however: condensation.

Even in well-insulated homes, condensation can lead to problems — dripping windows, wet sills, damp walls, mold, wet insulation, wood rot, and corrosion of metal. According to University of Minnesota extension specialists, even with reasonable indoor humidity of 30 to 50%, condensation can result if moisture-laden air leaks into cool parts of the home. The flow of heated, humidified air leaking through missed openings can carry water vapor to cool areas such as attics. With prolonged dampness in cool areas, insulation can lose its insulating ability and wood rot can take place in studs, wall sheathing, and roof decking.

Specialists Roger A. Peterson and Lewis T. Hendricks at the university observe that preventing condensation requires a four-part strategy: 1) trying to keeping relative humidity no higher than 50%, 2) installing a warm-side vapor retarder and a continuous air-barrier system, 3) adding adequate corner insulation and thermally insulated windows and doors, and 4) controlling excessive moisture sources, such as wet basements, unvented clothes dryers or kerosene heaters, firewood stored indoors, overly frequent showers, or misused

Interior weather stripping, above, helps reduce condensation at door bottoms. Metal thresholds should have a complete thermal break.

humidifiers.

Vapor Retarders. The thermal envelope of a home consists of all the insulated walls and ceilings that enclose the heated and humidified space. A vapor retarder on the interior (heated) side of the envelope restricts interior water vapor from getting into the insulation layer, or into unheated areas, such as the attic. A vapor retarder can be polyethylene film, special paint or sealer, or other vapor-resistant material. Films, foils, sealers, or paints are considered adequate in some areas of the country.

Because water vapor tends to find openings and penetrate them, special effort should be made to seal the vapor retarder and install an air barrier to prevent air leakage. Potential leaks can include holes for wires, wiring boxes, and pipes. Special construction tape, rubber gaskets, and sealants are available to economically seal such leaks.

Surface Condensation. Even in today's better-insulated homes, surface condensation can takes its toll. It can occur where water vapor in inside air comes in contact with a cool surface, especially on window glass and frames during cold weather. This often results in dripping that can cause interior damage, such as peeling paint, swelled or splitting wood, window frame and sill rot, staining, and mold. The best solution in cold climates is to use triple-pane insulating windows (or either double-pane windows plus storm window, or high-performance double-pane insulating glass). Where that is not feasible, easily installed window insulating kits that use clear shrunk-in-place plastic may help.

Doors and Corners. The specialists also point out that newer energy-efficient doors have insulating core materials and thermal spacers at the edges that prevent condensation or

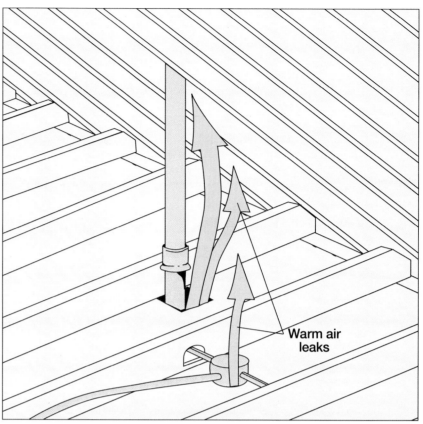

Warm air leaks

Holes in the ceiling for wires, pipes, and light fixtures should be sealed so humid air cannot leak into insulation or attic space.

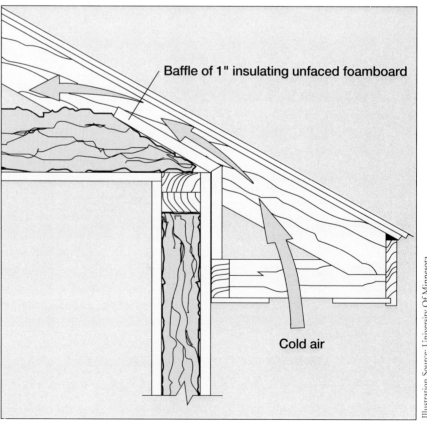

Baffle of 1" insulating unfaced foamboard

Cold air

Baffles and proper insulating can keep wind from entering ceiling insulation and causing damage or mildew on interior corners.

Illustration Source: University Of Minnesota

Special truss to allow full thickness of insulation without blocking ventilation

Roofing

Insulation

Air chute or baffle

Air movement

Air vent

Vapor retarder

Ceiling

In new construction, high-heel roof trusses provide space for adequate roof venting and for installing ceiling insulation full depth to the attic edge.

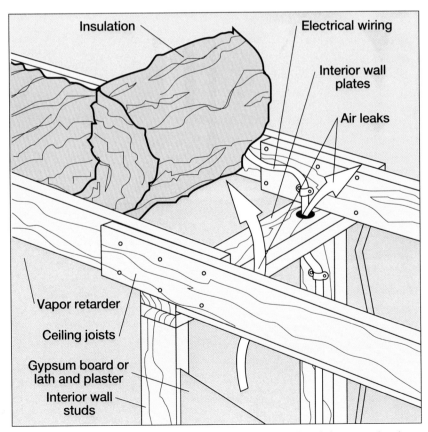

Insulation

Electrical wiring

Interior wall plates

Air leaks

Vapor retarder

Ceiling joists

Gypsum board or lath and plaster

Interior wall studs

Vapor retarders and air barriers can help keep moist interior air from condensing in wall, ceiling, and attic areas.

frost. High-quality weatherstripping can keep cold air from entering and also help prevent condensation or frost from forming on the door frame. Metal door thresholds should be avoided, the specialists say, unless they have a complete thermal break from inside to outside.

Condensation also can take place in cooler exterior corners of rooms, especially those constructed using 2x4s and standard sheathing. Exposure to cold on two sides of the exterior draws heat away rapidly, and warm air on the inside can't circulate into corners very well. If condensation occurs, it can result in stains, mold, mildew, and paint or wallpaper peeling.

To improve corner insulation, thick wall framing (such as 2x6s) and insulation should be used in new construction, or insulating foam sheathing should be added to the interior or exterior. In existing homes insulating sheathing can be added to the inside of the wall during interior remodeling. Tip: Foam sheathing installed on the exterior (cold side) should have a vapor retarding rating at least five times lower than the rating of the interior (warm side) vapor retarder.

Attic or Ceiling Holes. The holes where wires, pipes, ducts, or light fixtures go through the ceiling should be sealed so humid air can't leak through the ceiling into the insulation or attic space. The attic insulation must be adequate enough to provide warm interior surfaces and prevent condensation on ceilings.

In new construction, special "high-heel" roof trusses can be used to provide enough space to install ceiling insulation full depth to the edge of the attic, as well as proper venting space. Baffles to deflect the wind from entering the edge of the insulation in attics also are important.

Moisture Sources. In the war against condensation, the specialists also advise paying attention to sources of moisture. Ventilation exhaust fans or exhaust registers (for a central ventilation system) should be installed in rooms that regularly contribute high levels of household moisture, such as bathrooms, kitchens, and laundry rooms. Vents in these rooms should be positioned to draw moisture from the entire space.

In cold climates, the specialists say, it is particularly important to have triple-insulation glass (or its equivalent) in bathroom windows, and to have well-insulated walls and ceilings to keep surface temperatures as warm as possible. In new homes, extra insulation can be installed easily in bathroom walls with furred-in framing if the floor plan allows for extra space in tub enclosure areas.

Proper Venting. Peterson and Hendricks also point out that the

QUICK CONDENSATION FIXES

Energy-efficient doors combine core materials of high insulation value and thermal breaks. Newer weatherstripping materials, like this pre-formed caulking from 3M, also help keep cold air from entering and forming condensation on windows.

Insulating kits, such as this one from 3M, can help reduce air infiltration around window seals. After clear plastic is sealed down with tape, a hair dryer shrinks it to make it tight, smooth, and nearly invisible.

Photos: 3M

burning of fuel produces water vapor. This makes the proper venting of furnaces, water heaters, wood-burning stoves, and fireplaces important not only for humidity control, but also for safety and health reasons.

Proper venting, they advise, requires that the appliance area be kept at neutral air pressure with a constant supply of outside air. All exhaust fans, exhaust hoods, and exhaust appliances should be balanced with an adequate supply of outside air into the house or directly to the equipment if it is designed for direct outside air. They note that this is a problem especially with down-draft cooking ranges which have high airflows but typically have not been provided any air supply. Balanced vent fan systems, in which supply flow equals exhaust flow, help neutralize the air pressure in the home. ❧

The
BUCKET BRIGADE

*The Simple Bucket Offers New Ideas On
How To Get Organized And Stay That Way*

Sometimes the best ideas lay right under our noses, and are overlooked because they seem too simple to be of value. That is, until someone stops thinking that a complex problem always requires a complex solution.

One problem that has plagued do-it-yourselfers for years has been how to keep project tools, supplies, and equipment in order and ready to use at a moment's notice. You can have the most well-organized shop, with tools neatly hung on miles of pegboard, and still encounter the problem. When a hole is punched through a sheetrock wall, it can take twice as long to round up the tools and supplies you need as it does to actually make the repair.

The taping knives are in the basement, the tape and mud in the furnace room. But what happened to the saber saw, and who took the power drill?

Just a few short years ago, contractor Bob Fierek noticed that those who have this kind of problem almost every day — tradesmen such as carpenters, plumbers, and electricians — had figured out a primitive solution. Their answer was to use the basic unadorned, plastic 5-gallon bucket, the kind used for drywall mud, pickles, paint, and other commodities. Some would even use several of the lightweight buckets, filling each one with what was needed for a specific kind of job. A plumber, for example, might have one filled with tools for making pipe connections, another for faucet-fixing supplies, and still another for toilet installations.

With some possible improvements, Bob speculated, the simple bucket

Catskinner Mike Hoffield tests an early Bucket Boss before it hit the big time.

might be just the ticket to help do-it-yourself homeowners and others keep things organized and portable. The bucket, he thought, could become a prime example of a low-tech solution to a problem created by high tech. With its built-in handle, a simple bucket makes whatever it stores instantly transportable, a handy alternative to an 80-lb. toolbox. Without some system of organizing its contents, however, buckets can become a jumble of junk.

Bob and his brother Dave began experimenting with ways to develop the idea. They first tried string and wire around buckets to hold tools, then bungee cords. Later they began tying carpenter's aprons and old tool belts around the outside to hold tools and parts that otherwise fell to the bottom. By 1985, Dave had come up with something that worked, a red tool holder of tough nylon that easily slipped over the bucket rim to allow 16 pockets to hang down the outside, 11 on the inside.

They saw it as a Rolodex for project people, and the best thing since duct tape. They decided to call it the Bucket Boss.

Three years later Bob met Paul Maire, who convinced him he could start up a company on a shoestring in space above a marble processing factory. The firm, called Portable Products, tripled its business every year and by 1992 it was heading toward $5 million in sales by selling some 400,000 Bucket Bosses. It didn't hurt that at the 1991 National Hardware Show the Bucket Boss was chosen from among 150,000 new products to receive the Retailer's Choice Award as one most likely to succeed in the marketplace.

Paul Maire, now president, says that at first they were afraid they could only sell Bucket Bosses to tradesmen, including painters, mechanics, roofers, paperhangers, and drywallers. But they have been surprised at who else is buying the item and the jobs it's being used for, such as gardening, maintenance, cleaning, fishing, camping, boating, crafts, decorating, and dozens of other activities. "We get postcards back all the time from people who come up with new ideas for using the bucket with our product," says Paul. "It practically sells itself to a practical person who wants to save time."

In its short life, Portable Products has introduced four "bucket-mounted tool carriers," plus a "parachute bag" that fits into the bottom of a bucket to keep small parts organized, a "tool/chisel roll" for hand tools, a 30-pocket "rigger's bag" of cotton duck, and an add-on to the original Bucket Boss called "high pockets" that provides 10 more pockets. They also sell a special strap to keep longer tools outside the bucket in place, as well as a handle pad and what has become their trademark: pairs of red suspenders. Their main office is cluttered with prototypes of new ideas, including an experimental bucket cover lid to sit on while you eat lunch.

In their spartan, but adequate, headquarters in St. Paul, Bob and Paul can go on for hours speculating how a do-it-yourselfer could put the bucket concept to good use. When homeowners start setting up their own "bucket brigade," ideas seem to sprout from nowhere. The first step is to stash several buckets in the shop or garage, outfitted by type of activity. The buckets are easily held up out of the way on screw hooks and, when it is time to take them to the job, their round shape is easy to carry and won't damage walls or doors like a square-edged toolbox. Also, a bucket won't capsize like a toolbox if it must be lifted to a roof with rope.

You can begin to experiment with the bucket concept even without a

THE GENERAL-PURPOSE BUCKET

If you are a beginning bucket user, one or more fitted with a Bucket Boss can be set up to handle a special organizing problem, such as keeping general project tools together. Use it for assorted basic tools, such as pliers and adjustable wrenches, as well as hammers, saws, measuring tapes, marking tools, and perhaps an extension cord and other equipment often used for maintenance and repair around the home.

THE YARD AND GARDEN BUCKET

A special green and yellow version, called the Garden Boss, is designed to transform a 5-gallon bucket into a handy garden tote. With 27 pockets, 11 inside and 16 outside, it can store all needed gardening tools in one place instead of scattered all over the garage or yard. Pruners, small spades, bulb planters, weeders, even seeds, bulbs, ties, and other supplies are all candidates for a garden bucket.

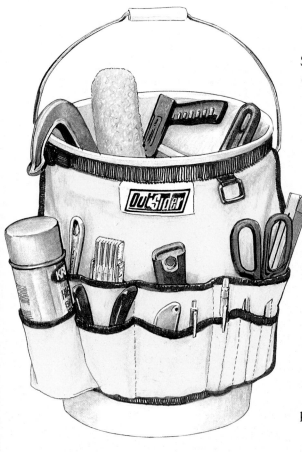

THE OUTDOOR PROJECT BUCKET

Setting up buckets for outside uses makes sense because what you need requires easy portability. This special version of the Bucket Boss provides 23 pockets outside and none inside so you retain the full use of the bucket's interior. It can be set up for general handyman work or for pursuits like hunting or fishing. Because the interior is open, things like nails, fasteners, and small parts can be conveniently stored in a parachute bag.

THE COLLAPSIBLE-BAG BUCKET

If you would like the convenience of a bucket, but need more flexibility, one option is the Rigger's Bag. This improvement on traditional mariner gear is 18" long, 10" high, and 6½" wide, and has 30 pockets of various sizes surrounding the exterior. With a triple bottom, it stows better than a bucket in a boat, for example, where space is at a premium. It is also ideal for such hobbies as knitting, sewing, or other craftwork.

Bucket Boss accessory, however. To start, commandeer buckets at little or no cost from such places as delicatessens, for example, which throw out their pickle pails. Buckets are also increasingly available at low cost from home center stores. (Portable Products sells them for $4.95.) You may want to start with one general-purpose bucket just for portable power tools, for instance, to find out how you like the idea. Once you discover how handy it can be, you can keep adding more buckets for increasingly specialized uses.

Some ideas for the average homeowner might include one bucket marked for Inside Jobs, one for Outside Jobs, one for General Cleaning, one for Automotive Work, and one for Gardening Work. Depending upon your project schedule, you also may find separate buckets handy for more specialized applications, such as Drywall Work, Plumbing Work, Electrical Work, Doors and Windows, Soldering and Brazing, General Woodworking, Heat Gun and Accessories, Small Engines, or Glass and Screen Repair.

Or you can organize buckets by the place where they are used: sailboat, camper, RV, cabin, or garage. The illustrations give more specific suggestions on how to outfit your "starter" buckets. Keep in mind that while your "bucket brigade" can be an excellent secondary method of organizing, storing, and transporting tools and supplies, a well-kept workshop still has its place for items that are used only occasionally, or are too bulky to fit inside a bucket.

Once you get used to the bucket concept, you may make interesting discoveries. Some canoe campers, for example, are finding that buckets are excellent replacements for extra backpacks. Fitted with lids, they provide waterproof storage for

ACCESSORIZING THE BASIC BUCKET

New converts to bucket organizing often get so enthused their minds churn for days on what further improvements could be made. A cabinet full of correspondence from bucket users at Portable Products headquarters testifies that there is no end to new concepts. The company has developed a few of these ideas, shown here, to make at-home customizing easier.

PARACHUTE BAG

One genetic defect of the bucket is that you still need to accommodate the many small parts and items that many projects require. One answer to this problem is the canvas parachute bag that can keep nuts, screws, bolts, washers, or nails in order without risk of spilling. The bag has six 5½"-deep compartments and an authentic military-spec drawstring closure; it's just the right size to slip inside a 5-gallon bucket. If you are a pack rat, you can stack as many as four parachute bags in a single bucket, giving you a total of 24 compartments.

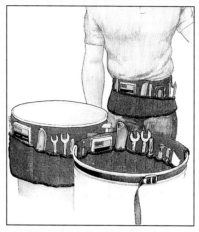

HIGH POCKETS

Let's say you need more pockets for hard-to-organize items and don't want to set up more buckets. One answer is this special organizer that instantly offers 10 additional pockets to either the interior or exterior of the bucket rim. (If you need to reserve the interior for small parts stored in a parachute bag, use the High Pockets on the outside.) The company designed it to be used with a strap that also makes it possible to remove and strap the pockets around your waist like a tool belt.

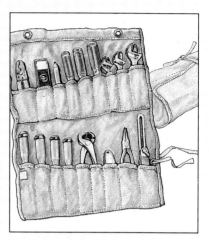

TOOL/CHISEL ROLL

This one is not a new idea; it's been a long-time favorite used by tradesmen for screwdrivers, wrenches, chisels, and fine hand tools that need special protection. Made of the same canvas that is used for boat covers, the 20" x 25" flexible tool kit makes an ideal bucket companion, or can be used alone as a tool kit for your car trunk, an organizer/carrier for camping utensils, or a place to stow craft and hobby tools or other items that would benefit from protective pockets. Utility/knife cases for single items like pens, gauges, knives, and small flashlights are also available.

food and other items that need to stay dry. Likewise, some do-it-yourselfers have picked up on the idea of converting plastic buckets into specialized "electric pails." With a GFCI-protected outlet bolted to the outside, a bucket provides an ideal way to store extension cords coiled inside, as well as small power tools. (Flat extension cords actually are easier to re-coil than round cords.) The electrified bucket is handy for

all types of outdoor jobs requiring power, and the portable GFCI receptacle is smart and needed safety protection.

A final tip: Bucket enthusiast Bill Simeon of Poplar, Wisconsin, has found that any newly recruited buckets can be made even more portable by mounting ball-bearing swivel casters to the bottom. So equipped, they become easy to nudge, pull, or push along as you work. Using the small

nylon or styrene wheels available at hardware stores will eliminate any danger of marring floors. You also can get casters with locking brakes. Top-heavy buckets, Bill says, work best with five casters, instead of three or four. ❧

Note: To get started with your own bucket organizing experiments, contact Portable Products at 58 East Plato Blvd., St. Paul, MN 55107 or call toll-free 800/688-2677 (612/221-0308 in Minnesota).

HOME WIRING

Tips On Tools, Supplies, And Procedures
For Adding A New Circuit In Your Home

The home looked big enough when you bought it. But after a few years the rooms seem to get smaller, or you need more storage space, or you want an extra bedroom either for new arrivals or for the grandkids. Such additions will likely require adding a new electrical circuit instead of just extending an existing circuit. Whether this provides an opportunity to save money by doing it yourself depends on a number of factors.

Most local codes will allow a homeowner to do the electrical work on any addition if you buy the materials and do the work yourself. A permit probably will be required, however, along with a couple of inspections: 1) when the electrical work is done, but before the walls or ceilings are covered, and 2) when the entire project is complete.

D-I-Y WIRING DECISIONS

Whether you tackle the job yourself may depend on how much you already know about electrical work, how much time you have to bone up on what you don't know, or how quickly you want to get the job done. It is a job that must be done right and one that can present serious safety hazards if you don't know what you are doing. (See *Caution: Safety First* at the end of this section.) However, it's likely you could save from $200 to $500 or more by adding the circuit yourself, depending on the size of the addition and its requirements.

Wiring a new addition with a single circuit is one of the more straightforward electrical projects. It is even simpler if you use Romex wire and nonmetallic boxes, and are able to connect the circuit to an existing 100-amp service panel. Besides testing devices, it's likely you will be able to get by with a minimum tool investment. Tools worth getting include an inexpensive cable ripper (about $2), a pliers-style wire stripper

TYPICAL CABLE ROUTING

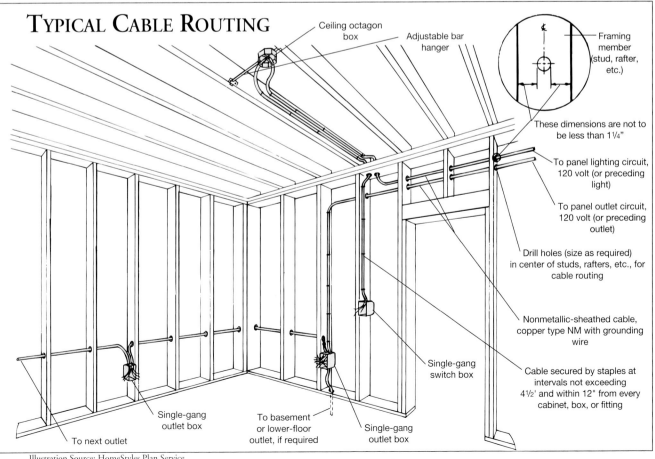

Ceiling octagon box

Adjustable bar hanger

Framing member (stud, rafter, etc.)

These dimensions are not to be less than 1¼"

To panel lighting circuit, 120 volt (or preceding light)

To panel outlet circuit, 120 volt (or preceding outlet)

Drill holes (size as required) in center of studs, rafters, etc., for cable routing

Nonmetallic-sheathed cable, copper type NM with grounding wire

Cable secured by staples at intervals not exceeding 4½' and within 12" from every cabinet, box, or fitting

Single-gang switch box

Single-gang outlet box

To next outlet

Single-gang outlet box

To basement or lower-floor outlet, if required

Single-gang outlet box

Illustration Source: HomeStyles Plan Service

THREE-WAY SWITCH INSTALLATION

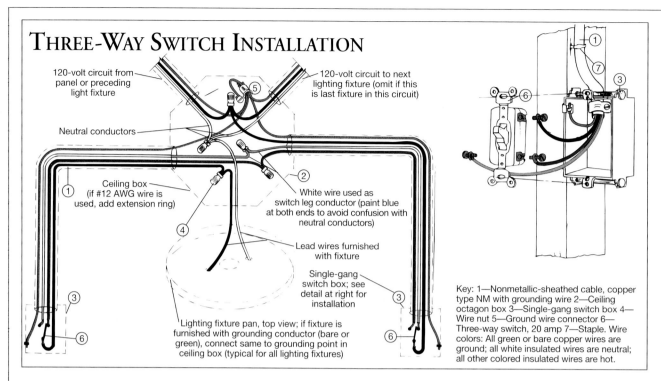

120-volt circuit from panel or preceding light fixture

120-volt circuit to next lighting fixture (omit if this is last fixture in this circuit)

Neutral conductors

Ceiling box (if #12 AWG wire is used, add extension ring)

White wire used as switch leg conductor (paint blue at both ends to avoid confusion with neutral conductors)

Lead wires furnished with fixture

Single-gang switch box; see detail at right for installation

Lighting fixture pan, top view; if fixture is furnished with grounding conductor (bare or green), connect same to grounding point in ceiling box (typical for all lighting fixtures)

Key: 1—Nonmetallic-sheathed cable, copper type NM with grounding wire 2—Ceiling octagon box 3—Single-gang switch box 4—Wire nut 5—Ground wire connector 6—Three-way switch, 20 amp 7—Staple. Wire colors: All green or bare copper wires are ground; all white insulated wires are neutral; all other colored insulated wires are hot.

(about $5), and a needle-nose pliers (about $7). These, plus the pliers, screwdrivers, and protective gear you probably already have, should get you through the project.

If you've never done any wiring before, consult some of the better do-it-yourself electrical books available, and consider taking a night class on wiring for beginners sometimes given at local home centers and tech schools. Then try to line up someone with electrical work experience who will be available if any questions come up. (One very good option is to consider hiring an electrician to plan out the job for you, answer your questions, and make sure you stay on the right track.)

Even before you start planning the job, check with local electrical code officials and tell them what you intend to do, and ask if you need a permit. Most local electrical codes are patterned after the National Electrical Code (NEC), but often vary to some extent between communities in interpretation. Your local electrical inspector also can tell you where to get a summary of the latest version of the NEC.

PLANNING IT OUT

Before you assemble materials, you need to map out what the electrical load will be on the new circuit, as close as you can figure it. Unless you plan to have a kitchen or heavy-duty appliance in a new one-room addition, chances are good you may be able to get by with a single circuit of either 12-gauge Romex wire, using a 20-amp circuit breaker, or the smaller 14-gauge Romex wire, which requires a breaker no larger than 15 amp.

Romex wire has insulated wires wrapped in a plastic sheathing, and will likely be coded NM (which stands for nonmetallic). Wire stamped Type NM 12-2 With Ground, for example, will be of 12-gauge wire and will have both white and black insulated wires, plus a bare ground wire, inside the sheathing. Wire stamped Type NMC is for use where moisture may be present; wire stamped Type UF is waterproof cable that can be buried directly in the ground (check your local code).

Whether you use 12-gauge or 14-gauge wire may depend on the load.

Some electricians will always favor the heavier 12 gauge, and some local codes require it. A general rule of thumb is that, except for kitchens and laundry rooms, a 20-amp circuit should take care of 500 sq. ft. of space, while a 14-amp circuit should handle 375 sq. ft. (At the maximum, the NEC specifies a 15-amp circuit may not be used to service more than 575 sq. ft. of floor area.) Another rule of thumb is that you can put about eight outlets on a circuit — but also confirm this with local officials.

Another method is to add up the total wattage for all lights and appliances that may be used on the circuit. (Two formulas to use are Volts x Amps = Watts, or Watts divided by Volts = Amps.) The maximum should be less than about 1,500 watts for one 15-amp circuit, and less than about 2,000 watts for a 20-amp circuit. The wattage requirements of various appliances can be found in some do-it-yourself reference books.

How many outlets do you need? The NEC requires an outlet for any wall space wider than 2'. Also, out-

Four-Way Switch Installation

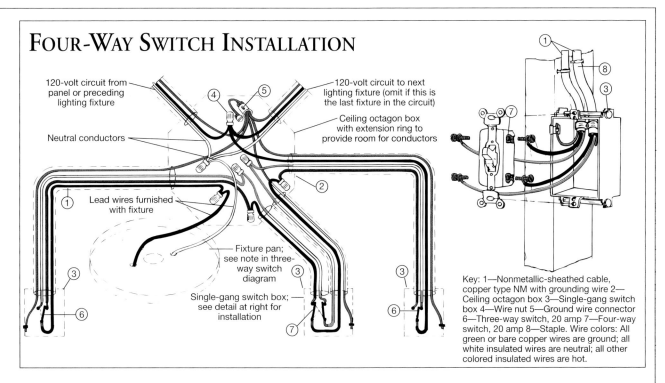

120-volt circuit from panel or preceding lighting fixture

Neutral conductors

Lead wires furnished with fixture

120-volt circuit to next lighting fixture (omit if this is the last fixture in the circuit)

Ceiling octagon box with extension ring to provide room for conductors

Fixture pan; see note in three-way switch diagram

Single-gang switch box; see detail at right for installation

Key: 1—Nonmetallic-sheathed cable, copper type NM with grounding wire 2—Ceiling octagon box 3—Single-gang switch box 4—Wire nut 5—Ground wire connector 6—Three-way switch, 20 amp 7—Four-way switch, 20 amp 8—Staple. Wire colors: All green or bare copper wires are ground; all white insulated wires are neutral; all other colored insulated wires are hot.

lets must be within 12' of each other around a general-purpose room. (Railings also count as "wall.") Generally, except for special requirements for kitchens, baths, or laundry rooms, you can put outlets and lighting on the same circuit. You can run power to a junction box, for example, and then branch off from it to outlets, or you can run power from one outlet to the next — whichever seems easiest and most economical.

If the new addition will have a window air conditioner that would draw more than half of the capacity of the circuit, you will need to add a separate circuit to service it. Also, if the circuit will run to areas where water is used, or be used for outdoor outlets, it will need the protection of a ground fault circuit interrupter (GFCI). This can be done with either a GFCI circuit breaker, or you can use a GFCI feed-through receptacle in the first outlet of the circuit. A GFCI receptacle is the less expensive way to go.

When buying supplies, you'll find a wide variety of boxes available, in both metal and the increasingly popular nonmetallic styles. Generally you'll use rectangular boxes for outlets, and round or octagonal boxes for ceiling light fixtures. If you are using Romex, look for boxes which have built-in clamping devices to secure the cable.

Doing The Installation

Watch that you don't put too many wires inside too small of a box. The NEC provides formulas for figuring the number of wires allowed in various size boxes, determined by the number of "wire ends" coming into the box. If you will have no more than two cables coming into the box, you should have no problem with this. But if you are feeding many outlets from one junction box, or will be using three-way or four-way switches, it's a good idea to prefigure how many wires will be in the box. If there's any question, go with larger boxes; you'll have more space for wires as you complete the installation.

Installing Boxes. The tops of outlets are generally installed at least 12" off the finished floor, with boxes positioned so their outer edge will be flush with the finished wall surface.

The code doesn't allow any splices outside boxes. If you need to make a splice in the middle of a cable run, for example, you have to use a junction box. It's permissible to use a box with a solid cover on it inside a wall or ceiling, but you must keep all boxes accessible.

Running Cable. To run wire for a new circuit to a new addition, you may need to get it through some existing walls. A fish tape can be helpful, but if the wire needs to be pulled through an area of 6' or less, you may not need it. Measure so you make sure where you are going. You can buy small-diameter "aircraft" drill bits, which are a foot or more long, to help you explore. You may be able to push the wire through; if not, try coat hangers, doweling, or even string with a washer at one end. Drop the string through, then pull back up a heavier string or rope attached to the wire cable.

Fastening Cable. You can run Romex through ⅝" to 1" holes drilled in the center of 2x4 studs. But where cable is installed closer than 1¼" to the edge of a joist or stud (other than in the center of a 2x4), it should be

SINGLE SWITCH INSTALLATION

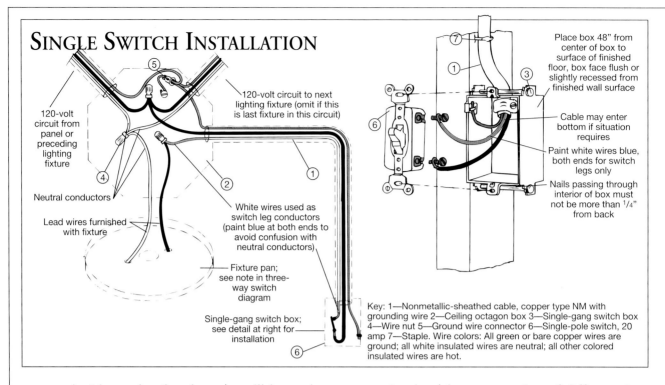

120-volt circuit to next lighting fixture (omit if this is last fixture in this circuit)

120-volt circuit from panel or preceding lighting fixture

Neutral conductors

Lead wires furnished with fixture

White wires used as switch leg conductors (paint blue at both ends to avoid confusion with neutral conductors)

Fixture pan; see note in three-way switch diagram

Single-gang switch box; see detail at right for installation

Place box 48" from center of box to surface of finished floor, box face flush or slightly recessed from finished wall surface

Cable may enter bottom if situation requires

Paint white wires blue, both ends for switch legs only

Nails passing through interior of box must not be more than $1/4$" from back

Key: 1—Nonmetallic-sheathed cable, copper type NM with grounding wire 2—Ceiling octagon box 3—Single-gang switch box 4—Wire nut 5—Ground wire connector 6—Single-pole switch, 20 amp 7—Staple. Wire colors: All green or bare copper wires are ground; all white insulated wires are neutral; all other colored insulated wires are hot.

protected with metal nailer plates. To provide support if you are bridging rafters, first tack down scrap lumber across the space and use plastic staples to fasten the cable to it. Unsupported Romex cable should be attached with plastic staples every $4\frac{1}{2}'$ or less along the run, and also attached within 12" of a plastic box. The wire must be secured at the box with either a self-locking tab or connector clamps.

Cutting Wire. From $\frac{1}{8}$" to $\frac{1}{4}$" of Romex sheathing must show beyond the clamps on the inside of the box. It's better not to be too stingy on wire. Leave a little slack in runs, and be sure to leave enough wire inside the box, generally at least 6" as measured from the outside edge of the box. This is something not well covered in electrical books, and can trip you up. Remember, leave enough wire inside the box. If you don't have enough wire coming into the box, you may find yourself re-doing all the box connections after an inspection, pulling wires and re-stapling. It's not a fun job.

Connecting Ground Wires. When using Romex cable with ground,

you'll have a bare copper wire that must be connected to run continuously throughout the circuit. The ground wire always connects to the green screw on a receptacle, using what is called a "pigtail" splice. (A short piece of bare wire goes under the green screw; the other end is fastened inside a wire nut along with the "incoming" bare ground wire and the "outgoing" bare ground wire.) If you have a number of ground wires coming into a box, they should all be connected together with a wire nut.

(In some cases you won't have anything to connect the ground wire to, such as a switch without a grounding screw used in a plastic box at the end of a run. In such cases, just carefully tuck the bare ground wire into the back of the box.)

Using Connectors. Splice connections used to have to be twisted, soldered, and covered with two kinds of tape. Now you must use electrical wire nuts over the ends of the wires. With some brands you may not need to pre-twist the wires together; the box or package should tell you. (If it doesn't, ask the supplier.) The box also should say

how many wires of different sizes you are allowed to use inside a particular size wire nut.

Installing Receptacles. With only one exception, the black "hot" wire connects to the brass or gold-colored screw on a receptacle or switch; the white "neutral" wire connects to the silver or light-colored screw. The bare ground wire connects to the green screw. The exception is when you branch off to switches that interrupt the flow of electricity in the black "hot" wire only. In this case, the white wire is used as a return "hot" wire, and its ends are painted or taped blue or black to indicate it is "hot."

Installing Switches. All single pole switches interrupt the black "hot" wire. Ends of the "hot" wire connect to the two brass-colored terminals on the switch. Switches are generally installed about 48" off the finished floor, and those near doors should be on the "door knob" side of the door. If you plan to use three-way switches (two switches controlling the same light fixture) or four-way switches (three or more switches controlling a light fixture) for the first time, use diagrams to guide you. (One good

SWITCHED OUTLET INSTALLATION

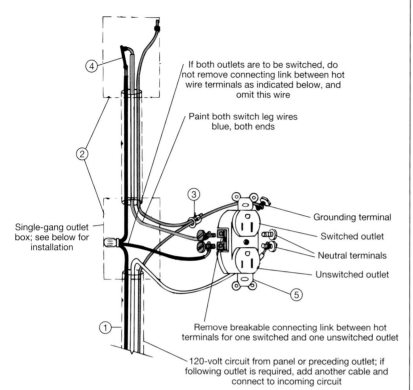

If both outlets are to be switched, do not remove connecting link between hot wire terminals as indicated below, and omit this wire

Paint both switch leg wires blue, both ends

Single-gang outlet box; see below for installation

Grounding terminal

Switched outlet

Neutral terminals

Unswitched outlet

Remove breakable connecting link between hot terminals for one switched and one unswitched outlet

120-volt circuit from panel or preceding outlet; if following outlet is required, add another cable and connect to incoming circuit

Key: 1—Nonmetallic-sheathed cable, copper type NM with grounding wire 2—Single-gang switch/outlet box 3—Ground wire connector 4—Single-pole switch, 20 amp 5—Duplex outlet, 15 amp. Wire colors: All green or bare copper wires are ground; all white insulated wires are neutral; all other colored insulated wires are hot.

OUTLET INSTALLATION

Place boxes uniformly 12" to center above finished floor and with box face flush or slightly recessed from finished wall surface

Connect neutral white wire(s) to silver terminal(s)

Connect hot leg black wire(s) to brass terminal(s)

Connect bare copper or green wire(s) to green terminal(s)

Key: 1—Nonmetallic-sheathed cable, copper type NM with grounding wire 2—Single-gang outlet box 3—Ground wire connector 4—Duplex outlet, 15 amp 5—Duplex outlet, 20 amp 6—Staple. Wire colors: All green or bare copper wires are ground; all white insulated wires are neutral; all other colored insulated wires are hot.

source is the set of low-cost how-to diagrams available from HomeStyles Plan Service, Inc.; see the end of this section for ordering information.)

Installing Fixtures. All fixtures must have an electrical box behind them, and today all recessed light fixtures must have thermal protection which cuts out the power if the fixture gets dangerously hot. Multiple light fixtures should be wired in parallel, with the black wire from one fixture connected to the black wire of the next fixture.

Connecting The Circuit. Once the circuit is completely wired and tested, it can be connected to the electrical service panel, providing it is an up-to-date 100-amp panel and there is space to accommodate another circuit. If all spaces for breakers are already in use, you will need to install an "add-on" panel. The job is relatively simple if a circuit breaker in the service panel is not being used, or if there is space to add a circuit breaker. If there is an outside disconnect, turn it off so there is no power coming into the panel. If there isn't, turn off the main switch on the panel, but be aware that there still are hot terminals inside the panel.

Make sure that you don't cut the cable too short near the service panel; leave 2' or 3' beyond where it will enter the panel. After the wires are connected inside, don't forget to fasten the cable within 12" of the panel, just like with boxes within a run. In a modern service panel, the black "hot" wire from the circuit connects under a screw on the circuit breaker. The white "neutral" wire connects under a screw on the neutral bus (a bar which will have other white wires running to it), and the bare ground wire connects under a screw either on the neutral bus or, if provided, on a ground bus (another

COUNTERTOP COOKING UNIT CONNECTION

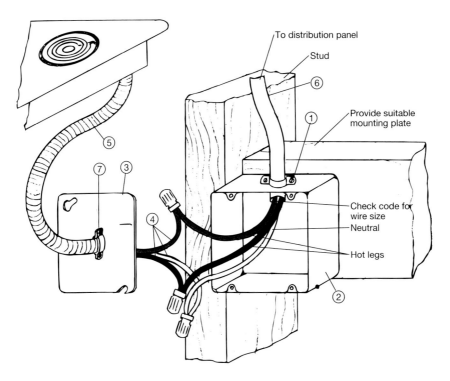

To distribution panel

Stud

Provide suitable mounting plate

Check code for wire size

Neutral

Hot legs

Key: 1—Box connector 2—Square box, 4 $^{11}/_{16}$" x 2 $^{1}/_{8}$" 3—Cover 4—THW wire, No. 8 AWG 5—Flexible metal conduit, $^{1}/_{2}$" 6—Type SE, three-conductor cable, copper 7—Conduit connector. Wire colors: All green or bare copper wires are ground; all white insulated wires are neutral; all other colored insulated wires are hot.

bar which will have other bare ground wires running to it).

If you are connecting wires from a new circuit to a service panel which is shut off only by the main switch on the panel, take all precautions to avoid shock, and don't attempt the job unless you are absolutely confident you can do it safely. Because of the possibility that the bare ground wire could contact a hot terminal, connect it first, being careful to watch the entire length of the bare wire. Then connect the other two wires.

As a doublecheck, you can use a small neon tester to make sure receptacles are properly grounded. Or, you can buy a special plug-in tester for under $10 which has three small lights. It will indicate problems such as open ground, open neutral, open hot, hot and ground

RANGE AND DRYER RECEPTACLE

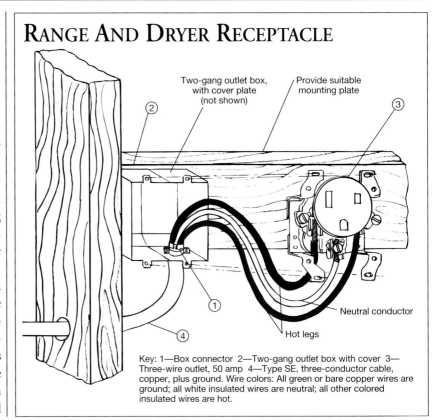

Two-gang outlet box, with cover plate (not shown)

Provide suitable mounting plate

Neutral conductor

Hot legs

Key: 1—Box connector 2—Two-gang outlet box with cover 3—Three-wire outlet, 50 amp 4—Type SE, three-conductor cable, copper, plus ground. Wire colors: All green or bare copper wires are ground; all white insulated wires are neutral; all other colored insulated wires are hot.

WATER HEATER RECEPTACLE

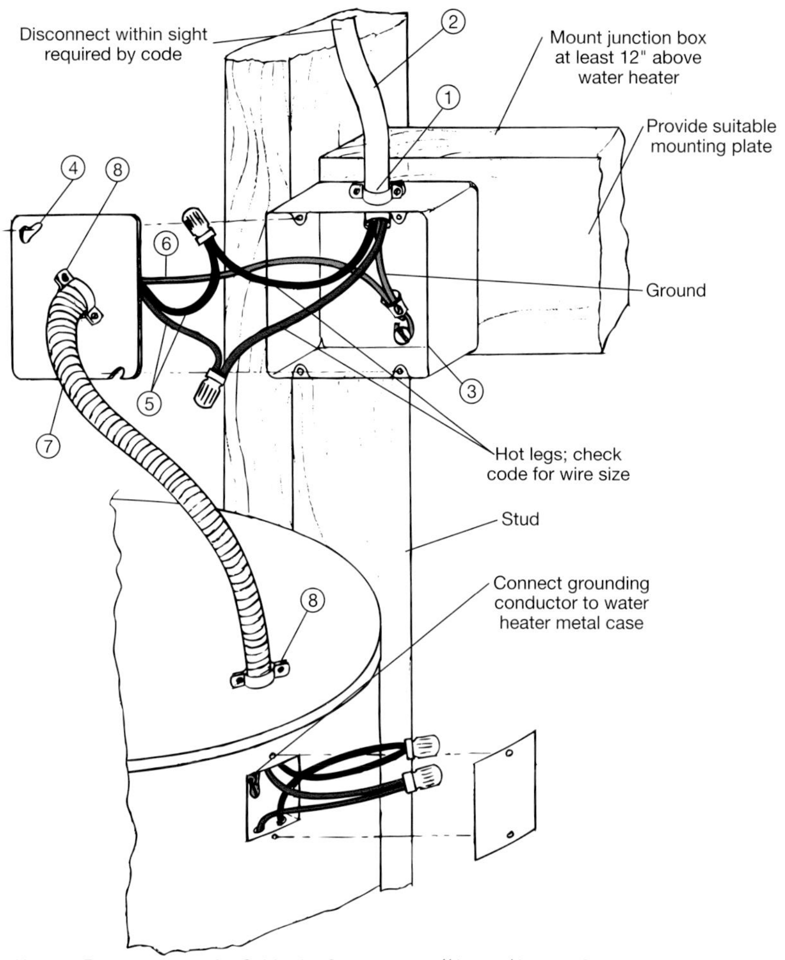

Disconnect within sight required by code

Mount junction box at least 12" above water heater

Provide suitable mounting plate

Ground

Hot legs; check code for wire size

Stud

Connect grounding conductor to water heater metal case

Key: 1—Box connector 2—Cable 3—Square box, 4$^{11}/_{16}$" x 2$^1/_8$" 4—Cover 5—THW wire, No. 8 AWG 6—Bare copper wire No. 8 AWG 7—Flexible metal conduit, $^1/_2$" 8—Conduit connector. Wire colors: All green or bare copper wires are ground; all white insulated wires are neutral; all other colored insulated wires are hot.

reversed, or hot and neutral reversed. The instructions that come with the unit will tell you how to use it. ❧

Note: The information presented here is not intended to serve as a complete guide to wiring a new electrical circuit, but to familiarize you with some of the basic procedures. If you intend to do your own wiring, seek out more complete and detailed sources of information on wiring procedures, including how to connect a new circuit at the service panel. One excellent resource for homeowners who want to learn more about home wiring is a special six-page, blueprint-style summary of typical residential wiring diagrams and procedures available from HomeStyles Plan Service Inc., 275 Market St., Suite 521, Minneapolis, MN 55405 (612/338-8155). Besides helpful diagrams (a sampling is shown here), the set provides valuable advice on completing home wiring projects. The company also markets a similar five-page, blueprint-format diagram summary on all aspects of home plumbing projects. The cost is $12.50 per set, or $23 for two sets, plus shipping and handling.

CAUTION: SAFETY FIRST

On any do-it-yourself electrical work, safety is an over-riding consideration. Make sure you know all electrical safety precautions before you start, and never guess. Electrical contact can be fatal. If you have any questions whatsoever, seek competent help through such sources as licensed electricians, local electrical code officials, or other qualified and knowledgeable persons.

When working on the electrical system, always shut off the current at the main switch on the service panel. Better yet, if the service panel is fed through a disconnect outside your home, turn that off before working on the system. It's best to always assume wires are hot, and always make sure your body is not grounded when working with electricity. Check and doublecheck your work before,

during, and after the project. Wiring can be tested while the current is off with a continuity tester, either a volt-ohm meter or a signal device.

Neon test lights can be used to see if wires, outlets, or switches are live. Keep in mind that just turning off switches and circuit breakers may not be enough. For example, switches may be fed from fixtures, or neutral wires may be shared by more than one circuit. In some cases you can be shocked by white neutral wires assumed to be off. You also can get a shock from neutral wires if you interrupt their path back to the service panel. Be sure you know what you are doing before attempting any electrical work.

INDEX

CREDITS & ADDRESSES

TEXT AND PHOTO CREDITS

Section Pages: Spread photos, Lindal Cedar Homes, Seattle. Inset photos: CONCEPTS, WGBH Boston. CHALLENGES, Monte Burch. CREATIONS, Thos. Moser Cabinetmakers. CLASSICS, Marvin Windows & Doors. CHECKPOINTS, Matt Straw, *In-Fisherman* Communications Network.

Features: Produced by North Coast Productions, with help from the following. **The Do-It-Yourself Payoff:** photo pages 8 and 9, Marlyn Rodi. **The New Yankee Workshop:** photos, Richard Howard and WGBH, Boston; illustration pages 14 and 15 adapted by Barbara Bowen from original illustration by Nina Coles. **Storage Projects:** text sources, photos, and illustrations, Western Wood Products Association. **The Functional Deck:** text sources and photos, California Redwood Association; inset photo, page 27, Marlyn Rodi. **Shop Sawyers:** text, Howard Silken; photos, Delta International Machinery Corporation. **Painted Surfaces:** text, Ed Jackson; photos, 3M Co. **Mechanized Painting:** text, Ed Jackson; photos, Wagner Spray Tech. **Kitchen Engineering:** text, pages 46, 47, and 55, Jim Krengel; text, pages 48–53, Ralph Wilson Plastics Co.; text, page 54, National Kitchen & Bath Association. **The Log Cabin:** text and photos, Monte Burch; illustration source, pages 62 and 63, Whispering Pines Log Homes. **Home Project Outfitters:** photos, pages 64 and 66, Wagner Spray Tech. **An Artist's Touch:** project photos, William Lemke; Tom Rauschke portrait, Mary Osmondsen. **Sensational Sun Rooms:** text source and photos, Lindal Cedar SunRooms. **Furniture Moser-Style:** text source and photos, Thos. Moser Cabinetmakers. **Cabin Carpenters:** photos, pages 90, 92, and 93, Lindal Cedar Homes. **The Whirlpool Bath:** text, Jean M. Fredensborg; photos and illustrations, Kohler Co. **Wild Projects:** text and illustration source, Minnesota Department of Natural Resources. **The Garden House:** text source and photos, Gardener's Supply Company. **Project Rules Of Thumb:** text source, members of National Association of Home and Workshop Writers and contributors to *Home Shop News* magazine. **French Doors:** text source and photos, Marvin Windows & Doors. **The Raised-Bed Garden:** text, Greg Northcutt; photos, Garden Way, Inc. **The Backyard Resort:** text by Monte Burch adapted with permission from *Decks & Backyard Projects* magazine, copyright 1992 Aqua-Field Publishing Co.; photos and illustration source, Monte Burch. **All-Star Do-It-Yourself Hints:** illustrations, Marlyn Rodi; text source, contributors to *Home Shop News* magazine; **File Know-How:** photos, Disston Inc.; illustration sources, CooperTools, division of Cooper Industries. **Home Emergency Repairs:** text adapted with permission from *The Home Repair Emergency Handbook,* Taylor Publishing Co., copyright 1992 Gene L. Schnaser; illustrations, Rebecca Gammelgaard. **Smart Boat Rigging:** text adapted with permission from *In-Fisherman* magazine, copyright 1992 *In-Fisherman* Communications Network; top photo, pages 160 and 161, Jan Couch; photo of Al Lindner and Jim Wentworth, page 161, Matt Straw; illustrations, *In-Fisherman* magazine. **Tool Power:** text sources, Skil Corporation and Stanley Tools, division of Stanley Works. **Head-Start Building:** text, Ed Jackson; photo and illustration, page 173, HomeStyles Plan Service Inc.; photos, page 174, Melroe Co. **Second-Generation Weatherproofing:** photos, page 175 and 177, 3M Co.; text and drawings adapted with permission from NR-FO-3567, *Humidity and Condensation Control in Cold Climate Housing,* copyright 1988 University of Minnesota Extension Service. **The Bucket Brigade:** text source, photo, and illustrations, Portable Products Co.; illustrations by Kollath Graphic Design. **Home Wiring:** illustration source, HomeStyles Plan Service Inc.

ADDRESSES

Below is a list of the addresses of companies and organizations that helped in major ways in the preparation of the 1993 edition of the *Homeowners' Do-It-Yourself Yearbook.*

California Redwood Association, 405 Enfrente Dr., Suite 200, Novato, CA 94949.

Delta International Machinery Corp., 246 Alpha Dr., Pittsburg, PA 15238.

Garden Way (Troy-Bilt), 102nd St. and 9th Ave., Troy, NY 12180.

Gardener's Supply Co., 128 Intervale Rd., Burlington, VT 05401.

Kohler Co., Kohler, WI 53044.

HomeStyles Plan Service Inc., 275 Market St., Suite 521, Minneapolis, MN.

In-Fisherman Magazine, P.O. Box 999, 651 Edgewood Dr., Brainerd, MN 56401.

Lindal Cedar Homes, 4300 S. 104th Pl., P.O. Box 24426, Seattle, WA 98124.

Marvin Windows & Doors, 2020 Silver Bell Rd., Suite 15, Eagan, MN 55122.

Maytag, Consumer Information Center, Newton, IA 50208.

Portable Products, 58 East Plato Blvd., St. Paul, MN 55107.

Ralph Wilson Plastics Co., 600 South General Bruce Dr. Temple, TX 76504.

Skil Corporation, 4300 W. Peterson Ave., Chicago, IL 60646.

Stanley Tools, Division of Stanley Works, New Britain, CT 06050.

Thos. Moser Cabinetmakers, 72 Wright's Landing, P.O. Box 1237, Auburn, ME 04211.

Wagner Spray Tech Corp., 1770 Fernbrook Lane, Plymouth, MN 55447.

Western Wood Products Association, Yeon Building, 522 SW Fifth Ave., Portland, OR 97204.

Whispering Pines Log Homes, Box 99, Hwy. 10 West, Verndale, MN 56481.